PROGRESS IN ECONOMICS RESEARCH

# PROGRESS IN ECONOMICS RESEARCH

## VOLUME 42

# PROGRESS IN ECONOMICS RESEARCH

Additional books and e-books in this series can be found on Nova's website under the Series tab.

PROGRESS IN ECONOMICS RESEARCH

# PROGRESS IN ECONOMICS RESEARCH

## VOLUME 42

ALBERT TAVIDZE
EDITOR

Copyright © 2019 by Nova Science Publishers, Inc.

**All rights reserved.** No part of this book may be reproduced, stored in a retrieval system or transmitted in any form or by any means: electronic, electrostatic, magnetic, tape, mechanical photocopying, recording or otherwise without the written permission of the Publisher.

We have partnered with Copyright Clearance Center to make it easy for you to obtain permissions to reuse content from this publication. Simply navigate to this publication's page on Nova's website and locate the "Get Permission" button below the title description. This button is linked directly to the title's permission page on copyright.com. Alternatively, you can visit copyright.com and search by title, ISBN, or ISSN.

For further questions about using the service on copyright.com, please contact:
Copyright Clearance Center
Phone: +1-(978) 750-8400        Fax: +1-(978) 750-4470        E-mail: info@copyright.com.

### NOTICE TO THE READER

The Publisher has taken reasonable care in the preparation of this book, but makes no expressed or implied warranty of any kind and assumes no responsibility for any errors or omissions. No liability is assumed for incidental or consequential damages in connection with or arising out of information contained in this book. The Publisher shall not be liable for any special, consequential, or exemplary damages resulting, in whole or in part, from the readers' use of, or reliance upon, this material. Any parts of this book based on government reports are so indicated and copyright is claimed for those parts to the extent applicable to compilations of such works.

Independent verification should be sought for any data, advice or recommendations contained in this book. In addition, no responsibility is assumed by the Publisher for any injury and/or damage to persons or property arising from any methods, products, instructions, ideas or otherwise contained in this publication.

This publication is designed to provide accurate and authoritative information with regard to the subject matter covered herein. It is sold with the clear understanding that the Publisher is not engaged in rendering legal or any other professional services. If legal or any other expert assistance is required, the services of a competent person should be sought. FROM A DECLARATION OF PARTICIPANTS JOINTLY ADOPTED BY A COMMITTEE OF THE AMERICAN BAR ASSOCIATION AND A COMMITTEE OF PUBLISHERS.

Additional color graphics may be available in the e-book version of this book.

## Library of Congress Cataloging-in-Publication Data

ISBN: 978-1-53615-120-6
ISSN: 1549-1552

*Published by Nova Science Publishers, Inc. † New York*

# CONTENTS

| | | |
|---|---|---|
| **Preface** | | vii |
| **Chapter 1** | WTO Global E-Commerce Policy Discussions and the Challenge of Developing Country Participation<br>*Farrokh Farrokhnia and Cameron K. Richards* | 1 |
| **Chapter 2** | How Do Stages of Economic Development Affect China's Competitiveness? Efficiency Analysis: China's Position as a Global Player in Comparison with the WTO Members<br>*Lenka Fojtíková and Michaela Staníčková* | 37 |
| **Chapter 3** | A Review of the Challenges to Political and Socio-Economic Development in Kenya<br>*Daniel N. Sifuna and Ibrahim Oanda* | 101 |
| **Chapter 4** | Growing Market Economy and Institutions: Evidence from the Former Soviet Republics<br>*Enrico Ivaldi, Marta Santagata and Riccardo Soliani* | 137 |

| | | |
|---|---|---|
| **Chapter 5** | Some Aspects of Taxation in the Former Soviet Union<br>*Sergei V. Jargin* | **171** |
| **Chapter 6** | Evolution and Trends in a Spanish Fishery of Anchovies<br>*Raquel Fernández-González, Marcos Pérez-Pérez, Ana Lemos Nobre and M. Dolores Garza-Gil* | **191** |
| **Contents of Earlier Volumes** | | **217** |
| **Index** | | **225** |

# PREFACE

In relation to the perspectives of World Trade Organization members, *Progress in Economics Research. Volume 42* examines key policy requirements involved in developing countries' participation in future global e-commerce. This is based on a policy analysis of World Trade Organization e-commerce policies using grounded theory tools of deep-level inquiry.

The authors go on to evaluate economic competitiveness in China, and its position as a global player in comparison with other World Trade Organization members using the Data Envelopment Analysis method.

The dynamics behind socioeconomic inequality in Kenya are examined based on a reinterpretation of previously published works and existing data. In terms of political approaches to economic planning, Kenya has moved from the centralized statist approach in 1963 to a "district focus" strategy in the 1980s; an era of devolved funding from the 1990s and, since 2010, a devolved governance structure. Data from social sectors is highlighted to illustrate trends.

Later, to assess the relationship between development paths and institutions in the Republics of the former Soviet Union, the authors build an index of development based on World Bank data. They consider the impact of governance on economic growth through a new index, also created from World Bank data.

Also in relation to the former Soviet Union, the authors demonstrate that exemptions from taxation can be arbitrarily denied by fiscal authorities under invented pretexts. A stockholder and investor should know that, even in the course of simple transactions, he or she can encounter decisions of authorities contradictory to the law, misquoting of the legal codes by civil servants in their correspondence, backdating of official letters and embezzlement of registered letters.

The closing chapter studies the Spanish fishing and processing sector of anchovy, analyzing its trade balance and prices for preparation to characterize the current situation of this sector at the national level. Production and economic performance are analyzed in the local, European and global context to define trends affecting the management of this species.

Chapter 1 - The option for developing countries to share in the growth of global trade has been always an integral part of WTO different declarations. This should also include developing country participation in global e-commerce. However, e-commerce studies show a significant non-uniform development of this mode of trade between developed and developing countries. In relation to the perspectives of WTO members, this paper will examine the key policy requirements and barriers involved in developing countries participating in future global e-commerce. This will be based on a policy analysis of WTO e-commerce policies using grounded theory tools of deep-level inquiry. The study will focus on the range of relevant issues raised in WTO member proposals and discussions on e-commerce since 1998. These suggest that contrary to the defined WTO's objectives, double standards and asymmetries against developing countries exist in e-commerce too as well as in conventional trade and commerce. It will propose that the WTO needs to adopt a more inclusive approach to the challenging issues of e-commerce which can and should bring the benefits of e-commerce to developing countries.

Chapter 2 - Globalization generally refers to the process of the broadening and deepening of interrelationships in international trade and foreign investment. The outcome is the creation of a global marketplace for goods and services that is largely indifferent to national borders and governmental influence. Openness to trade, investment and even the movement of people is vital for prosperity, peace and individual freedom. Also, there have been few better moments in history where trade played the central role in global growth, job creation and development. The current economic circumstances are full of challenges. Rapid technological change coupled with falls in barriers to international trade, have driven it. Also, the World Trade Organization (WTO) agreements and regional treaties forced domestic markets to open up. This development and the current wave of globalization of the economy has generated widespread interest among countries and within countries in the development and upgrading of national competitiveness. The current economic circumstances are full of challenges, especially in the meaning of new global economic powers such as China. China has come a long way since the 1978 election of President Deng Xiaoping heralded a new era of market-oriented reforms. From 1980 to 2010, its economy grew 18-fold, averaging 10 percent a year. It progressed from low-income to upper-middle income country status, lifting hundreds of millions out of poverty: by 2011 just 6 percent of people were in extreme poverty, compared with 61 percent in 1990. Recent developments – including the weakening of the yuan, the stock market crash, rapid credit growth, and a stalling property market – have cast some doubt on China's economic prospects. Yet a hard landing of the Chinese economy still seems unlikely. China has the opportunity to be a global leader in a number of important areas that will be the cornerstones of global growth in the next decades and this is also challenging as well as the threat for the other WTO members and their competitiveness. The chapter focuses on evaluating the Chinese competitiveness and its position as a global player in comparison with the WTO members with using the Data Envelopment Analysis (DEA) method. Efficiency analysis is based on countries belonging to the relevant stage of economic development. Countries face very different challenges and priorities as they move from resource-based via investment-based to knowledge-based economies, which influences their competitive advantages and also disadvantages. The applicability and efficacy of the suggested approach are illustrated by a real data set involving 137 WTO members (from the whole 164 WTO members) within the factors of competitiveness (6 inputs and 6 outputs) based on the Global Competitiveness Index (GCI) in the period from 2007 to 2017, i.e., pre-in-post crises years. A quantitative score of competitiveness will facilitate WTO members in identifying possible weaknesses together with factors mainly driving these weaknesses.

Chapter 3 - Development policy in Kenya after independence sought to improve the socio-economic conditions of citizens. The leadership of the nationalist movement aimed to redress the racial, ethnic and gender inequalities that characterized society during the colonial period. The government has since independence in 1963, engaged different approaches to achieve these objectives through periodic national development plans. The emphasis and focus of the development policy have shifted over time due to persistent internal challenges and the exigencies of the external environment. The shifts in policy planning, however, have not redressed socio-economic challenges. Instead, each subsequent policy has produced contradictions, causing a small percentage of growth sectors and wealthy individuals, while informalizing production processes in many sectors of the economy and widening socio-economic marginalization of most of the population. In terms of political approaches to economic planning, Kenya has moved from the centralized statist approach in 1963 to an experimentation with a 'district focus' strategy in the 1980s; an era of devolved funding from the 1990s and, since 2010, a devolved governance structure. Shifts in approaches to socio-economic development and political organization have only exacerbated the problem of socio-economic inequalities. This chapter seeks to examine the dynamics behind these persistent challenges. The chapter is based on a re-interpretation of already published works and existing data. Data from social sectors that most manifest socio-economic inequalities will be highlighted to illustrate the trends.

Chapter 4 - Twenty-five years ago, the Soviet Union broke up and its 15 Republics gained independence. The present paper analyses their respective levels of development and quality of governance. To assess the relation between development paths and institutions in the Republics of the former Soviet Union, the authors build an index of development, FSD, based on the World Bank data. Then the authors consider the impact of governance on economic growth through a new index, the FSG, elaborated from World

Bank data as well. The two indices are highly correlated. Not unexpectedly, FSG shows a significant correlation also with the Adjusted Human Development Index (AHDI): human development can be encouraged by fair institutions. On the contrary, rate of growth and FSD have a weak correlation; apparently, the latter conveys more information than the mere growth of GDP.

Chapter 5 - According to Russian legislation, the income-tax is collected from funds obtained from selling of securities. There have been exemptions, depending on the time the property had been owned by a taxpayer, and newly also on the date when it was acquired. The legislation has been modified several times being hardly transparent for non-professionals. The aim of this chapter was to demonstrate that exemptions from taxation can be arbitrarily denied by fiscal authorities under invented pretexts. A stockholder and investor should know that, even in the course of simple transactions, he or she can encounter decisions of authorities contradictory to the law, misquoting of the legal codes by civil servants in their correspondence, backdating of official letters, embezzlement of registered letters etc. Stockholders receive numerous letters and telephone calls from brokers prompting to sell the stock sometimes at prices below the market value. Brokers dispose of confidential information about stockholders: not only their names, addresses and telephone numbers but also names and quantities of their securities etc., which indicates that they have access to databases of depositaries. Besides, some aspects of taxation of immobile property (owner-occupied apartments) are discussed.

Chapter 6 - Anchovy (*Engraulis encrasicolus*) is a widespread pelagic species in the East Central Atlantic, the Mediterranean and the Black Sea. It is a species of great commercial importance, which presents great fluctuations depending on environmental conditions. Spain is the EU country with the largest catch of anchovy, and there is also an important processing and canning sector in this country, where some fishing ports have specialized in preparations such as salting or marinating. The Spanish fisheries for anchovy include ICES sub-area VIII (Bay of Biscay), where the French fisheries also operate, and Division IXa (Iberian Atlantic waters), where the Portuguese fleets also operate. It is important to note that the

Spanish fisheries operate mainly with purse seiners in Sub-area VIII and with purse seiners and trawlers in Division IXa. Anchovy is the target species in Sub-area VIII and Sub-area IXa-S, while occasionally it is targeted (when abundant) in the northern part of Division IXa (southern Galicia), where sardine is the target species. The management of this type of fisheries has also presented challenges for the Spanish fishing community, for example, when the fisheries in the Bay of Biscay were closed between 2005 and 2009, due to extremely poor stock conditions. This chapter studies the Spanish fishing and processing sector of anchovy, analyzing with special attention its trade balance and prices for preparation to characterize the current situation of this sector at national level. Production and economic performance are analyzed in the local, European and global context to define trends affecting the management of this species.

In: Progress in Economics Research
Editor: Albert Tavidze
ISBN: 978-1-53615-120-6
© 2019 Nova Science Publishers, Inc.

*Chapter 1*

# WTO GLOBAL E-COMMERCE POLICY DISCUSSIONS AND THE CHALLENGE OF DEVELOPING COUNTRY PARTICIPATION

*Farrokh Farrokhnia*[1,*,†], *PhD*
*and Cameron K. Richards*[2], *PhD*

[1]The Perdana School of Science, Technology and Innovation Policy, University Technology Malaysia, Johor Bahru, Malaysia
[2]Cameron Richards, Faculty of Education, Southern Cross University, Lismore, Australia

## ABSTRACT

The option for developing countries to share in the growth of global trade has been always an integral part of WTO different declarations. This should also include developing country participation in global e-commerce. However, e-commerce studies show a significant non-uniform

---

[*] Corresponding Author Email: farokhnia@ymail.com.
[†] This article partly reflects the focus of Farrokh Farroknia's doctoral thesis on "A Constructivist Grounded Theory Study of WTO's Negotiations on E-commerce Policy and Regulation" completed at the University Technology Malaysia.

development of this mode of trade between developed and developing countries. In relation to the perspectives of WTO members, this paper will examine the key policy requirements and barriers involved in developing countries participating in future global e-commerce. This will be based on a policy analysis of WTO e-commerce policies using grounded theory tools of deep-level inquiry. The study will focus on the range of relevant issues raised in WTO member proposals and discussions on e-commerce since 1998. These suggest that contrary to the defined WTO's objectives, double standards and asymmetries against developing countries exist in e-commerce too as well as in conventional trade and commerce. It will propose that the WTO needs to adopt a more inclusive approach to the challenging issues of e-commerce which can and should bring the benefits of e-commerce to developing countries.

# INTRODUCTION

The 1998 *WTO Declaration on Global E-commerce* highlighted the necessity of "taking into account the economic, financial, and development needs of developing countries" (WTO, 1998d). As Datta (2011) has reinforced, there has been a long-term recognition of the potential benefits of e-commerce for this category of countries. The benefits cited for online trade by developing countries in the WTO meetings include: the combating of poverty (WTO, 2011e, 7), the stimulation of economic growth and development (WTO, 2003c, 11), improved bargaining power through greater access to information, and the enhanced ability to better judge market conditions (WTO, 2013b, 14). Accordingly, developing countries might develop e-commerce capacity as part of a wider strategy to fully realize their economic potential (WTO, n.d.-b, para. 7).

Different WTO members have thus agreed that there is a need to enhance the participation of the 'least-developed' developing countries in global e-commerce (WTO, 2011d, 2; WTO, 2002b, 6; WTO, 2012a, 1; WTO, 2013c, 2; WTO, 2013c, 2; WTO, 2012b, 1; WTO, 2012d, 1). Nonetheless, subsequent studies have shown a non-uniform development of e-commerce between developed and developing countries (UNCTAD, 2010). In other words, developing countries have notably lagged behind developed countries in e-commerce (Molla and Heeks, 2007). Consequently, there is general recognition in the WTO that such a challenge needs to be addressed and urgently so (WTO, 2011f).

The aim of this paper is to be able to better understand and also address the key requirements and barriers of participation by developing countries in global e-commerce. It will proceed in terms of a deep-level exploring and interpreting of the policy issues implicit in the WTO members' proposals and discussions on e-commerce issues since the establishment of the WTO Work Program on e-commerce in 1998. Such an approach is supported by the use of the key grounded theory tools such as *coding* and *theoretical sampling*) as a basis of policy analysis (Farrokhnia & Richards, 2016; Richards & Farrokhnia, 2016). The analysis will focus on statements by WTO members regarding both requirements and barriers to increasing the participation of developing countries to global e-commerce. A juxtaposing of these two main policy emphases shows that the existing WTO approach to e-commerce is not in line with the WTO *Declaration on Global E-commerce*. This declaration proclaims that a fundamental objective of this organization should be to assist developing countries with increasing their participation in global e-commerce.

The framework of the study here is as follows. Section two briefly describes the background of the central focus of the paper on how the advantages of e-commerce should also be relevant and applicable to developing countries wishing to participate in global e-commerce. Section three explains the methods used in this study for data gathering and analysis. The fourth section addresses the requirements of helping to increase the participation of developing countries in global e-commerce based on different proposals sent to the WTO Work Program so far. This is followed in section five by an overview (based on statements made by different delegations) of the extent to which the requirements of increasing the participation of developing countries to global e-commerce have been addressed or emphasized by the WTO Work Program and during WTO members' negotiations about related e-commerce issues. On this basis the sixth section concludes that the requirements of increasing participation of developing countries to global e-commerce have not been effectively addressed. Finally, section seven outlines a proposal that there is a need for a fresh and comprehensive approach within the WTO to promoting the participation of developing countries in global e-commerce.

## DEVELOPING COUNTRIES, THE WTO AND GLOBAL GOVERNANCE OF E-COMMERCE

In its second Ministerial Conference in 1998, the WTO adopted a related *Declaration on Global Electronic Commerce*. The Declaration proposed "to establish a comprehensive work program to examine all trade-related issues relating to global e-commerce, taking into account the economic, financial, and development needs of developing countries" (WTO, 1998d). This recognition that developing countries (and associated developmental issues) should be a key pivot of WTO program on global e-commerce partly reflects the related idea that e-commerce should also benefit the participation of developing countries in global trade (Datta, 2011).

E-commerce has thus been considered in a range of WTO policy discussions as a potential stimulator of economic development and sustainable growth in developing countries (WTO, 2002b, 3; WTO, 2003c, 11; WTO, 2001a, 2; WTO, 2002a, 22) as well as a means to combat poverty (WTO, 2007a, 5; WTO, 2011c, 7; WTO, 2002b, 3). These benefits of e-commerce might be obtained by contributing to the "efficiency of economic activities" (WTO, 1999b, 3) and also increasing "opportunities and links with strategies for the future" (WTO, 2009a, 2).

Furthermore, e-commerce has been projected in these related discussions to have an important role to play in the "deeper integration of developing countries and economies in transition into the framework of trade rules" (WTO, 2003c, 10). Online trade is an opportunity for developing and least-developed countries to gain a stronger foothold in the multilateral trading system (WTO, 2001b, 1; WTO, 2013b, 22). E-commerce can empower less developed countries with increased bargaining power through greater access to information and the ability to better judge market conditions (WTO, 2013b, 14) which in turn might or should lead to the promotion and enhancement of exports (WTO, 2001d, 1; WTO, 1998c, 2). Accordingly, it has long been projected in the WTO that developing countries might develop e-commerce to fully realize their economic potential (WTO, n.d.-b, para. 7).

However, while e-commerce has an important potential capacity to sustain economic development in every developmental situation, some WTO Members believe that "the pace of e-commerce evolution and its technological dynamism is beyond the capacity of many developing countries" (WTO, 1999b, 2-3; WTO, 2003a, 3). This is a view reinforced by how developed countries are generally still much more advanced in online trade (Molla & Heeks, 2007). It is a view which also partly reflects the non-uniform development of e-commerce between different countries which has increasingly become recognised as a key challenge for global e-commerce (UNCTAD, 2010).

According to the WTO, the failure of less developed countries to exploit the possibilities of e-commerce provided by the internet has become an urgent challenge in recent years (WTO, 2011f). Narrowing the gap between developed and developing countries has long been considered as "important and urgent" as well as "beneficial to both developed and developing countries alike" (WTO, 1999h, 2). Such an outcome would also lead to the "balanced development of the global economy" (WTO, 1999b, 3) and an effective harnessing of opportunities presented by online trade (WTO, 1999b, 3; WTO, 2003a, 4-5). Likewise, different WTO Members agree that there is a need to enhance the participation of those developing countries 'least-developed' in global e-commerce (WTO, 2011d, 2; WTO, 2002b, 6; WTO, 2012a, 1; WTO, 2013c, 2; WTO, 2013c, 2; WTO, 2012b, 1; WTO, 2012d, 1). In addition, it has been stated that any relevant body of the Work Program should explore appropriate mechanisms to address the relationship between e-commerce and development (WTO, 2013d).

## POLICY ANALYSIS OF WTO DOCUMENTS

Addressing the main research question of this paper requires a deep-level exploring and interpreting of the policy issues implicit in the WTO documents examined. Such an approach is assisted here by the use of the key grounded theory tools *Coding*[1] and *Theoretical Sampling*[2] as part of a strategy of constructive policy analysis. To discover the major requirements and barriers of participation of developing countries to Global E-commerce perceived within WTO Member policy discussions about this since 1998, sets of related WTO documents were analysed through an applied *coding* of the key ideas and concepts informing various discussions and statements. This provided a basis for additional as well as related analytical thoughts and insights about how these codes inform WTO documents, discussion and also policy directions. The result of this process is a network of relationships between different issues and concepts involved in the classification of e-commerce products (Figure 1). Finally, analytical ideas written on this network of policy perspective relationships helped frame the emergence of a more abstract and conceptual code which presents what is happening in the data and can be considered as a basis for interpreting a response to the main research question.

---

[1] Coding refers to sorting, comparing and classifying the segments of relevant data under the emergent categories according to what they indicate for the research problem (See Kathy Charmaz, *Constructing grounded theory: A practical guide through qualitative analysis* (London: Sage Publications Limited, 2014, 45). Throughout this process, new segments of data are constantly compared with existing codes to be categorized under them or to be used as the basis for creating a new code. Coding makes fundamental processes explicit and render hidden assumptions visible (Id, at.133). Codes thus emerge as the data and their meanings are scrutinized (Id, at.133). Coding requires moving beyond concrete statements in the data to analytic interpretations in the form of different levels of abstraction (See Id, at 42 & 45).

[2] Theoretical sampling is defined as "the process of data collection for generating theory whereby the analyst jointly collects, codes and analyses his data and decides what data to collect next and where to find them" (See Barney G. Glaser & Anselm L. Strauss, *The discovery of grounded theory: strategies for qualitative research* 45 (London: AldineTransaction, 1967). The general procedure of theoretical sampling is to elicit codes from the raw data from the start of data collection through constant comparative analysis as the data pour in. Then one uses the codes to direct further data collection, from which the codes are further developed theoretically, with properties and theoretically coded connections with other categories until each category is saturated (See Barney G Glaser, *Emergence vs forcing: Basics of grounded theory analysis* 102 (Sociology Press, 1992).

The WTO documents employed in this study derived from different meetings, discussions, negotiations and proposals on the global e-commerce regulation and governance – items all collected on the WTO online database (WTO Documents Online).[3] The content of these documents therefore reflect the activities of this intergovernmental organization on the global governance of e-commerce, also touching on results achieved and problems faced. The WTO documents are a kind of typical if not definitive archival data or extant text on e-commerce policy that can give the researcher insights into perspectives, practices, and events not easily obtained through other sources or by other qualitative methods (Charmaz, *supra* n.34, 39). This source of data is generally considered "a rich and unique source of research material" (Corti et al., 2012).

The following sections include statements made by delegations from different countries in the meetings of the WTO work program These sections include: 1) statements regarding the requirements of increasing the participation of developing countries to global e-commerce based on different proposals sent to the Work Program; and 2) statements made by delegations mainly from developed countries which are seemingly not in favour of developing countries. However, not all of these statements explicitly address developing country issues and demands. Rather, interpreting and linking these statements to the mentioned demands and desires of developing countries can help depict the barriers as well as requirements which developing countries need to address in order to enhance their participation to the global e-commerce. Juxtaposing these two types of statements can assist with showing the extent to which the requirements of increasing the participation of developing countries to global e-commerce have been addressed or emphasized during the WTO Members' negotiations on e-commerce issues.

---

[3] docsonline.wto.org.

# REQUIREMENTS FOR ENHANCING THE PARTICIPATION OF DEVELOPING COUNTRIES IN GLOBAL E-COMMERCE

This part includes the statements made by different WTO Members regarding the requirements of increasing the participation of developing countries to global e-commerce in the form of different proposals sent to the Work Program or discussions in the WTO meetings.

## Effective Policy Space for Domestic Regulation on E-Commerce

E-commerce development in developing countries, in addition to the technical assistance, requires "an appropriate legal framework" which is "coherent" and "predictable" (WTO, 1998c, 2; WTO, 1998a, 11; WTO, 2003a, 3). Domestic policy and regulation on e-commerce can improve the governments' "revenues" (WTO, 2003d, 4) and market access for enterprises in developing countries through affecting "capacity building," "competition" and "free flow of information" (WTO, 2002c, 4). Accordingly, many WTO Members have mentioned issues like domestic regulatory regimes, national strategies (WTO, 2001a, 3) and "policy frameworks" (WTO, 1998b, 9) as important to e-commerce development in developing countries (WTO, 1998f, 4).

Given "the global and trans-frontier nature of the new communication systems," establishment of "a coherent, predictable, legal and regulatory framework" is vital (WTO, 1998c, 2). Therefore, "the possibility of ensuring appropriate policy spaces" (WTO, 1999f, 1) and establishment of "adequate legal systems" related to the development of e-commerce in developing countries should be guaranteed (WTO, 2003c, 11). Based on this, Cuba, Ecuador, Nicaragua, Bolivia and Venezuela (WTO, 2011e) in their submissions to the WTO Work Program one-commerce have emphasized that implementation of targeted public policies and promotion of "regulatory environments and analysis of best public (government) support practices" are needed to "guarantee the full participation of developing countries in the global market for ICT enabled services" and related activities of e-commerce (WTO, 2011c, 3).

In order to address the above issues, delegations have made further suggestions. For instance, they have recommended "creating a list of policy objectives in the context of Article VI:4 which justifies domestic regulatory measures with restrictive effects in the area of e-commerce" (WTO, 1999k, 10). Another delegation called for an improvement in developing countries' technical capacity "in the formulation of e-commerce-related public policies, laws and regulations resulting from the rights and obligations established in the WTO covered agreements" (WTO, 2011c, 6).

## Fair and Equitable Access to Technology

There is a correlation between the "level of a country's infrastructure development and technology capacity" and the "benefits" which that country can get from e-commerce (WTO, 2000a, 1-2; WTO, 2003a, 2-3 & 7). Hence, "the deeper integration of developing countries into the framework of trade rules" (WTO, 2003f, 2) and filling "the huge digital gaps" (WTO, 2011d, 2) in developing nations require technological improvement, technical assistance and capacity-building projects relating to e-commerce (WTO, 1999k, 10). Access to new technologies is also necessary for developing countries "to incorporate technical standards necessary for ensuring international trade and use national resources to apply them" (WTO, 1999e, 2). Based on this, "a better," "fair," "equitable," "facilitated" and "anon-discriminatory access" to relevant technology as well as "transparent" technical assistance programs are needed to increase the participation of developing countries in global e-commerce (WTO, 2003c, 10; WTO, 1999b, 4; WTO, 2013b, 13-14; WTO, 2011b, 3).

Therefore, "the elimination of all commercial and technological restrictions" regarding access to the technology required for implementation of national plans to develop e-commerce is "a vital condition" for any decision within the WTO in favour of unlimited e-commerce (WTO, 2003c, 10). The need for a non-discriminatory access to e-commerce technology has also been emphasized by the Council for Trade in Services, the World Telecommunication Standardization Assembly and the Article 7 of the TRIPS Agreement (WTO, n.d.-e). Without "a meaningful level of cooperation and assistance" for capacity building in developing countries which lack required resources (WTO, 1999i, 2), such countries "risk being left behind in the technology race" as other countries move ahead with modern systems (WTO, 1999i, 3). Certain measures and "international cooperation" are thus necessary for encouraging technology transfer to least-developed countries and dealing with "anti-competitive practices" (WTO, 2003b, 4; WTO, 2007a, 2-3). Moreover, public policies should be implemented "to secure adequate investment" in key relevant industries (WTO, 1998c, 2) and guarantee the full participation of developing countries in the global market for ICT enabled services (WTO, 2011c, 3).

In line with the above needs, some WTO Members have proposed different solutions (WTO, 1999i, 1; WTO, 1998e, para. 12; WTO, 2011c, 7-8; WTO, 1999g, 3). For instance, both Indonesia and Singapore have suggested that the WTO should have a stronger role in providing developing countries with access to the requisite technology. Venezuela has also suggested that the WTO Ministers should "guarantee the need to access to and transfer of technology" to developing countries (WTO, 1999f, 1). Cuba has put on record its view that the WTO Working Group on Transfer of Technology (as well as the Work Programme on E-Commerce) should consider the growing use of new technologies in e-commerce and the related problems facing developing countries with regard to the transfer of these technologies (WTO, 1999e, 2).

## Sharing Information and Experiences

WTO Members have also pointed out that e-commerce can be beneficial to developing countries in terms of sharing experience through the documentation of innovative solutions and success stories in developing countries (WTO, 1999k, 4). In this context, future work on "successful partnerships between developed countries and developing countries" (WTO,

1999b, 5; WTO, 1999k, 4) and on "collection of information on the present situation in Members (WTO, 2000b, 2) have been suggested by different delegations.

Cuba, Ecuador and Nicaragua (as well as Bolivia and Venezuela (WTO, 2011e) have proposed the establishment of a Working Group for sharing and analyzing experiences as well as "a permanent notification mechanism" for cases in which non-discriminatory access to technology needed for e-commerce development "has been obstructed" (WTO, 2011c, 5-6). Japan has also recommended that developed countries should provide relevant information to extend cooperation toward the smooth participation of developing countries in e-commerce-related markets (WTO, 1999g, 1).

However, it should be mentioned that in the current WTO legal frame work and under the GATS Article IV:2, developing countries service suppliers have access to contact points which are required to provide information related to the commercial and technical aspects of the supply of services - including by electronic means. Developing country suppliers can also obtain information on the availability of relevant services technology, which may be particularly useful in the context of e-commerce (WTO, 1998f, 4).

## Participation by Developing Countries in Global E-Commerce Policymaking

WTO Members have generally emphasized the importance of participation by all countries in global as well as local establishment of an environment that supports the development and adoption of e-commerce (WTO, 2003f, 7; WTO, 2011c, 2; WTO, 2013b, 23). In this context, one delegation has stated that "developing countries should be fully integrated" in the development of standards on e-commerce in order to ensure that such standards do not create barriers to entry for developing countries' firms (WTO, 2001a, 3) and to ensure interoperability, connectivity and their access to e-commerce platforms (WTO, 1999j, 8). A representative of WIPO has also highlighted the need for the participation of developing countries in the discussion of the issues arising as a result of the impact of e-commerce on the intellectual property system (WTO, 2000b, 1).

## Cooperation with UNCTAD

The need to take advantages of work on e-commerce which is being done in other international organizations has been emphasized in different WTO meetings on e-commerce by different Members (WTO, 1999k, 6-7; WTO, 2001a, 3; WTO, 2012a, 1). However, there has been particular attention on the role the WTO cooperation with UNCTAD takes among different international organizations as a step which addresses the developing countries' needs in the global e-commerce (WTO, 1999i, 3). According to some Members, the WTO cooperation with UNCTAD can address the "digital divide" between developed and many developing countries and the need for promoting developing countries' participation in e-commerce (WTO, 2000a, 1). It will also result in "deeper integration of developing countries into the framework of trade rules" by providing technical assistance and capacity-building projects relating to e-commerce (WTO, 2003c, 10) and access to the requisite technology for developing countries (WTO, n.d.-c). This cooperation can be facilitated through "a platform for systematic cooperation and coordination" with inter alia UNCTAD (WTO, 1999i, 4).

In this context, Cuba, Ecuador and Nicaragua have proposed work in conjunction with UNCTAD, ITU and WIPO "to monitor solutions to the problems faced by developing countries in using e-commerce as a tool for development" and assess "the adoption of any other decisions or measures within the WTO framework" (WTO, 2011c, 6) [Bolivia and Venezuela later requested to be added as a co-sponsor of this document (WTO, 2011e]. Indonesia and Singapore have also expressed the opinion that the WTO cooperation with UNCTAD will clarify the types of technical assistance and capacity building programs that need to be provided for developing countries (WTO, 2003a, 2).

## Liberalization in Areas of Export Interest for Developing Countries

A number of WTO Members believe that liberalization in areas of export interest for developing countries (especially in terms of the implementation of Article IV of the GATS) can enhance the participation of developing countries in the global trade (WTO, 2005a, 4; WTO, 1999e, 1; WTO, 2001d, 1). In the same context, the WTO has stated that liberalization through cross-border delivery involving the trading partners of developing countries' (Mode 1under the GATS) facilitates sales of certain labour-intensive services in which developing countries have a comparative advantage. However, they have so far been unable to exploit such a proposed advantage because of restrictions on the movement of natural persons (WTO, 1998f, 4; WTO, 1999a, 2). Moreover, to this end, developing countries should be helped to build the capacity to exploit the "further liberalization of telecommunications services under the GATS" (WTO, n.d.-c, para. 3).

## An Efficient Special and Differential Treatment for Developing Countries

Cuba has stated that the application or consideration of provisions to guarantee Special and Differential Treatment (SDT) for developing countries is necessary for the continued liberalization of trade on a fair and equitable basis should be one of the key aims of the WTO, and also global e-commerce (WTO, 1999e, 2). Venezuela has also suggested that the "Ministers should agree to guarantee the particular needs of developing countries including Special and Differential Treatment" (WTO, 1999f, 1). In the same vein, Uganda and China have emphasized the importance of this issue (WTO, 2006, 1). They have proposed that provisions on Special and Differential Treatment should be without delay "operative and obligatory" (WTO, 2006, 1).

It is worth noting that the state of implementation of Special and Differential Treatment in traditional trade has not been efficient enough for developing countries – but rather has been regarded as "a deep source of concern" (Babu, 2011). To many developing countries SDT is "meaningless and is thus fundamentally flawed," without a "clear scope" and "has not promoted development but rather discouraged developing countries to engage in the process of reciprocal liberalization of trade" (Hoekman et al., 2004). Utilizing SDT by small developing countries has also resulted in an "insignificant" increase in their exports (Shafaeddin, 2010). There are thus many proposals, mostly from LDCs, suggesting that the SDT needs to "be made mandatory" and "easier to implement" (Kobori, 2003) "as a rule not as an exception" (Shafaeddin, 2010). Many scholars thus believe that the "long-term viability" of the WTO (Hoekmanet al., 2004) - including maintaining it and consequently the "stability of the world economy" (Mah, 2011) - is not possible without "recasting" or improving the SDT.

## Adequate Human Resources and Training

In the field of e-commerce, one of the main concerns of policy makers in developing countries has been that many businesses lack an adequate "understanding of the implication of the world trading body" and also of the role and function "market destination, with respect to trade and non-trade barriers, as well as business and social culture" (WTO, n.d.-c; paras. 10&15). Developing countries thus need to adjust their education systems to prepare young people for e-commerce as a "new reality" (WTO, 2013a, 3). Therefore, policies are required to ensure adequate levels of digital literacy globally (WTO, 2011a, 3), and to address "the problem of human resource training" (WTO, 1999e, 2; WTO, 2003a, 5). Moreover, then, investment in human infrastructure including "specialized education and training" is important for e-commerce development in developing countries (WTO, 1998a, 11).

## Contribution of Other WTO Programs or Bodies

In various WTO Members' discussions and proposals on governance of global e-commerce, other WTO committees, working groups or Agreements have been mentioned as contributions to the WTO work program on how to enhance the participation of developing countries in global e-commerce. This includes the Committee on Trade and Development, the Committee on Trade and Development (CTD), the Agreement on Technical Barriers to Trade and the WTO Aid for Trade initiative.

The role of CTD in strengthening the capacity of countries to take advantage of e-commerce and also narrow the digital divide has been emphasized on the WTO website (WTO, n.d.-c). The delegation from Egypt has also suggested that it is appropriate to discuss the issue of electronic trade in goods and services in the CTD (WTO, 2003a, 2). The General Council should thus request the CTD to examine the developmental implications of e-commerce taking into account the economic, financial and development needs of developing countries. Such an inquiry should focus on the benefits that e-commerce can bring to developing countries (WTO, 1999k; WTO, 2002c, 1; WTO, 1999k, 10). It has been also recommended to create a Working Group under the CTD to comprehensively address the developmental dimension of the Work Programme on e-commerce (WTO, 2011c, 5).

The Agreement on Technical Barriers to Trade tries to ensure these regulations do not create unnecessary obstacles, while also providing Members with the right to implement measures to achieve legitimate policy objectives. This is particularly important because technical regulations and product standards may vary from country to country. Also, if regulations are set arbitrarily, they could be used as an excuse for protectionism (WTO, n.d.-d, paras. 1-2). As Cuba has suggested, the involvement of this Agreement in the Work Programme on E-commerce might emphasise how technical standards should not become trade barriers for developing countries. The access to the technologies required to apply these standards should be guaranteed (WTO, 1999e, 2).

The WTO Aid for Trade initiative encourages developing country governments and donors to recognize the role that trade can play in national and global development. In particular, the initiative seeks to mobilize resources to address the trade-related constraints identified by developing and least-developed countries (WTO, n.d.-a, para.1). Some developing countries believe that incorporation of e-commerce in the Aid-for-Trade initiative can help enhance their participation in the global e-commerce (WTO, 2011d, 3).

Finally, given the implications of e-commerce for developing countries, Cuba, Ecuador and Nicaragua have proposed setting up a working group on the relationship between e-commerce and development. The proposed working group would be open to the participation of all Members and operate under the auspices of the Committee on Trade and Development "to promote the use of e-commerce by developing countries as a tool for development and poverty reduction" (WTO, 2011c, 5) Bolivia and Venezuela later requested to be added as a co-sponsor of this document (WTO, 2011e). This Working Group should provide inter alia actions such as the sharing and analysis of experiences, the analysis of best government support practices, the consideration of new alternatives and regulatory issues, and the study of institutional issues.

## Issues Requiring Further Studies

In addition to the issues discussed above, there are two additional points regarding the enhancements of participation by developing countries in global e-commerce which the WTO Members have suggested to be studied further:

### *The Role of Institutional Capacity*

In their discussion on the factors limiting e-commerce in developing countries, Cuba, Ecuador, Nicaragua, Bolivia and Venezuela have mentioned institutional and infrastructure capacity as an item which should be promoted through more study in "a working group on the relationship between e-commerce and development" (WTO, 2011c, 6; WTO, 2011e). The importance of institutional issues for e-commerce development has been also generally mentioned in some other meetings and documents (WTO, 2005a, 9; WTO, 2007b, 1&44; WTO, 2013a, 1).

### *E-Commerce and SMEs in Developing Countries*

The use of e-commerce by micro, small, and medium-sized enterprises can lead to achieving the benefits that e-commerce can bring to developing countries to enhance their trade. Accordingly, different WTO members have commented on the need for "facilitating discussions" on this issue (WTO, 1999j; WTO, 2011c, WTO, 2012a, 1; WTO, 2013c, 2; WTO, 2012b, 1; WTO, 2012c, 1). The CTD (Committee on Trade and Development) has also proposed further study on impact of e-commerce on "supply and demand for particular goods and services," "domestic producers," "competition" and "inter-firm relations" of enterprises in developing countries in order to achieve the potential benefits of e-commerce for these countries (WTO, 2000a, 2). Similarly, the delegation of Egypt has pointed out that further examination should be made of the impacts of e-commerce and recent proposals on a possible global framework for e-commerce on "the supply and demand of goods and services," the market structure, labour markets and competition (WTO, 2003a, 3).

# BARRIERS TO THE PARTICIPATION OF DEVELOPING COUNTRIES IN GLOBAL E-COMMERCE

This part includes an analysis and discussion of statements made by delegations in the meetings of the WTO work program which are not in favour of developing countries. However, there are few explicit statements about developing countries in the relevant documents. Rather, in order to depict the conflicts between developed and developing countries, the discussions are interpreted and compared with mentioned demands and desires of developing countries in WTO meetings discussed in section 4.

## Challenges in Fulfilling Domestic Regulatory Objectives for Electronic Transactions

An analysis of various WTO member statements on the topic of global e-commerce shows that, despite the vital role of domestic policy and regulation for e-commerce development, discussions on this area tended to be mainly limited to the likely restrictive effects of domestic regulations on trade (WTO, 2003c, 10; WTO, 2003f, 2). Some WTO members claim that "the adoption of WTO trade rules in services reduces the areas of domestic policies which can be manoeuvred particularly in developing countries" (WTO, n.d.-c, paras 6 & 11). In the same document mention is made of the "challenge of "reconciling the need to protect the national interest with the need to benefit from services liberalization" in the field of e-commerce. The WTO rules confront developing countries with "constraints" or "challenges" in creating "legal underpinning for electronic transactions" and "fulfilling legitimate domestic regulatory objectives" (WTO, 1999l, 3; WTO, 2001c, 19). "The need to protect society and the rights of individuals" (WTO, 2002c, 4) or the incapability of the GATS Article XVI to address "all the measures governments may take" have been mentioned by some WTO Members in relevant discussions as further instances of the diverse voices which make up the WTO discussion on e-commerce.

It is worth noting that in the area of traditional trade (vis-à-vis e-commerce) different scholars have already emphasized the need for the WTO in general to better consider and provide appropriate policy space for the socio-economic differences of developing countries (Wolfe, 2004, Wade, 2005, Bown and McCulloch, 2007, Karapinar, 2011). Nonetheless, it seems that the WTO has a history of tending to be either ignorant or resistant about the required policy space to better support the local imperatives of developing countries (Wade, 2003, Gallagher, 2005, UNDP, 2005, Khan, 2007, Natsuda and Thoburn, 2014, He, 2011, Moon, 2011, Qin, 2012). While the proposals submitted to the WTO by poor and middle-income countries have largely emphasized the need for more flexibility and 'policy space' (Hoekman et al., 2004), the proposals from developed countries during the Doha Round were to encourage poor nations to give up their "sovereignty to deploy effective development policies" for insignificant potential benefits (Gallagher, 2008). These proposals could thus "limit the policy space of developing countries" and "lock lower-income countries, with little industrial capacity, in exports of commodities with little effect on economic development (Shafaeddin, 2010). On this basis, the policy options permitted under the WTO agreements have been called "developed country friendly" (Mah, 2011).

## Limited and Discriminatory Access to Relevant Technology

Despite different WTO Members emphasising the important role of technical barriers to e-commerce development in developing countries, access of these countries to the technology required for e-commerce is typically limited. Different WTO Members have considered the limited and discriminatory access to the internet and the necessary telecommunication and information technology infrastructure as a "problem" or even "the major obstacle" to expansion of e-commerce in developing countries and "participation of developing countries in global e-commerce" (WTO, 1999e, 1; WTO, 2013b, 24; WTO, 2011c, 3). One delegation has argued that due to the lack of access to technology, online trade is "almost non-existent for many developing countries" (WTO, 2003c, 10). The limited access by companies from developing countries to technologies, ideas or solutions which have already been patented is further inhibiting the expansion of e-commerce and preventing the use of some related technologies. This issue is a key factor in the "unequal competition imposed by developed countries" and subsequently "the late entry of developing countries" into e-commerce (WTO, 1999e, 1).

In their discussion on the factors limiting e-commerce in developing countries Cuba, Ecuador and Nicaragua have pointed out the significant difference between the infrastructural development (broadband connections and prices, fixed telephones, mobile telephones, number of personal computers) in the region of eighteen Latin American countries[4] comparing to developed countries. Together with Bolivia and Venezuela (WTO, 2011e), these countries, believe in "the discriminatory conditions relating to international access to technology needed for e-commerce (WTO, 2011c, 3). This general obstacle is mainly created by issues of "concentration of technological resources within a few international companies," "monopolies and cartels in the telecommunications equipment market" as well as "the high cost of technologies" (WTO, 2001c, 25; WTO, 2011c, 3). In this context, one WTO Member has stated that:

The main networks, known as 'backbones', are controlled by the largest telecommunications operators which establish fee waiver agreements among similar companies and apply discriminatory access conditions and costs for internet service providers of developing countries passing through their network (WTO, 2011c, 3). According to a communication from a developing country, "several developing country members of the WTO have been prevented from participating in the Global Project of the International Telecommunication Union (ITU), owing to the United States unilateral and coercive policy." These restrictions are "further widening the digital gap between countries" "hampering international trade" and have many negative consequences for both the developing countries (WTO, 2001d, 2).

The relevant technologies mentioned by different WTO members include technologies required for data protection (WTO, 2001d, 1; WTO, 2011c, 3), payment systems (WTO, 2011c, 3), authentication of documents (WTO, 1999e, 2; WTO, 2011c, 3), digital signature and encryption techniques (WTO, 2001c, 21) and content and privacy regulation and the fiscal implications of e-commerce (WTO, 2011c, 3). In addition, developing countries need appropriate data storage hardware (WTO, 2001d, 2) and secure servers (WTO, 2002a, 14; WTO, 2013b, 25).

---

[4] Argentina, Bolivia, Brazil, Chile, Colombia, Dominican Republic, Ecuador, Guatemala, Honduras, Mexico, Nicaragua, Panama, Peru, Puerto Rico, Paraguay, El Salvador, Uruguay and Venezuela.

## An Unjustified Extension of the Moratorium on the Imposition of Custom Duties on E-Commerce

Since the establishment of the WTO Work Program on E-commerce, many members have agreed to "maintain the current practice of not imposing customs duties on electronic transmissions until our next session." This is in fact a constant part of the Ministerial Declarations at the Second Ministerial Declaration in Geneva, Switzerland in 1998 (WTO, 1998d, 1), at the Fourth Ministerial Declaration in Doha in 2001 (WTO, 2001b, 7) at the sixth Ministerial Declaration in 2005 (WTO, 2005a, 8) at the seventh Ministerial Declaration in 2009 (WTO, 2009c, 1) at the eighth Ministerial Declaration in 2011 (WTO, 2011f, 1) and at the last or the Ninth Ministerial Declaration in 2013 (WTO, 2012e, 1).

However, the issue of the extension of the Moratorium on customs duties on electronic transmissions has been one of the controversial issues in the WTO members' discussions on e-commerce (WTO, 2013c, 2). Some members firmly believe that the Moratorium should become permanent because it is a step through which the e-commerce benefits extend to all economies (WTO, 2003f, 6; WTO, 2005c, 1; WTO, 2009b, 4). However other members have a view that the Moratorium and its implications for developing countries is not a straightforward issue and requires a deeper examination of the related issues (WTO, 2005c, 1).

Critics of making the Moratorium permanent (who are mainly from developing countries) believe that the Moratorium has "important implications" for their revenues and fiscal policies (WTO, 2001a, 3; WTO, 2000a, 2; WTO, 2003d, 4). They state when "cross-border e-commerce has developed throughout the world…it is probably important not to forgo sales taxes on it" (WTO, 2003d, 6). The revenue loss resulting from the Moratorium can be thus "substantial" particularly when the "technological means of applying customs duties" on electronic transmissions have "changed substantially" (WTO, 2003d, 4). In this situation, "the question is no longer one of technology but whether a Member wishes to impose customs duties on e-commerce" (WTO, 2003d, 5).

Accordingly, there is a need for "a deeper examination of the long-term impact of the Moratorium" (WTO, 2001a, 4). Also, the "implications" of the practice of not imposing custom duties on e-commerce "should be clarified" and "considered carefully" before becoming "permanent and binding" (WTO, 2005b, 2; WTO, 2009b, 3). Particularly, "the development dimension" of the Moratorium, as a "highly sensitive and important" issue, requires a "comprehensive and substantive work" (WTO, 2011d, 4). On this basis, developing countries such as Indonesia and Mongolia have expressed their concerns regarding the implications of Moratorium on their "economic, financial and development needs" and have asked for "a comprehensive examination" in this regard (WTO, 1999c, 5) and "developing clearer and more specific rules" (WTO, 1999d, 2).

The delegations from some developing countries have also stated that sales taxes are the bulk of their fiscal revenues - and foregoing them on e-commerce can mean "a substantial loss of revenue." Thus, there are revenue implications for developing countries where companies doing business online often do not pay tax - unlike most service suppliers operating conventionally. While this "loss" might not involve large sums of money, in many developing countries a little revenue goes a long way (WTO, 2003d, 5). On this basis, some delegations from African countries agree in essence with the imposition of custom duties on e-commerce and have stated their reluctance or hesitation to make the Moratorium permanent (WTO, 2003c, 14). This is to the extent that one delegation has clearly said "there should be no extension of the Moratorium" (WTO, 2009b, 3).

Developing countries thus see necessary substantive work on justifying any extension of the Moratorium. Any decision on this issue should thus include the right of Members to regulate and to implement development policies (WTO, 2009b, 3; WTO, 2005b, 4).

## A Political Approach to E-Commerce Issues

According to some WTO members, barriers to the enhancement of developing countries in the global e-commerce have in some cases been politically motivated. For example: several developing country members of the WTO have been prevented from participating in the Global Project of the International Telecommunication Union (ITU), owing to the United States unilateral and coercive policy" in violation of the rules and principles of international trade (WTO, 2001d, 2). Similarly, the issues of classification (WTO, 2002c, 4) and the Moratorium on the imposition of customs duties on electronic transmissions have been seen as influenced by "political" decisions by Ministers (WTO, 1999k, 10; WTO, 2003c, 12). This issue raises a question mark about the competency of the WTO Work Program (WTO, 2003c, 12). As earlier discussed in Section 3, it also might have other implications for developing countries. For instance, as a developing country Cuba has stated that:

We underline the necessity and importance of eliminating across the board all types of politically motivated restrictions, whether commercial or technological, including those affecting the purchase and free use of encryption technologies and hardware available on the market, as they constrain the development of global e-commerce and the full incorporation of all developing countries as an indispensable condition for reaching a multilateral agreement or decision within the WTO framework in favour of unrestricted e-commerce (WTO, 2001d, 2).

## Exaggerating the Role of Market Openness in Digital Trade

A thorough analysis of the WTO documents on e-commerce depicts how developed countries'[5] tend to exaggerate the role of liberalization in global e-commerce development. This approach considers the "highest level" of market openness for e-commerce products as a "crucial step," "a key consideration" and as a condition for "promotion" of global trade that "creates a win-win situation" for "economies at all levels of development" (WTO, 2003f, 3-5). As a result of such an approach the European Union (EU) and the United States have jointly designed a set of principles to

---

[5] The United States, Japan, Canada and EU.

enhance the development of e-commerce with an exaggerated focus on liberalization as a pretext for often avoiding mention of the particular needs of developing countries (WTO, 2003e). The tendency to overemphasize the role of market openness in digital trade is particularly evident when the United States proposed that greater liberalization should be the main objective of the WTO Work Program on e-commerce (WTO, 1999m, 1). It should be kept in mind that in the WTO Marrakesh Agreement "more liberalization" is mentioned as merely a way to contribute to the main objectives of this organization. Inter alia this includes the commitment "to ensure that developing countries and especially the least developed among them, secure a share in the growth in international trade commensurate with the needs of their economic development" (WTO, 1994, 1).

Some scholars believe that there is no reliable and sustained evidence about the benefits of deregulation and liberalization for economic growth in all conditions (Friedman, 2002, Cordoba et al., 2005, Stiglitz, 2005, Subramanian and Wei, 2007, Lewis, 2007, Koester, 2008, Eicher and Henn, 2011). On the contrary, it is becoming clearer over time that some kinds of regulation appropriate to different situations are necessary for sustained economic growth (Stiglitz, 2005). The proposed liberalization recommended by some developed countries is not "optimized relative to development" (Winters, 2007). Rather this has caused some developing countries to lose control of domestic industries and resulted in "indirect discriminatory impacts" in countries like Nicaragua and Ghana (Friedman, 2002). However, such adverse effects are not usually detected in straightforward fashion (Moon, 2011). Besides, further borrowing for covering the "unpredictable economic and social costs" of liberalization and "minimizing the burden of adjustment" are not usually the first priority for the nations which are "already highly indebted" and are losing more tariff revenues. In other word, for developing countries the disadvantages of liberalization often outweigh the advantages (Cordoba et al., 2005).

## THE INADEQUATE ADDRESSING OF THE GLOBAL E-COMMERCE NEEDS OF DEVELOPING COUNTRIES

The analysis of the proposals and discussions on e-commerce issues by WTO Members since the establishment of WTO Work Program on e-commerce provides the basis for identifying the emergence of fourteen Initial Codes. These can be further categorized in terms of two sets of issues considered as Focused Codes in the sense of the grounded theory method: 1) *Requirements for enhancing the participation of DCs to the global e-commerce* and 2) *Barriers to enhancement of the participation of DCs in global e-commerce*. The first Focused Code reflects the requirements of e-commerce development in developing countries which have been left unaddressed (not encountered opposition nor been supported by developed countries during the negotiations). In contrast, the second Focused Codes is made up of the issues which have been explicitly criticized by developing countries and to this end have been identified as barriers or obstacles. Juxtaposing these two Focused Codes can give us a picture of the extent to which developing countries needs and conditions have been addressed during the WTO course of negotiations on e-commerce issues since 1998.

Figure 1 shows the relationships between the Initial Codes, Focused Codes and the Analytical Category which emerged during data collection and analysis. This Figure depicts the inadequate attention paid to the requirements of increasing the participation of developing countries to global e-commerce during the WTO negotiations on e-commerce. This is further evidenced by proposals submitted to the WTO Work Program on E-commerce which in general "contains practically nothing regarding development and developing countries per se as a group" (WTO, 2003c, 10). Such a situation can be implicitly linked to the digital divide or gap between developed and developing countries in the field of e-commerce which has been pointed out by different WTO Members (WTO, 2013b, 5; WTO, 2011c, 2; WTO, 2011a, 3; WTO, 2003a, 5; WTO, 2013b, 7; WTO, 2005a, 2). As illuminated by Cuba "the adverse consequences of cases of discrimination in e-commerce" affects "development in underdeveloped country Members" in a way that is inconsistent with WTO rules" (WTO, 2006, 1-2).

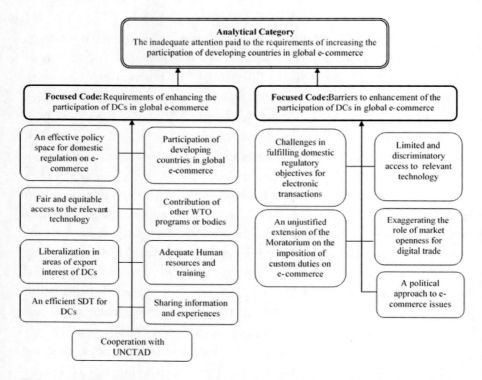

Figure 1. Requirements and barriers affecting the participation of developing countries in global e-commerce: A grounded theory framework for analysing WTO policy discussions and directions.

This appears to repeat the negative history of the WTO when it comes to policy frameworks for the role of developing countries in conventional trade (REF). In the realm of conventional trade (vis-à-vis e-commerce), the WTO has been also accused of creating "implicit discrimination" against developing countries and allowing developed countries to refuse the unpleasant demands of developing countries and even forcing them to liberalize some sectors (Braga, 2005). This has resulted in a sense of dissatisfaction expressed by many of developing countries (Shafaeddin, 2010) and has made the "presumed beneficiaries" of the WTO its main critics (Smith, 2004). This is particularly so because the functions of the

WTO framework do not include looking for the "best policies for the global public interest" (Lafont, 2010). Rather it appears to include little regard for the socio-economic characteristics of developing countries (Stiglitz, 2005). And such a condition for conventional trade therefore appears to many to be repeated in the domain of e-commerce – which some WTO Members believe should be considered as a new phenomenon requiring new rules.

## CONCLUSION: THE NEED FOR A COMPREHENSIVE APPROACH TO THE GLOBAL E-COMMERCE NEEDS OF DEVELOPING COUNTRIES

As was indicated above, an analysis of the proposals and discussions on e-commerce issues involving WTO members (since the establishment of WTO Work Program on e-commerce) depicts the inadequate attention paid to the requirements of increasing the participation of developing countries in global e-commerce. In other words, the current WTO approach to e-commerce cannot ensure that developing countries, and especially the least developed among them, secure a share in the growth of not only global e-commerce but international trade generally. Therefore, the WTO is not assisting such countries with their various economic development needs. Also, it is not fulfilling some key promises or assurances of its organisational charter and related fundamental objectives. Imbalances and asymmetries between developed and developing countries in the WTO can threaten the legitimacy and survival of the WTO (Narlikar and Wilkinson, 2004). This would also have adverse socio-political consequences for the international community with little or no hope for fair treatment in the future (Shafaeddin, 2010).

In this paper we have discussed how the current WTO approach to e-commerce is not in line with the WTO's own Declaration on Global E-commerce. In other words, the dominant WTO policy approach to e-commerce has been at odds with one of the fundamental objectives of this organization: the commitment to better support and encourage greater participation by developing countries in global e-commerce. A deep-level exploring and interpreting of the policy issues implicit in the proposals and discussions of WTO Members on e-commerce issues reveals that requirements for and barriers to enhancing the participation of developing countries in global e-commerce have generally been left unaddressed by the WTO Work Program on E-commerce. The existing approach and process cannot thus guarantee that developing countries secure a share in the growth in international online trade commensurate with their economic development needs.

Furthermore, it seems that similar to conventional trade, double standards and asymmetries against developing countries also exist in terms of e-commerce too. The WTO is not providing sufficient or adequate assurance that proposed rules designed in favour of developing countries in this domain will be effectively implemented without being nullified by political motivations. As developing countries represent some three quarters of the WTO's membership, the multilateral trading system can only function when fully taking into account the needs and priorities of those very same countries (Smeets, 2013).

In conclusion, the WTO thus requires a more comprehensive and coordinated approach on e-commerce regulation which is able to better address the mentioned requirements for and barriers to the enhancement of the participation of developing countries in global e-commerce. In its future negotiations for a better WTO framework for global e-commerce, the WTO should adopt a more holistic approach to e-commerce challenging issues. Such an approach might better recognise and engage with key socio-economic and political factors for bringing about the benefits of e-commerce to developing countries, and to also narrow the gap between developed and developing countries in overall international trade. This might lead to a more balanced development of global e-commerce which can and should be beneficial to both developed and developing countries alike.

## REFERENCES

Babu R. R. 2011. "Cause and effect of 'differentiation' between developing countries in the WTO." *International Journal of Private Law* 4(3):342-53.

Bown C. P. and McCulloch R. 2007. "Trade adjustment in the WTO system: are more safeguards the answer?" *Oxford Review of Economic Policy* 23(3):415-39.

Braga C. A. P. 2005. "E-commerce regulation: New game, new rules?" *Quarterly Review of Economics and Finance* 45(2-3):541-58.

Cordoba D., Fernandez S., Laird S. and Vanzetti D. 2005. "Trick or treat? Development opportunities and challenges in the WTO negotiations on industrial tariffs." *The World Economy* 28(10):1375-400.

Corti C., Thompson P., Seal C., Gobo G., Jaber, Gubrium F. and Silverman D. 2012. "Secondary analysis of archived data." In *SAGE Secondary Data Analysis*, edited by J. Goodwin, 243-269. London: SAGE Publications.

Datta P. 2011. "A preliminary study of ecommerce adoption in developing countries." *Information Systems Journal* 21(1):3-32.

Eicher T. S. and Henn C. 2011. "In search of WTO trade effects: Preferential trade agreements promote trade strongly, but unevenly." *Journal of International Economics* 83(2):137-153.

Farrokhnia F. and Richards C. 2016. "E-Commerce products under the World Trade Organization Agreements: Goods, services, both or neither?" *Journal of World Trade* 50(5):793-817.

Friedman B. M. 2002. "Globalization: Stiglitz's case, review of 'Globalization and its discontents' by Joseph E. Stiglitz." *The New York Review of Books, August 15th.*

Gallagher K. P. 2005. "Globalization and the nation-state: reasserting policy autonomy for development." In *Putting development first: the importance of policy space in the WTO and IFIs*, edited by K. P. Gallagher, Londres: Zed Books.

Gallagher K. P. 2008. "Understanding developing country resistance to the Doha round." *Review of International Political Economy* 15(1):62-85.

He J. 2011. "Developing countries' pursuit of an intellectual property law balance under the WTO TRIPS Agreement." *Chinese Journal of International Law* 10(4):827-63.

Hoekman B., Michalopoulos C. and Winter L. A. 2004. "Special and differential treatment of developing countries in the WTO: Moving forward after Cancun." *The World Economy* 27(4):481-506.

Karapinar B. 2011. "Export restrictions and the WTO Law: How to reform the 'degulatory deficiency'." *Journal of World Trade* 45(6):1139-1155.

Khan S. R. 2007. "WTO, IMF and the closing of development policy space for low-income countries: A call for neo-developmentalism." *Third World Quarterly* 28(6):1073-1090.

Kobori S. 2003. "Post-Doha challenges for the WTO." *Asia Pacific Review* 10(1):72-81.

Koester U. 2008. "Poverty & the WTO. Impacts of the Doha Development Agenda." *European Review of Agricultural Economics* 35(1):108-10.

Lafont C. 2010. "Accountability and global governance: challenging the state-centric conception of human rights." *Ethics & Global Politics* 3(3):193-215.

Lewis T. M. 2007. "Impact of globalization on the construction sector in developing countries." *Construction Management and Economics* 25(1):7-23.

Mah J. S. 2011. "Special and differential treatment of developing countries and export promotion policies under the WTO." *The World Economy.* 34(12):1999-2018.

Molla A. and Heeks R. 2007. "Exploring e-commerce benefits for businesses in a developing country." *The Information Society* 23(2):95-108.

Moon G. 2011. "Fair in form, but discriminatory in operation—WTO law's discriminatory effects on human rights in developing countries." *Journal of International Economic Law* 14(3):553-592.

Narlikar A. and Wilkinson R. 2004. "Collapse at the WTO: a Cancun post-mortem." *Third World Quarterly* 25(1):447-460.

Natsuda K. and Thoburn J. 2014. "How much policy space still exists under the WTO? A comparative study of the automotive industry in Thailand

and Malaysia." *Review of International Political Economy*, 21(6):1346-1377.
Qin J. Y. 2012. "Reforming WTO discipline on export duties: Sovereignty over natural resources, economic development and environmental protection." *Journal of World Trade* 46(5):1147-1190.
Richards, C. and Farroknia, F. 2016. "Optimizing grounded theory for policy research: A knowledge-building approach to analyzing WTO e-commerce policies." *International Journal of Qualitative Research* 15(1) DOI: 10.1177/1609406915621380.
Shafaeddin M. 2010. "The political Economy of WTO with special reference to NAMA Negotiations." *European Journal of Development Research* 22(2):175-196.
Smeets M. 2013. "Trade capacity building in the WTO: Main achievements since Doha and key challenges." *Journal of World Trade* 47(5):1047-1190.
Smith J. 2004. "Inequality in international trade? Developing countries and institutional change in WTO dispute settlement." *Review of International Political Economy* 11(3):542-573.
Stiglitz J. E. 2005. "Development policies in a world of globalization," In *Putting development first: The importance of policy space in the WTO and IFIs*, edited by K. P. Gallagher, Londres: Zed Books.
Subramanian A. and Wei S. J. 2007. "The WTO promotes trade, strongly but unevenly.'", *Journal of International Economics* 72(1):151-175.
UNCTAD 2010. *Information economy report 2010: ICTs, enterprises and poverty alleviation.* UN Publication, Switzerland.
UNDP 2005. *E-commerce for development: The case of Nepalese artisan exporters.* Accessed June 25, 2017 http://sdnhq.undp.org/e-gov/e-comm/nepal-artisans-exec-summ.pdf.
Wade R. H. 2003. "What strategies are viable for developing countries today? The World Trade Organization and the shrinking of 'development space'." *Review of International Political Economy* 10(4):621-644.
Wade R. H. 2005. "What strategies are viable for developing countries today? The WTO and shrinking the development space." In *Putting*

*development first: the importance of policy space in the WTO and IFIs*, edited by K. P. Gallagher, Londres: Zed Books.

Winters L. A. 2007. "Coherence and the WTO." *Oxford Review of Economic Policy* 23(3):461-480.

Wolfe R. 2004. "Crossing the river by feeling the stones: Where the WTO is going after Seattle, Doha and Cancun." *Review of International Political Economy* 11(3):574-596.

WTO 1994. *Marrakesh Agreement Establishing the World Trade Organization.*

WTO 1998a. "*Committee on Trade and Development - Development implications of electronic commerce - Note by the Secretariat.*" WT/COMTD/W/51, 11.

WTO 1998b. "*Electronic commerce in goods and services: Communication from the delegation of Egypt*", WT/COMTD/W/38.

WTO 1998c. "*Global electronic commerce communication from Australia.*" WT/GC/W/86.

WTO 1998d. "*Ministerial conference: Declaration on global electronic commerce.*" WT/MIN(98)/DEC/2, 1.

WTO 1998e. "*Work programme on electronic commerce.*" No. 20/1/2014.

WTO 1998f. "*The work programme on electronic commerce - Note by the Secretariat."* S/C/W/68.

WTO 1999a. "*Committee on Trade and Development - Seminar on electronic commerce and development*, 19 February 1999, Summary Report." WT/COMTD/18, 23.

WTO 1999b. "*Contribution by the Committee on Trade and Development to the WTO work programme on electronic commerce: Communication from the Chairperson.*" WT/COMTD/19.

WTO 1999c. "*Ministerial conference: Third Session, Indonesia: Statement by H.E. Mr. Jusuf Kalla Minister of Industry and Trade.*" WT/MIN(99)/ST/94.

WTO 1999d. "*Ministerial conference: Third Session, Mongolia: Statement by H. E. Ms. Nyamosor Tuya, Minister for External Relations.*" WT/MIN(99)/ST/124.

WTO 1999e. "Preparations for the 1999 Ministerial Conference - Communication from Cuba." *WT/GC/W/380*.
WTO 1999f. "Preparations for the 1999 Ministerial Conference - Communication from Venezuela." *WT/GC/W/376*.
WTO 1999g. "Preparations for the 1999 Ministerial Conference - Electronic Commerce- Communication from Japan." *WT/GC/W/253*.
WTO 1999h. "Preparations for the 1999 Ministerial Conference - Electronic Commerce - Communication from Canada." *WT/GC/W/339*.
WTO 1999i. "Trade facilitation and electronic commerce: Communication from the European Community." *G/C/W/138*.
WTO 1999j. "Work programme on electronic commerce - Information provided to the General Council." *G/C/W/158*.
WTO 1999k. "Work programme on electronic commerce - Interim report to the General Council." *S/C/8*.
WTO 1999l. "Work programme on electronic commerce - Progress report to the General Council - Adopted by the Council for Trade in Services on 19 July 1999." *S/L/74*.
WTO 1999m. "Work programme on electronic commerce: Submission by the United States." *WT/GC/16, G/C/2, S/C/7, IP/C/16, WT/COMTD/17*.
WTO 2000a. "Committee on Trade and Development - Work programme on electronic commerce - Contribution by the Committee on Trade and Development - Report by the Chairman." *WT/COMTD/26*.
WTO 2000b. "Council for trade-related aspects of intellectual property rights - Work programme on electronic commerce - Progress Report by the Chairman to the General Council." *IP/C/20*.
WTO 2001a. "Dedicated discussion on electronic commerce under the auspices of the General Council on 15 June 2001." *WT/GC/W/436*.
WTO 2001b. "Ministerial Conference: Declaration on global electronic commerce, Fourth session, Adopted on 14 November 2001." *WT/MIN(01)/DEC/1*.
WTO 2001c. Minutes of meeting - Held in the William Rappard Centre on 8 and 9 May 2001." *WT/GC/M/65*, 51.

WTO 2001d. "Need for unrestricted global electronic commerce: Communication from Cuba." *WT/GC/W/435, G/C/W/264, S/C/W/193, IP/C/W/264, WT/COMTD/W/87.*

WTO 2002a. "Committee on Trade and Development - Thirty-Sixth Session - Note on the Meeting of 26 November 2001." *WT/COMTD/M/36,* 22.

WTO 2002b. "Second dedicated discussion on electronic commerce under the auspices of the General Council on 6 May 2002 - Summary by the Secretariat of the Issues Raised." *WT/GC/W/475.*

WTO 2002c.'Third dedicated discussion on electronic commerce under the auspices of the General Council on 25 October 2002 - Summary by the Secretariat of the Issues Raised." *WT/GC/W/486.*

WTO 2003a. "Work on electronic commerce in the Committee on Trade and Development - Background Note by the Secretariat." *WT/COMTD/W/110.*

WTO 2003b. "Council for trade-related aspects of intellectual property rights - The work programme on electronic commerce - Background Note by the Secretariat – Addendum." *IP/C/W/128/Add.1.*

WTO 2003c. "Fifth dedicated discussion on electronic commerce under the auspices of the General Council on 16 May and 11 July 2003 - Summary by the Secretariat of the Issues Raised." *WT/GC/W/509.*

WTO 2003d. "Fourth dedicated discussion on electronic commerce under the auspices of the General Council on 27 February 2003 - Summary by the Secretariat of the Issues Raised." *WT/GC/W/492.*

WTO 2003e. "Work programme on electronic commerce - Classification Issue - Submission from the European Communities." *WT/GC/W/497.*

WTO 2003f). "Work programme on electronic commerce - Submission from the United States." *WT/GC/W/493.*

WTO 2005a. "Ministerial Conference: Declaration on global electronic commerce, Sixth Session, Hong Kong, Adopted on 18 December 2005." *WT/MIN(05)/DEC.*

WTO 2005b. "Sixth dedicated discussion on electronic commerce under the auspices of the General Council on 7 and 21 November 2005 - Summary by the Secretariat of the Issues Raised." *WT/GC/W/556.*

WTO 2005c. "Work program on electronic commerce: Communication from the United States." *WT/GC/W/551*.

WTO 2006. "Ministerial Conference: Summary Record of the Twelfth Meeting, Hong Kong, 13 - 18 December 2005." *WT/MIN(05)/SR/12/Add.1*.

WTO 2007a. Council for trade-related aspects of intellectual property rights - Priority needs for technical and financial cooperation - Communication from Uganda." *IP/C/W/500*, 11.

WTO 2007b. "Council for trade related aspects of intellectual property rights - Priority needs for technical and financial cooperation - Communication from Sierra Leone." *IP/C/W/499*, 12.

## BIOGRAPHICAL SKETCHES

### *Farokh Faroknia*

**Affiliation:** Perdana School of Science, Technology and Innovation Policy, Universiti Teknologi Malaysia

**Research and Professional Experience:** Farrokh Farroknia has recently completed his PhD at the Perdana School of Science, Technology and Innovation Policy, Universiti Teknologi Malaysia – where he was the president of the faculty postgraduate association. His dissertation focused on a policy analysis of WTO e-commerce polices. His recent funded research projects include a study of Tehran's ranking as a world city for the Tehran Urban Planning and Research Centre.

**Publications from the Last 3 Years:**

1) Farrokh Farrokhnia, Cameron Keith Richards (2016), E-Commerce Products under the WTO Agreements: Goods, Services, Both or Neither? *Journal of World Trade*, Issue 50 (1), (ISI).

2) Cameron Richards & Farrokh Farroknia (2015) Optimizing grounded theory for policy research: A knowledge-building approach to analyzing WTO e-commerce policies, *International Journal of Qualitative Methods* (ISI).
3) Farrokh Farrokhnia and Cameron Keith Richards (2013), The Accountability Challenge to Global E-commerce: The Need to Overcome the Developed-Developing Country Divide in WTO E-commerce Policies, in Liam Leonard, Maria Alejandra Gonzalez-Perez (ed.) *Principles and Strategies to Balance Ethical, Social and Environmental Concerns with Corporate Requirements* (*Advances in Sustainability and Environmental Justice*, Volume 12), Emerald Group Publishing Limited, pp.161-181 (Scopus Indexed).

## Cameron Richards

**Affiliation:** Faculty of Education, Southern Cross University

**Research and Professional Experience:** Includes – past Professor of Policy Studies, *The Perdana School of Science, Technology and Innovation Policy, University Technology Malaysia*

Dr. Cameron Richards' is a semi-retired Australian professor of interdisciplinary studies with extensive experience in the Asia-Pacific region - including at Nanyang Uni. Singapore, Hong Kong Institute of Education, Uni. of Western Australia, and UTM in Malaysia. He has a multi-disciplinary background which also includes sustainability studies, policy research, organizational learning, and intercultural communication. He is currently a Visiting Professor at Chulalongkorn Uni. in Bangkok. He also works as a consultant with NGOs and other agencies on 'sustainable policy' projects and proposals in South-East Asia focused on the global and local challenges of better reconciling economic, social and environmental sustainability.

In: Progress in Economics Research
Editor: Albert Tavidze

ISBN: 978-1-53615-120-6
© 2019 Nova Science Publishers, Inc.

*Chapter 2*

# How Do Stages of Economic Development Affect China's Competitiveness? Efficiency Analysis: China's Position as a Global Player in Comparison with the WTO Members

*Lenka Fojtíková[*] and Michaela Staníčková*
Department of European Integration, Faculty of Economics
VŠB - Technical University of Ostrava, Ostrava, Czech Republic

## Abstract

Globalization generally refers to the process of the broadening and deepening of interrelationships in international trade and foreign investment. The outcome is the creation of a global marketplace for goods and services that is largely indifferent to national borders and governmental

---

[*] Corresponding Author Email: lenka.fojtikova@vsb.cz.

influence. Openness to trade, investment and even the movement of people is vital for prosperity, peace and individual freedom. Also, there have been few better moments in history where trade played the central role in global growth, job creation and development. The current economic circumstances are full of challenges. Rapid technological change coupled with falls in barriers to international trade, have driven it. Also, the World Trade Organization (WTO) agreements and regional treaties forced domestic markets to open up. This development and the current wave of globalization of the economy has generated widespread interest among countries and within countries in the development and upgrading of national competitiveness. The current economic circumstances are full of challenges, especially in the meaning of new global economic powers such as China. China has come a long way since the 1978 election of President Deng Xiaoping heralded a new era of market-oriented reforms. From 1980 to 2010, its economy grew 18-fold, averaging 10 percent a year. It progressed from low-income to upper-middle income country status, lifting hundreds of millions out of poverty: by 2011 just 6 percent of people were in extreme poverty, compared with 61 percent in 1990. Recent developments – including the weakening of the yuan, the stock market crash, rapid credit growth, and a stalling property market – have cast some doubt on China's economic prospects. Yet a hard landing of the Chinese economy still seems unlikely. China has the opportunity to be a global leader in a number of important areas that will be the cornerstones of global growth in the next decades and this is also challenging as well as the threat for the other WTO members and their competitiveness. The chapter focuses on evaluating the Chinese competitiveness and its position as a global player in comparison with the WTO members with using the Data Envelopment Analysis (DEA) method. Efficiency analysis is based on countries belonging to the relevant stage of economic development. Countries face very different challenges and priorities as they move from resource-based via investment-based to knowledge-based economies, which influences their competitive advantages and also disadvantages. The applicability and efficacy of the suggested approach are illustrated by a real data set involving 137 WTO members (from the whole 164 WTO members) within the factors of competitiveness (6 inputs and 6 outputs) based on the Global Competitiveness Index (GCI) in the period from 2007 to 2017, i.e., pre-in-post crises years. A quantitative score of competitiveness will facilitate WTO members in identifying possible weaknesses together with factors mainly driving these weaknesses.

**Keywords:** advantage, China, competitiveness, DEA, disadvantage, efficiency, effectiveness, international trade, stage of economic development, super-efficiency, WEF, WTO

# INTRODUCTION

In an increasingly global economy, the future prosperity of a country depends more and more on the international competitiveness of its firms and industries. Policy-makers at all levels have been swept up in this competitiveness fever. This growing interest may perhaps be partly attributable to their awareness of the fact that all countries are having to contend with raised standards of economic efficiency as a result of the globalization of goods and factor markets. The economy may be competitive but if the economic, social and environmental society suffers too much the country will face major difficulties and vice versa. Therefore governments, in the long run, cannot focus alone on the economic competitiveness of their country; instead they need an integrated approach to govern the country. Indeed, governments consistently may view these types of domestic policies as isolationist and limited approaches to economic efficiency (Hančlová and Melecký, 2016). Some of the evidence of these changes includes some countries' implementation of economic policies that are designed to attract global investment, the prominent role of cross-border mergers and alliances, and the cooperation among national and sub-national governments. These features of the globalization process point to the need to examine the growing importance of a nation's competitiveness by investigating the combination of specific competitive advantages as well as a nation's comparative advantages (it is reflected in its ability to create an environment conducive for trade and development).

Therefore, changes in the global economy have intensified competition in the international and internal markets of developed and developing countries. The current economic situation is causing why the governments of countries worldwide aim to streamline their processes in terms of collecting revenue from the state budget and then redistributing it on the principle of economic efficiency. Comparative analysis of efficiency in the public sector is thus the starting point for studying the role of efficiency, effectiveness and performance regarding the economic governance of resource utilization by public management for achieving the short/medium-term objectives of economic recovery and sustainable development of national economies (Mihaiu, Opreana and Cristescu, 2010, 132). Increasing performance is generally considered as the only one sustainable way of improving living standards in the long-term. Statistical evidence to help policymakers to understand the routes to performance growth can help to lead to better policy. To get empirical applications for economic policy, the Data Envelopment Analysis (DEA) approach is used in this chapter.

The aim of the chapter is to propose a DEA application in order to evaluate efficiency changes and to analyze a level of productivity depending on each country's stage of development. DEA approach applies in the form of output-oriented Banker-Charnes-Cooper model of efficiency with variable returns to scale (OO BCC VRS) with the balanced number of inputs and outputs (6 inputs and 6 outputs). Subsequently, output-oriented Andersen-Petersen model of super-efficiency with variable returns to scale (OO APM VRS) is applied for ranking. The calculation is verified on the sample of 137 World Trade Organization (WTO) members in the reference period 2007–2017 (including all the years inside this range). Variables of inputs and outputs present the factors of competitiveness based on Global Competitiveness Index (GCI), which is part of the Global Competitiveness Reports (GCR) published by the World Economic Forum (WEF) every year. Special attention is dedicated to the Chinese position within an evaluated sample. China in recent years has also been very active in the global economy. It firmly supports globalization and is against trade protectionism. China's accession to the WTO in 2001 was widely regarded as a major milestone in the development of the Chinese economy as well as the multilateral trading system for the world economy influencing global economic growth, international trade, transparency of trade policy, regional trade arrangements, foreign direct investment, banking sector liberalization, exchange rate reform, agricultural trade and energy demand. What are the implications of China's incorporation into the world market as well as global trade for the competitiveness of the other WTO members? WTO competitiveness and the impacts on the Chinese economy will be evaluated.

## LITERATURE REVIEW

Globalization generally refers to a process of broadening and deepening of interrelationships in international trade, foreign investment and portfolio flows. The outcome is the creation of a global marketplace for goods and services that is largely indifferent to national borders and governmental influence. Globalization since the 1960s have altered the production, export and employment structure of the world economy but many barriers to full integration still remained. Although analysts seem to differ on the policy implications of globalization, most would concur that the post-1980s episode is likely to herald more rapid international economic integration than previous episodes. Rapid technological change coupled with falls in barriers to international trade (through the implementation of the Uruguay Round Agreements and economic liberalization in developing countries), have driven it. Also, other WTO agreements and regional treaties forced domestic markets to open up. China's accession to WTO is a landmark event in China's economic reform and in the evolution of the international trading system, i.e., this accession also has a significant impact on all players in the world economy. China's leaders expect to leverage the increased foreign competition inherent in its WTO commitments to transform the country's inefficient, money-losing companies and hasten the development of a commercial credit culture in its banking system. This development and the current wave of globalization of the economy has generated widespread interest among countries and within countries in the development and upgrading of national competitiveness. Globalization and national competitiveness are popular issues in economic policy debates. Economic theory suggests that globalization will lead to greater convergence in economic performance (including competitiveness performance) between open economies.

## Globalization and International Trade

Foreign trade is one of the oldest and historically most important elements of economic relations. Currently, the foreign trade, resp. international trade is one of the most dynamic characters of the globalized world economy due to the result of technological progress, the promotion of financial and trade liberalization that has led to the internationalization of production that has become an important tool for global development and growth. The term of globalization means an international interconnection of markets, which is caused due to the increasing mobility of factors of production and decreasing the distance between markets, that makes the national economy more dependent on each other. The impact of globalization is then higher, the greater the openness of national economies. Academics and practitioners have discussed this problem in many theoretical and empirical studies.

Recent studies deal with the foreign trade based on most of the neoclassical theory approach of foreign trade. The comparative advantages of trade by David Ricardo, as well as the neoclassical Heckscher and Ohlin model dealing with the factor intensity of foreign trade and a new theory of foreign trade created by Paul Krugman, who work with different types of market structures in an environment of rising revenues of scale are used as a basic tools for research and recommendations to modern trade policy. The thoughts of classical political economy´s representatives as Adam Smith, David Ricardo or John Stuart Mill, are based primarily on criticism of mercantilist doctrine. A faith of classical economists in the ability of the free market and specialization increase the wealth of the country became the basis for nowadays appearance of most foreign trade relations and it is the main reason for the liberalization of world trade. The original theory of comparative advantage shows the advantages of integration into the international trade on the basis of terms of profitability ratios. During the last century, the theory was subjected to many studies.

The neoclassical economists founded the theory of international trade on expanding the comparative advantages of additional factor of production - capital. The most important neoclassical theory is the Heckscher-Ohlin model, which works with both factors of production. Their theorem says that the country will specialize in the production of the goods, which is relatively intensive for the production factor (e.g., capital), which has an economy relatively more in comparison to the second factor of production (e.g., labor). However, the truth of this theory was denied by the American economist Wassily Leontief based on empirical research of the American economy. However, this work has had its critics as well. Many other authors have dealt with the validity of Heckscher-Ohlin model, e.g., Bagicha (1962), Jones (1956), Vanek (1963), Keesing (1966), Baldwin (1971), Leamer (1984) and Trefler (1995). Rybczynski (1955) referred to the situation that increases production of goods intensive in one kind of factor endowment under the influence of an unexpected growth of that factor, while the production of goods intensive in another factor of production decrease, whose abundance has remained the same. Stolper and Samuelson (1941) point to the fact that the economy's opening to foreign trade raises prices of goods of an intensive factor, the price of goods also increases and vice versa. This theory was then examined by Metzler (1949), McKenzie (1955) or Chipman (1966). Among other criticisms of neoclassical theory is the fact that it doesn't work with the mobility of production endowments, transaction costs or mutual substitution of production factors. New trade theory is based on the standard model of international trade, which was created by Paul Krugman. This model responds primarily to the fact that each of neoclassical theory is narrowly focused on specific issues of foreign trade, but never affects the international trade as a whole. The second reason is a response to non-existent assumptions of perfect competition. A new theory of foreign trade is based on assumptions of economies of scale and monopolistic competition. This model was later extended to other economic aspects typical of the globalizing economy. Among the best-known studies can be included Ethier (1982), Brander and Spencer (1985), Eaton and Grossman (1986), Krugman (1994), Grossman and Horn (1987) or Grossman and

Helpman (1992). The Melitz model (2003) working with heterogeneous firms is the last significant entry into the field of international trade theories.

It is evident that opinions and ideas regarding foreign trade and its benefits were continuously changed and evolved over time. Nowadays, among the most important channels of global integration are international trade and capital flows. Strong cross-border capital flows have been a major phenomenon in the new global economy as more and more countries embrace free markets and undertake trade and investment liberalization. Foreign direct investment (FDI) has strengthened the integration of individual national markets and has been a driving force in world trade and economic growth. Today the most modern and dynamic industries are transnational in scope since they are the result of an integrated system of global trade and production. Therefore, the development options for many countries depend, to a significant degree, on the kind of export roles they assume in the global economy and their ability to proceed to more sophisticated, high-value industrial niches.

Technological changes and the continuous fall in communication and transport costs have been a major factor behind global integration, and most countries are reversing import-substitution policies designed to prevent the need for trade. Governments are increasingly seeking to improve the international competitiveness of their economy rather than shield it behind protective walls. Most countries have made tremendous progress in education and steady improvements in physical capital and infrastructure, thus boosting their productive capacity and enabling them to compete in world markets. This shift in development strategy has been reinforced by communication technologies, which have made the world easier to navigate. Goods, capital, people and ideas travel faster and cheaper today than ever before.

International trade has come to occupy the centre stage in the economic activity, growth, and development processes of most modern societies. Today's world economic order (disorder) has simply rendered almost every modern economy to be heavily dependent on its foreign trade sector. And in no aspect is this trend more remarkable than the aspect of international competitiveness and the immense importance it now holds for the prospects of survival or failure of nations in their ability to obtain the maximum economic potentials from international trade. It can be stated that where international trade may be an engine that drives the economic growth of nations, international competitiveness represents the fuel that empowers that engine (Ezeala-Harrison, 1999, 3).

## International Trade and Competitiveness

In recent years, the topics about measuring and evaluating competitiveness have enjoyed economic interest. Although there is no uniform definition and understanding of competitiveness, this concept remains one of the basic standards of performance evaluation and it is also seen as a reflection of the success of area (company, country, region) in a wider (international, interregional) comparison. Competitiveness is monitored characteristic of national economies which is increasingly appearing in evaluating their performance and prosperity, welfare and living standards. The exact definition of competitiveness is difficult because of the lack of mainstream view for understanding this term. Competitiveness remains a concept that can be understood in different ways and levels despite widespread acceptance of its importance. The concept of competitiveness is distinguished at different levels – microeconomic, macroeconomic and regional. Anyway, there are some differences between these three approaches; see e.g., Krugman (1994).

The need for a theoretical definition of competitiveness at the macroeconomic level emerged with the development of the globalization process in the world economy as a result of increased competition between countries. In order to understand what the competitiveness is in a national perspective, it is the best way to look at definition given by the President's Commission on Industrial Competitiveness (1985): "Competitiveness is the degree to which a nation can, under free and fair market conditions, produce goods and services that meet the test of international markets while simultaneously maintaining or expanding the real incomes of its citizens." This is the most quoted definition in this area and defines competitiveness from a macro perspective. Many writers (Barrell, Mason and O´Mahony, 2000; Krugman, 1994; Starr and Ullmann, 1988; Tyson, 1988) have also referred to this definition of competitiveness of nations. The definition points out that the ultimate goal of competitiveness is to maintain and increase the real income of its citizens, usually reflected in the standard of living of the country. From this perspective, the competitiveness of a nation is not an end but a means to an end; its ultimate goal is to increase the standard of living of a nation under free and fair market conditions (through foreign trade, production, and investment). It "refers to a country's ability to create, produce, distribute, and/or service products in international trade while earning rising returns on its resources" (Scott and Lodge, 1985, 3). Arguably, national governments' principal goal is to establish an environment that fosters a high standard of living for its citizens by addressing health, safety, laws, and environmental issues. This goal can be achieved, in part, through effective management and allocation of resources for producing the highest attainable level of products. Therefore, it becomes imperative that governments coordinate a comprehensive approach towards trade and investment that incorporates a competition orientation (Feketekuty, 1996). Indeed, many nations are very cognizant of the fact that internal growth depends upon their ability to sustain trade and attract foreign investment.

The concept of international competitiveness of nations makes sense only within a national economic context. Nations adopt economic and trade policies that directly affect the ability of enterprises and industries engage in international trade and investment. This concept is thus often used in analyzing countries' macroeconomic performance. It compares, for a country and its trading partners, a number of salient economic features that can help explain international trade trends. There have been several studies devoted to the competitiveness of international trade. Authors focus either on one particular country and its foreign relations or discuss the situation of a certain union of countries with respect to its environment or the situation within it. In his book, The Competitive Advantage of Nations, Porter (1990) observes that national competitiveness is measured by two sets of indicators: (1) the presence of substantial and sustained exports to a wide array of other nations, and/or (2) significant outbound foreign investment based on skills and assets created in the home country. He notes that the competitive advantage of nations is determined by the strength of their factor endowments; their demand conditions; the competitiveness of firm strategies, structures, and rivalries in major industries; and the strength and diversity of related and supporting industries.

It should be emphasized here that openness to global markets and the internationalization of economies play an increasing role in productivity and competitiveness enhancement (Fojtíková and Staníčková, 2017).

# METHODS

Efficiency measurement has been the challenge of many subjects which have the interest to improve their productivity. In 1957, Farrell investigated the question of how to measure efficiency and highlighted its relevance for economic policymakers (Farrell, 1957). One of the reasons that all attempts to solve the problem have been failed is the failure in combining the measurement of multiple inputs into any desirable outputs (Cook and Seiford, 2009). Since that time techniques to measure efficiency, i.e., one dimension of performance concept, have become more frequent and improved.

## Conceptual Issue

In recent years, the topics about measuring and evaluating competitiveness have enjoyed economic interest. Macroeconomic competitiveness is monitored by many institutions, however, two well-known international institutes, i.e., Institute for Management Development (IMD) and World Economic Forum (WEF) publish most reputable competitiveness reports. To compare a level of competitiveness of separated countries in the paper, we use the database performed by WEF. The first reason for choosing the WEF approach is its long-term continuity and international recognition of stakeholders. Since 1979, WEF publishes Global Competitiveness Report (GCR) that produces annual Global Competitiveness Index (GCI) to rank national economies. GCR aims to serve as a neutral and objective tool for governments, the private sector, and civil society to work together on effective public-private collaboration to boost future prosperity (WEF, 2017). By benchmarking each year's progress on different factors and institutions that matter for future growth, GCR keeps competitiveness on the public agenda, provides a focal point for the discussion of long-term competitiveness policies, and helps to keep stakeholders accountable. The ability to compare economies on a variety of indicators helps them to assess gaps and priority areas and to construct joint, public-private agendas to address them.

Competitiveness taxonomy provides a framework for action for countries that wish to improve their competitiveness. However, do all countries have the same opportunities in terms of competitiveness? GCR emphasizes an increasingly important theme confronting many nations – countries face very different challenges and priorities as they move from resource-based to knowledge-based economies, what influences their competitive advantages and also disadvantages. It is generally accepted that the level of economic development is not uniform across territories. On the contrary, it substantially differs. As an economy develops, so do its structural bases of global competitiveness. This process can be described as a sequence of stages, each with a different set of economic characteristics and challenges (Porter, 1990, 555–565):

- factor-driven stage: competitive advantage is based exclusively on endowments of labour and natural resources,
- investment-driven stage: efficiency in producing standard products and services becomes the dominant source of competitive advantage,
- innovation-driven stage: the ability to produce innovative products and services at the global technology frontier using the most advanced methods becomes the dominant source of competitive advantage.

Successful economic development is thus a process of successive upgrading, in which businesses and their supporting environments co-evolve, to foster increasingly sophisticated ways of producing and competing. Seeing economic development as a sequential process of building not just macroeconomic stability but also interdependent factors such as quality of governance, the societal capacity to advance its technological capability, more advanced modes of competition, and evolving forms of firm organizational structure, helps to expose important potential pitfalls in economic policy orientate on competitiveness.

Nowadays, competitiveness is monitored characteristic of national economies which is increasingly appearing in evaluating their performance and prosperity, welfare and living standards. The need for a theoretical definition of competitiveness at the macroeconomic level emerged with the development of the globalization process in the world economy as a result of increased competition between countries. It should be emphasised here that openness to global markets and the internationalisation of economies play an increasing role in productivity and competitiveness enhancement. Therefore, competitiveness is one of the fundamental criteria for evaluating economic performance and reflects the success of the area. Territories need highly performing units in order to meet their goals, to deliver the products and services they specialised in, and finally to achieve competitive advantage. Low performance and not achieving the goals might be experienced as dissatisfying or even as a failure. Moreover, performance, if it is recognised by others, is often rewarded by benefits, e.g., a better market position, higher competitive advantages, financial condition etc. Differences in performance across territories are seen by the government as important policy targets. For a number of years, government objectives have been set not only in terms of improving national productivity performance against other countries but also in creating conditions to allow less productive countries to reduce the 'gap' between themselves and the most productive ones.

Comparative analysis of performance in public sector is thus starting point for studying the role of efficiency/productivity and effectiveness, i.e., two aspects of performance regarding economic governance of resources utilization by public management for achieving medium/long-term objectives of economic recovery and sustainable development of national economies (Mihaiu, Opreana and Cristescu, 2010). Increasing productivity is generally considered to be the only sustainable way of improving living standards in the long term. Statistical evidence to help policymakers understand the routes to productivity growth, especially those which can be influenced by government, can help lead to better policy. Productivity is thus a central issue in analyses of economic growth, effects of fiscal policies, pricing of capital assets, level of investments, technology changes and production technology, etc. Based on Porter (1990), competitiveness is usually linked to productivity. Figure 1 illustrates the conceptual framework of efficiency (inputs-outputs) and effectiveness (outputs-outcomes). Efficiency can be achieved under conditions of maximising results of an action in relation to resources used, and it is calculated by comparing effects (outputs) obtained in their efforts (inputs). In a competitive economy, therefore, the issue of efficiency can be resolved by comparing these economic issues. Effectiveness is more difficult to assess than efficiency since the outcome is influenced by political choice and often linked to welfare or growth objectives. Drucker (2001) stated there is no efficiency without effectiveness because it is more important to do well what you have proposed than to do well something else that was not necessarily a concern.

Based on the Institute for Management and Development, competitiveness is a field of economic knowledge, which analyzes the facts and policies that shape the ability of a nation to create and maintain an environment that sustains more value creation for its enterprises and more prosperity for its people (IMD, 2012, 502). In other words, competitiveness measures how a nation manages the totality of its resources and competencies to increase the prosperity of its people (IMD, 2012, 502). Understanding of competitiveness is thus closely linked with an understanding of efficiency and effectiveness concepts, see Figure 1.

Using interconnections between competitiveness – productivity and WEF's meaning of competitiveness, it´s possible to make a decision about a quantitative method to competitiveness measuring and evaluating.

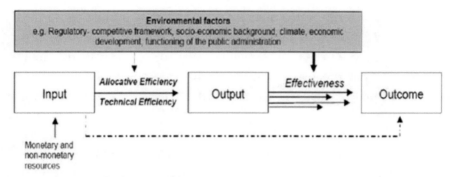

Source: Mandl, Dierx and Ilzkovitz, 2008.

Figure 1. Performance Dimensions and their Relationship.

## Methodological Issue

Performance management is one of the major sources of sustainable organisational efficiency, and a systematic understanding of the factors that affect productivity is very important. Measurement and analysis of efficiency change present a controversial topic enjoying a great deal of interest among researchers and practitioners. The primary problem in creating an evaluation of any system is establishing clear performance standards and priorities at the beginning of the performance cycle. The early research work on this problem focused on separate measures of productivity, and there was a failure to combine the measurements of multiple inputs into any satisfactory measure of efficiency. These inadequate approaches included forming the average productivity for a single input (ignoring all the other inputs) and constructing an efficiency index in which a weighted average of the inputs is compared with the outputs. Responding to these inadequacies of separate indices of labour productivity, capital productivity and so on, Farrell (1957) proposed an activity analysis approach that could deal more adequately with the problem. Farrell had already investigated the question of how to measure efficiency and highlighted its relevance for economic policymakers. Since that time, the techniques to measure efficiency have improved and investigations of efficiency have become more frequent. Twenty years after Farrell's model, and building on those ideas, Charnes, Cooper and Rhodes (1978), responding to the need for satisfactory procedures to assess the relative efficiencies of multi-input/multi-output production units, introduced a powerful methodology that has been titled as the Data Envelopment Analysis (DEA). The approach is based on the simple model of Farrell (1957) for measuring the efficiency of units with one input and one output initially expanded in 1978 by Charnes, Cooper, and Rhodes (CCR model) assuming constant returns to scale (CRS), and later modified in 1984 by Banker, Charnes and Cooper (1984), in the form of BCC model assuming variable returns to scale (VRS). DEA approach also includes advanced additive models, such as Slacks-Based Model (SBM) introduced by Tone (2002) and Free Disposal Hull (FDH) and Free Replicability Hull (FRH) models, which were first formulated by Deprins, Simar and Tulkens (1984).

DEA is an approach for providing a relative efficiency assessment and evaluating the performance of a set of peer entities called decision-making units (DMUs), which convert multiple inputs into multiple outputs. DEA is thus a multi-criteria decision-making method for evaluating the efficiency of a group of DMUs. The definition of a DMU is generic and flexible. DEA is convenient for determining the efficiency of DMUs that are mutually comparable – using the same inputs and producing the same outputs but with different efficiencies. DEA thus can categorise DMUs into two mutually exclusive sets: efficient and inefficient. Determining whether a DMU is efficient from the observed data is equivalent to testing whether the DMU is on the frontier of the production possibility set. A DMU is efficient if the observed data correspond to testing whether the DMU is on the imaginary production possibility frontier (Cooper, Seiford and Zhu, 2004). All other DMUs are inefficient. The best-practice units are used as a reference for the evaluation of the other group units. Therefore, the aim of this method is to decide if DMU are efficient or inefficient by the size and quantity of consumed resources and by the produced outputs. The efficiency score of DMU in the presence of multiple input and output factors is defined by the following equation (1) (Cook, Seiford and Tone, 2007):

$$Efficiency = \frac{weighted\ sum\ of\ outputs}{weighted\ sum\ of\ inputs}. \tag{1}$$

Various types of DEA models can be used, depending upon the problem at hand. Used DEA model can be distinguished by the scale and orientation of the model. If one cannot assume that economies of scale change, then a variable returns to scale (VRS) type of DEA model, the one selected here, is an appropriate choice (as opposed to constant returns to scale, (CRS) model). Furthermore, if in order to achieve better efficiency, governments' priorities are to adjust their outputs (before inputs), then an output-oriented (OO) DEA model, rather than an input-oriented (IO) model, is appropriate. Therefore, for calculations of macroeconomic efficiency, it is used output oriented BCC model with VRS in the chapter. The way in which DEA program computes efficiency scores can be explained briefly using mathematical notation in the model (2) (Cook, Seiford and Tone, 2007):

$$\min g = \phi_q + \varepsilon(\mathbf{e}^T \mathbf{s}^+ + \mathbf{e}^T \mathbf{s}^-), \tag{2}$$

subject to

$$\mathbf{X}\lambda + \mathbf{s}^- = \mathbf{x}_q,$$
$$\mathbf{Y}\lambda - \mathbf{s}^+ = \phi_q \mathbf{y}_q,$$
$$\mathbf{e}^T \lambda = 1,$$
$$\lambda, \mathbf{s}^+, \mathbf{s}^- \geq \mathbf{0},$$

where $g$ is the coefficient of efficiency of unit $U_q$; $\phi_q$ is radial variable indicates the required rate of increase of output; is infinitesimal constant; $\mathbf{e}^T \lambda$ is convexity condition; $\mathbf{s}^+$, and $\mathbf{s}^-$ are vectors of slack variables for inputs and outputs; $\lambda$ represent the vector of weights assigned to individual units; $x_q$ means vector of input of unit $U_q$; $y_q$ means vector of output of unit $U_q$; $\mathbf{X}$ is the input matrix; $\mathbf{Y}$ is the output matrix. In the BCC model aimed at outputs, the coefficient of efficient DMU equals 1, but the coefficient of inefficient DMU is greater than 1.

In the BCC model, the coefficients of efficient DMUs equal to 1. Depending on the chosen model, but also on the relationship between the number of units and number of inputs and outputs, a number of efficient units can be relatively large. Due to the possibility of efficient units' classification, it is used Andersen-Petersen's model (APM) of super efficiency. Following a variable return to scale (VRS) model is an output-oriented dual version of APM (3) (Andersen and Petersen, 1993):

$$\max g = \phi_q + \varepsilon(\mathbf{e}^T\mathbf{s}_i^+ + \mathbf{e}^T\mathbf{s}_i^-), \qquad (3)$$

subject to

$$\sum_{j=1}^{n} x_{ij}\lambda_j + s_i^- = x_{iq},$$

$$\sum_{j=1}^{n} y_{kj}\lambda_j - s_i^+ = \phi_q y_{kq},$$

$$\lambda_q = 0,$$

$$\lambda_j, s_k^+, s_i^- \geq 0,$$

$$j = 1,2,...,n, j \neq q; k = 1,2,...,r; i = 1,2,...,m.$$

where $x_{ij}$ and $y_{kj}$ are $i$-th inputs and $k$-th outputs of $DMU_j$; $\phi_q$ is efficiency index (intensity factor) of observed $DMU_q$; $\lambda_j$ is the dual weight which shows $DMU_j$ significance in the definition of an input-output mix of the hypothetical composite unit, $DMU_q$ directly comparing with. The coefficient of inefficient units is identical to model (2), i.e., ($\phi_q > 1$); for units identified as efficient in the model (2), provides OO APM (3) the coefficient of super-efficiency lower than 1, i.e., $\phi_q \leq 1$.

In Table 1, the characteristics of OO BCC-APM VRS are displayed.

**Table 1. Characteristics of Efficiency and Super-Efficiency Models**

| DEA Model | Score of Coefficient | |
| --- | --- | --- |
| OO BCC VRS – efficiency model | = 1 (efficient DMU) | > 1 (inefficient DMU) |
| OO APM VRS – super-efficiency model | < 1 (efficient DMU) | > 1 (inefficient DMU) |

Source: Own elaboration, 2018.

Suppose there are $n$ DMUs which consume $m$ inputs to produce $s$ outputs. If a performance measure (input/output) is added or deleted from consideration, it will influence the relative efficiencies. Empirically, when the number of performance measures is high in comparison with the number of DMUs, then most of the DMUs are evaluated efficiently. Hence, the obtained results are not reliable. There is a rough rule of thumb suggested by Cooper, Li, Seiford and Zhu (2004) which expresses the relation between the number of DMUs and the number of performance measures sufficient for DEA to be used, as follows (4), resp. in simplification (5):

$$n \geq \max\{m \times s, 3(m+s)\}, \tag{4}$$

$$n \geq 3(m+s). \tag{5}$$

The following section examines a real data set involving 137 WTO members (for each of six inputs and six outputs) to validate the proposed approach. In the chapter, the rule of thumb is met in all the cases of DEA empirical analysis – classification of countries into stages of development based on WEF approach (WEF, 2017, 320), i.e.:

- 137 WTO members: 137 $\geq$ 3 (6 + 6), 137 $\geq$ 3 (12), 137 $\geq$ 36;
- 56 WTO members: 56 $\geq$ 3 (6 + 6), 56 $\geq$ 3 (12), 56 $\geq$ 36;
- 45 WTO members: 45 $\geq$ 3 (6 + 6), 45 $\geq$ 3 (12), 45 $\geq$ 36;
- 36 WTO members: 36 $\geq$ 3 (6 + 6), 36 $\geq$ 3 (12), 36 $\geq$ 36.

## RESULTS AND DISCUSSION

In a relatively short period, DEA has grown into a powerful quantitative, analytical tool for measuring and evaluating performance. DEA has been successfully applied to a host of different types of entities engaged in a wide variety of activities in many contexts worldwide, also in the territorial analysis (see e.g., Melecký, 2018; Staníčková, 2017). DEA measures intended to be applicable to any productive organisation, i.e., to a whole economy too.

### Analysis Background

In the chapter, research is interested in determining efficiency among various DMUs (i.e., 137 countries) within the chosen WTO group. Essentially, the DEA approach determines the productivity of each country by comparing its productivity with others in the group of WTO members, i.e., territorial aspects of empirical analysis. WTO consists of 164 members since 29 July 2016 (WTO, 2016), but not all of these countries are part of the empirical analysis because of data non-availability with respect to selected approach for a database of indicators, i.e., WEF. Territorial aspect of the analysis is thus dedicated to 137 countries divided into three groups depending on each economy's stage of development, as proxies by its GDP per capita and the share of exports represented by raw materials (WEF, 2017, 320). Although all of GCI pillars described below will matter to a certain extent for all economies, it is clear that they affect different economies in different ways. In line with the well-known economic theory of stages of development, GCI assumes that, in the first stage, the economy is Factor-driven and countries compete based on their factor endowments (in this case primarily unskilled labour and natural resources). As a country becomes more competitive, productivity will increase and wages will rise with advancing development. Countries will then move into the Efficiency-driven stage of development when they must begin to develop more efficient production processes and increase product quality because wages have risen and they cannot increase prices. Finally, as countries move into the Innovation-driven stage, wages will have risen by so much that they are able to sustain those higher wages and the associated standard of living only if their businesses are able to compete using the most sophisticated production processes and by innovating new ones. Two criteria are used to allocate countries into stages of development. The first is the level of GDP per capita at market exchange rates. A second criterion is used to adjust for countries that, based on income, would have moved beyond stage 1, but where prosperity is based on the extraction of resources. This is measured by the share of exports of mineral goods in total exports (goods and services), and assumes that countries with more than 70 percent of their exports made up of mineral products (measured using a five-year average) are to a large extent factor driven. Countries that are resource driven and significantly wealthier than economies at the technological frontier are classified in the innovation-driven stage (WEF, 2016, 37). The breakdown of countries into three stages of development is evident from Tables 6–8. It is necessary to mention that in the chapter – in order to fulfil criteria of the rule of thumb expresses the relation between the number of DMUs (countries) and the number of performance measures (input and output indicator) – only the main stages of development are applied without two transition stages. Classification of countries into stages of development is as follows (WEF, 2017, 320):

- factor-driven stage (56 countries): GDP per capita (USD) threshold <2.999;
- efficiency-driven stage (45 countries): GDP per capita (USD) threshold 3.000–17.000;
- innovation-driven stage (36 countries): GDP per capita (USD) threshold >17.000.

The second reason for choosing WEF is its approach to perceiving competitiveness and suitability in terms of the used quantitative method in line with the used database. Indicators represent twelve GCI pillars are crucial for evaluation of productivity among WTO members by DEA approach. GCI pillars represent both sides of the required indicators, i.e., input and output size. Indicators come from WEF's database published within GCR in period 2007–2017 (WEF, 2018 a,b). In GCR, WEF defines competitiveness as the set of institutions, policies, and factors that determine the level of productivity of a country. Level of productivity, in turn, sets the level of prosperity that can be reached by an economy. Level of productivity also determines the rates of return obtained by investments in an economy, which in turn are the fundamental drivers of its growth rates. In other words, a more competitive economy is one that is likely to grow faster over time. This open-mindedness is captured within the GCI by including a weighted average of many different components, each measuring a different aspect of competitiveness. The components are grouped into 12 categories, the pillars of competitiveness, which are not independent, they tend to reinforce each other, and a weakness in one area often has a negative impact on the others (WEF, 2017). GCI pillars may be grouped according to the different dimensions (input versus output aspects) of competitiveness they describe. The terms 'inputs' and 'output' are meant to classify pillars into those which describe driving forces of competitiveness, also in terms of long-term potentiality, and those which are direct or indirect outputs of a competitive society and economy. It is not easy to make a decision on which GCI pillars are the economic drivers in terms of competitiveness (i.e., inputs) and which are the results of activities in the economy (i.e., outputs). For this purpose, we use the appropriate classification based on the EU Regional Competitiveness Index (RCI), created partly in line with GCI construction (Annoni and Kozovska, 2010), for detail see Table 2. Although all of GCI pillars matter to a certain extent for all economies, it is clear that they affect different economies in different ways what confirms the importance on application different stage of development concept.

## Table 2. Background of DEA Empirical Analysis

| GCI pillars – Inputs (II 1-6) | DMUs | GCI pillars – Outputs (OI 1-6) |
|---|---|---|
| 1. Institutions | 137 WTO members | 1. Goods market efficiency |
| 2. Infrastructure | | 2. Labour market efficiency |
| 3. Macroeconomic environment | | 3. Financial market development |
| 4. Health and primary education | | 4. Market size |
| 5. Higher education and training | | 5. Business sophistication |
| 6. Technological readiness | | 6. Innovation |
| Time-series | | |
| *GCI editions* | *Annual and periodical changes* | *Total period change* |
| 11 editions from GCR 2007-2008 to GCR 2017-2018 | 2007, 2008, 2009, 2010, 2011, 2012, 2013, 2014, 2015, 2016, 2017; 2007-2010, 2011-2013, 2014-2017 | Total changes across years in period 2007-2017 |

Source: Own elaboration, 2018.

## Table 3. Descriptive Statistics of Indicators for 2007-2017 Period

| Indicators | N | Minimum | Maximum | Mean | Std. Deviation |
|---|---|---|---|---|---|
| II1 | 137 | 2.29734 | 6.08443 | 4.06037 | 0.87098 |
| II2 | 137 | 1.77250 | 6.61933 | 3.91090 | 1.23002 |
| II3 | 137 | 2.93416 | 6.44984 | 4.68316 | 0.79212 |
| II4 | 137 | 3.09679 | 6.75518 | 5.37018 | 0.93484 |
| II5 | 137 | 2.00877 | 6.12250 | 4.09505 | 1.00708 |
| II6 | 137 | 2.07533 | 6.17780 | 3.88723 | 1.11527 |
| OI1 | 137 | 2.88599 | 5.69690 | 4.29115 | 0.55266 |
| OI2 | 137 | 2.91710 | 5.82244 | 4.31523 | 0.51681 |
| OI3 | 137 | 2.24275 | 5.85182 | 4.10263 | 0.72633 |
| OI4 | 137 | 1.27273 | 6.90862 | 3.69132 | 1.21527 |
| OI5 | 137 | 2.64469 | 5.80658 | 4.04927 | 0.72770 |
| OI6 | 137 | 1.97722 | 5.70584 | 3.40906 | 0.84357 |

Source: Own elaboration based on the calculation in IBM SPSS Statistics, 2018.

It is important to keep in mind that GCI pillars are not independent: they tend to reinforce each other, and a weakness in one area often has a negative impact on others. Input indicators (II) represent pillars of Institutions (II1), Infrastructure (II2), Macroeconomic environment (II3), Health and primary education (II4), Higher education and training (II5), and Technological readiness (II6). Output indicators (OI) represent pillars of Goods market efficiency (OI1), Labour market efficiency (OI2), Financial market development (OI3), Market size (OI4), Business sophistication (OI5), and Innovation (OI6). In Table 3, descriptive statistics of input and output indicators are shown.

The reference period 2007–2017 includes years of growth dynamics and economic downturn and stagnation, effects of the economic crisis and subsequent stagnation can be considered as the other milestones (i.e., pre-in-post crises years). Time-series is set with respect to the GCI concept – including convenient input-output indicators to DEA – because data prior to the GCR 2006 edition are not available due to changes in the GCI methodology. DEA calculates year-on-year efficiency scores in all years of period 2007–2017, as well as periodically changes for years of pre-crisis period (2007–2010), crises period (2011–2013) and post-crisis period (2014–2017). Background for DEA interpretation are results based on the trend of year-on-year efficiency scores in period 2007–2017 and overall efficiency scores for the whole reference period, as shown in Table 2. Empirical analysis includes calculations for the sample of all countries (137 WTO members), and then calculations for countries divided into a group of each stage of development, i.e., 1$^{st}$ stage of development (56 countries), 2$^{nd}$ stage of development (45 countries) and 3$^{rd}$ stage of development (36 countries).

## Efficiency and Super-Efficiency Analysis

Openness to trade, investment and even the movement of people is vital for prosperity, peace and individual freedom. And there have been few better moments in history to reconfirm the role of trade as central to global growth, job creation and development. Today's economic circumstances are full of challenges, especially after the year 2007. Ten years ago, the global financial crisis interrupted a period of sustained economic growth dating back to the 1960s. Since then, despite unorthodox monetary policy and fiscal stimulus packages, advanced economies have experienced prolonged comparatively sluggish growth. In emerging markets, the impact of the global financial crisis was lessened in part by interest rate differentials, with advanced economies fuelling capital inflows in the form of foreign direct investment, the commodity super-boom, and – related to this – the rapid growth of China. The growth of the Chinese economy has been tremendous. Only recently have advanced and emerging economies begun to show signs of recovery. These threats and opportunities have also intensified competition in global markets, which, in turn, implies a greater need to be competitive to generate additional market opportunities and economic links in the presence of many more participants vying for the same space. China has the opportunity to be a global leader in a number of important areas that will be cornerstones of global growth in the next decades and this is also challenging for its biggest competitors.

As we approach the 10th anniversary of the global financial crisis, the world economy is showing encouraging signs of recovery, with GDP growth accelerating to 3.5% in 2017. Despite this positive development, leaders are facing major predicaments when it comes to economic policy. Uneven distribution of the benefits of economic progress, generational divides, rising income inequality in advanced economies, and increasing environmental degradation have heightened the sense that the economic policies of past years have not served citizens or society well. Coupled with growth rates that remain below historical levels, these quandaries put many prevalent models of economic growth and related policies into question. Major technological disruption and the new fault lines emerging in the global economic and political order add further uncertainty about the types of policies that will make economies future-proof. Taken together, all of these factors are challenging decision makers to find new approaches and policies to advance economic progress. Emerging consensus is that economic growth once again needs to focus more on human well-being. Such human-centric economic progress is multi-dimensional by nature – it is broad-based by benefitting the vast majority of people, environmentally sustainable, and equitable in terms of creating opportunities for all and not disadvantaging future generations. Competitiveness remains an important contribution to the broader goal of human-centric economic progress by creating resources needed for increased well-being, including better education, health, security, and higher per capita income (WEF, 2017).

The aim of evaluation of the countries' operation is correction, improvement and promotion of performance. Considering the increasing importance of economic growth in the society and presence in a competitive world, evaluation of the territorial performance has been remarkably considered and various measures are brought up as a criterion for evaluation of territorial performance. Evaluation and comparison the performance of similar units is an important part of the complex organisation' management. DEA is one of the power management techniques empowering to estimate territorial performance in comparison with other competitors and make the decision for a better future. The empirical strategy of measuring WTO members' productivity consists of two procedure:

- firstly, in the processing phase, a database of relevant indicators are created and their descriptive statistics are analyzed,
- secondly, application of DEA to assess the efficiency score of WTO members in use of six inputs for production of six outputs in the field of competitiveness. The second step consists of evaluating such rankings with OO BCC VRS, resp. OO APM VRS in order to assess the relative importance of and rank the evaluated countries.

Performance is a major prerequisite for future development and success in broader comparison. In the chapter, a comparison of one dimension of performance is processed, i.e., efficiency. Purpose of the chapter is to map competitive efficiency at the macroeconomic level for WTO members. The expected results are of great variation within the whole sample because countries with low levels of competitiveness locate among strongly competitive countries – a higher degree of heterogeneity is thus foreseen. Disparities are diminishing in the assessment of countries within stages of development, which operate as more homogeneous groups.

From the main descriptive statistics of OO BCC VRS and OO APM VRS for the whole sample of 137 countries as well as for countries based on the stage of development and reference period 2007–2017 (see Table 4).

Figures 2–5 constitute the box-plots of OO BCC VRS and OO APM VRS for the whole sample of 137 countries as well as for countries based on the stage of development and reference period 2007–2017. Box-plots of each both models show data skewness and kurtosis to mean values; it is reflected by equal location of the median ($X_{50}$) between upper ($X_{75}$) and lower ($X_{25}$) quartiles. Data are skewed to the upper levels, so the median is shifted to the upper quartile ($X_{75}$). The shapes of box-plots also indicate the symmetry layout. Box-plots signalize that explored data set come from the normal distribution, not only due to its symmetry but also due to the position of the median, which lies almost in the middle of the interquartile range. Interesting is the position of the outliers and extreme values due to the highest or lowest OO BCC VRS and OO APM VRS scores in comparison to OO BCC VRS and OO APM VRS scores of other countries in the evaluated data sample.

**Table 4. Descriptive Statistics of OO BCC-APM VRS**

| Model | Minimum | Maximum | Mean | Std. Deviation |
|---|---|---|---|---|
| \multicolumn{5}{c}{137 countries} ||||
| OO BCC VRS | 1.00000 | 1.16569 | 1.02616 | 0.03499 |
| OO APM VRS | 0.62592 | 1.16569 | 0.99101 | 0.08077 |
| \multicolumn{5}{c}{Factor-driven stage = 56 countries} ||||
| OO BCC VRS | 1.00000 | 1.14256 | 1.01336 | 0.02577 |
| OO APM VRS | 0.62592 | 1.14256 | 0.95453 | 0.08920 |
| \multicolumn{5}{c}{Efficiency-driven stage = 45 countries} ||||
| OO BCC VRS | 1.00000 | 1.12369 | 1.01257 | 0.02324 |
| OO APM VRS | 0.75800 | 1.12370 | 0.96030 | 0.07210 |
| \multicolumn{5}{c}{Innovation-driven stage = 36 countries} ||||
| OO BCC VRS | 1.00000 | 1.03074 | 1.00486 | 0.00824 |
| OO APM VRS | 0.70935 | 1.02512 | 0.93437 | 0.07551 |

Source: Own elaboration based on the calculation in IBM SPSS Statistics, 2018.

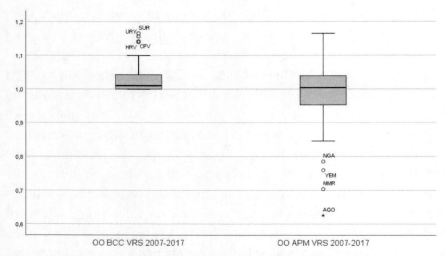

Source: Own elaboration based on the calculation in IBM SPSS Statistics, 2018.

Figure 2. Box-plots of OO BCC-APM VRS (137 countries).

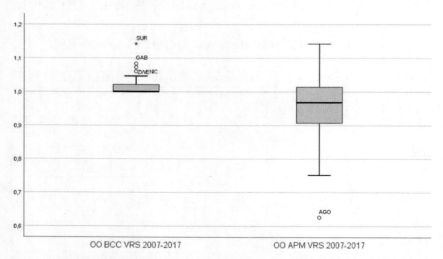

Source: Own elaboration based on the calculation in IBM SPSS Statistics, 2018.

Figure 3. Box-plots of OO BCC-APM VRS (56 countries).

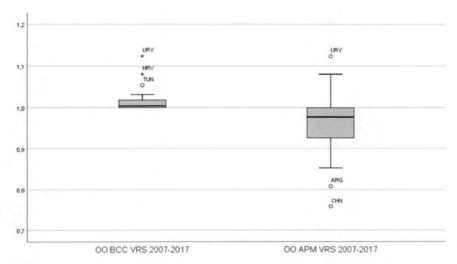

Source: Own elaboration based on the calculation in IBM SPSS Statistics, 2018.

Figure 4. Box-plots of OO BCC-APM VRS (45 countries).

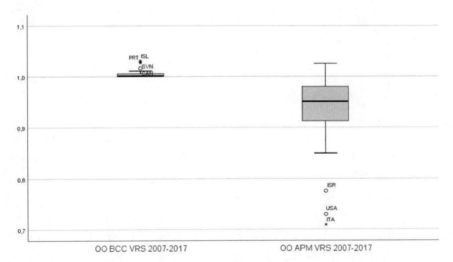

Source: Own elaboration based on the calculation in IBM SPSS Statistics, 2018.

Figure 5. Box-plots of OO BCC-APM VRS (36 countries).

## Table 5. Results of OO BCC-APM VRS in 2007–2017

| WTO Members | OO BCC VRS Model of Efficiency ||||||||||||
|---|---|---|---|---|---|---|---|---|---|---|---|
| | 2007 | 2008 | 2009 | 2010 | 2011 | 2012 | 2013 | 2014 | 2015 | 2016 | 2017 |
| 137 countries | 1.033 | 1.024 | 1.024 | 1.023 | 1.023 | 1.023 | 1.027 | 1,030 | 1,028 | 1,026 | 1,032 |
| | 1.026 |||| 1.024 ||| 1.029 ||||
| 1st stage | 1.014 | 1.012 | 1.013 | 1.009 | 1.011 | 1.013 | 1.014 | 1.018 | 1.014 | 1.013 | 1.018 |
| (56 countries) | 1.012 |||| 1.013 ||| 1.015 ||||
| 2nd stage | 1.020 | 1.016 | 1.011 | 1.009 | 1.012 | 1.008 | 1.011 | 1.012 | 1.015 | 1.015 | 1.010 |
| (45 countries) | 1.014 ||||||||||||
| 3rd stage | 1.007 | 1.009 | 1.007 | 1.004 | 1.003 | 1.003 | 1.008 | 1.004 | 1.003 | 1.004 | 1.002 |
| (36 countries) | 1.007 |||| 1.005 ||| 1.003 ||||
| WTO Members | OO APM VRS Model of Super-Efficiency ||||||||||||
| | 2007 | 2008 | 2009 | 2010 | 2011 | 2012 | 2013 | 2014 | 2015 | 2016 | 2017 |
| 137 countries | 1.007 | 0.993 | 0.994 | 0.988 | 0.994 | 0.994 | 1.048 | 1.008 | 0.998 | 1.000 | 1.012 |
| | 0.996 |||| 1.013 ||| 1.005 ||||
| 1st stage | 0.963 | 0.963 | 0.959 | 0.950 | 0.964 | 0.963 | 0.966 | 0.981 | 0.960 | 0.970 | 0.985 |
| (56 countries) | 0.959 |||| 0.964 ||| 0.974 ||||
| 2nd stage | 0.967 | 0.959 | 0.957 | 0.956 | 0.968 | 0.967 | 0.974 | 0.971 | 0.982 | 0.984 | 0.973 |
| (45 countries) | 0.960 |||| 0.970 ||| 0.978 ||||
| 3rd stage | 0.961 | 0.954 | 0.955 | 0.923 | 0.922 | 0.926 | 0.934 | 0.947 | 0.941 | 0.935 | 0.969 |
| (36 countries) | 0.949 |||| 0.927 ||| 0.948 ||||

Source: Own elaboration based on the calculation in DEA Frontier, 2018.

Table 5 presents annual and periodical efficiency changes of OO BCC VRS and OO APM VRS for the whole sample of 137 evaluated countries gained in the form of averages based on efficiency scores for the whole reference period 2007–2017. Table 5 also presents results for countries divided into stages of development for annual and periodical efficiency changes of OO BCC VRS and OO APM VRS gained in the form of averages based on efficiency scores. Level of efficiency measured by both models of efficiency and super-efficiency does not show extreme diversity and variability in the whole sample of evaluated across individual years as well as changes among three crises-periods. Across all three stages of development, differences in efficiency and super-efficiency scores are not so large, typically best results have recorded countries within the 3rd stage of development, i.e., the most developed countries.

Broader aspects enter into the overall evaluation of economics and these aspects are unnoticeable for DEA, i.e., part of the qualitative evaluation in line with the evaluation of overall performance. Performance is linked with respect to competitiveness sense: a good performance in the Innovation group (Technological readiness, Business sophistication, Innovation) is expected to also be a good performance in the Efficiency group (Higher education and training, Goods market efficiency, Labour market efficiency, Financial market development, Market size) and the Basic group (Institutions, Infrastructure, Macroeconomic environment, Health and primary education) as they are instrumental to increasing levels of competitiveness. The first Basic group represent the key basic drivers of all types of economies. As the economy develops, other factors enter into play for its advancement in competitiveness and are grouped in the second Efficiency group of pillars. At the most advanced stage of development of the economy, key drivers for improvement are pillars included in the third Innovation group. As countries move along the path of development, their socio-economic conditions change and different determinants become more important for the macroeconomic competitiveness, as subsequently explained by WEF (WEF, 2001) and as follows. As a result, the best way to improve the competitiveness of more developed countries will not necessarily coincide with the way to improve less developed countries.

These facts were also reflected in the results of the empirical analysis in the chapter. Development potentials or development weakness are inherent in the national diversity that characterizes a sample of all 137 evaluated WTO members. Part of the explanation of efficiency results has to do with differences in competitiveness. An economic entity in the country with low level of competitiveness may not have similar opportunities as an economic entity in the highly competitive country. This fact remains and can be confirmed. What does it mean for efficiency? In the chapter, DEA results efficiency differ from GCI results in competitiveness. Why? Is a high level of competitiveness necessarily associated with a high level of efficiency and vice versa? It may not always be the case of evaluated countries based on classification to the stage of development, as present results in Tables 6–8. In GCR, in some cases, the country can achieve lower GCI score, and in DEA higher score of efficiency or super-efficiency and seems to operate more efficiently in the whole reference period. Such a conclusion is relevant by comparing values of inputs and outputs in DEA, and the fact that outputs are achieved with given inputs. If the input-output ratio is low on both sides, countries could be considered efficient in the transformation process. Such results are not linked with overall competitiveness evaluation which does not depend primarily on efficiency, but the effectiveness of overall economic processes (see Figure 1).

In Tables 6–8, countries are classified based on their belonging to the relevant stage of development. Therefore, in the 1$^{st}$ factor-driven stage, 56 countries are evaluated within the sample. In the 2$^{nd}$ efficiency-driven stage, 45 countries are evaluated within the sample. Finally, in the 3$^{rd}$ innovation-driven stage, 36 countries are evaluated within the sample. In the first step, the OO BCC VRS model of efficiency was calculated for all stages of development and countries were divided into two groups – efficient and inefficient ones. In OO BCC VRS, the coefficient of efficient DMU equals 1, but the coefficient of inefficient DMU is greater than 1. Depending on the chosen model, but also on the relationship between the number of units and number of inputs and outputs, a number of efficient units can be relatively large. Due to the possibility of efficient units' classification and ranking from the best to the worst, in the second step, OO APM VRS model of super-efficiency was calculated for all stages of development and countries were divided into two groups again – efficient and inefficient ones. The coefficient of inefficient units is identical to OO BCC VRS model ($\phi_q > 1$); for units identified as efficient in OO APM VRS, the model provides the coefficient of super-efficiency lower than 1, i.e., $\phi_q \leq 1$.

## Table 6. OO BCC-APM VRS Scores, Ranks of WTO Members for 1st Stage of Development (56 Factor-Driven Countries)

| OO BCC VRS* | | | | | OO APM VRS* | | | | |
|---|---|---|---|---|---|---|---|---|---|
| Rank | DMU | Country | Score | Category | Rank | DMU | Country | Score | Category |
| 1 | AGO | Angola | 1.0000 | Efficient | 1 | AGO | Angola | 0.6259 | Efficient |
| | BFA | Burkina Faso | 1.0000 | | 2 | MMR | Myanmar | 0.7516 | |
| | GIN | Guinea | 1.0000 | | 3 | NGA | Nigeria | 0.7758 | |
| | MMR | Myanmar | 1.0000 | | 4 | IND | India | 0.7795 | |
| | BGD | Bangladesh | 1.0000 | | 5 | YEM | Yemen | 0.8559 | |
| | BDI | Burundi | 1.0000 | | 6 | MWI | Malawi | 0.8597 | |
| | KHM | Kyrgyzstan | 1.0000 | | 7 | PAK | Pakistan | 0.8693 | |
| | TCD | Chad | 1.0000 | | 8 | LBR | Liberia | 0.8879 | |
| | GMB | Gambia | 1.0000 | | 9 | NPL | Nepal | 0.8895 | |
| | GHA | Ghana | 1.0000 | | 10 | KEN | Kenya | 0.8917 | |
| | IND | India | 1.0000 | | 11 | BGD | Bangladesh | 0.8999 | |
| | KGZ | Kyrgyzstan | 1.0000 | | 12 | GIN | Guinea | 0.9004 | |
| | LBR | Liberia | 1.0000 | | 13 | RUS | Russian Federation | 0.9062 | |
| | MDG | Madagascar | 1.0000 | | 14 | RWA | Rwanda | 0.9072 | |
| | MWI | Malawi | 1.0000 | | 15 | UGA | Uganda | 0.9202 | |
| | NPL | Nepal | 1.0000 | | 16 | MDG | Madagascar | 0.9253 | |
| | RWA | Rwanda | 1.0000 | | 17 | GMB | Gambia | 0.9307 | |
| | UGA | Uganda | 1.0000 | | 18 | UKR | Ukraine | 0.9314 | |
| | YEM | Yemen | 1.0000 | | 19 | GHA | Ghana | 0.9350 | |
| | ZMB | Zambia | 1.0000 | | 20 | ZMB | Zambia | 0.9363 | |
| | KAZ | Kazakhstan | 1.0000 | | 21 | TZA | Tanzania | 0.9364 | |
| | NGA | Nigeria | 1.0000 | | 22 | BFA | Burkina Faso | 0.9431 | |

## Table 6. (Continued)

### OO BCC VRS*

| Rank | DMU | Country | Score | Category |
|---|---|---|---|---|
| 1 | RUS | Russian Federation | 1.0000 | |
| | UKR | Ukraine | 1.0000 | |
| | VEN | Venezuela | 1.0000 | |
| | MLI | Mali | 1.0000 | |
| 2 | PHL | Philippines | 1.0001 | Inefficient |
| 3 | TZA | Tanzania | 1.0007 | |
| 4 | HTI | Haiti | 1.0008 | |
| 5 | KEN | Kenya | 1.0010 | |
| 6 | LAO | Lao PDR | 1.0013 | |
| 7 | MRT | Mauritania | 1.0014 | |
| 8 | VNM | Vietnam | 1.0043 | |
| 9 | SEN | Senegal | 1.0053 | |
| 10 | PAK | Pakistan | 1.0058 | |
| 11 | CIV | Côte d'Ivoire | 1.0063 | |
| 12 | SLE | Sierra Leone | 1.0069 | |
| 13 | MOZ | Mozambique | 1.0082 | |
| 14 | MNG | Mongolia | 1.0093 | |
| 15 | BRN | Brunei Darussalam | 1.0097 | |
| 16 | LSO | Lesotho | 1.0130 | |
| 17 | BWA | Botswana | 1.0201 | |
| 18 | SYC | Seychelles | 1.0211 | |
| 19 | CMR | Cameroon | 1.0214 | |

### OO APM VRS*

| Rank | DMU | Country | Score | Category |
|---|---|---|---|---|
| 23 | MRT | Mauritania | 0.9497 | |
| 24 | BDI | Burundi | 0.9634 | |
| 25 | KAZ | Kazakhstan | 0.9651 | |
| 26 | KGZ | Kyrgyzstan | 0.9652 | |
| 27 | KHM | Cambodia | 0.9687 | |
| 28 | HTI | Haiti | 0.9689 | |
| 29 | MLI | Mali | 0.9690 | |
| 30 | CIV | Côte d'Ivoire | 0.9703 | |
| 31 | MOZ | Mozambique | 0.9707 | |
| 32 | PHL | Philippines | 0.9745 | |
| 33 | SEN | Senegal | 0.9798 | Inefficient |
| 34 | MNG | Mongolia | 0.9837 | |
| 35 | LAO | Lao PDR | 0.9926 | |
| 36 | VNM | Vietnam | 0.9940 | |
| 37 | BRN | Brunei Darussalam | 0.9943 | |
| 38 | SWZ | Swaziland | 1.0027 | |
| 39 | HND | Honduras | 1.0043 | |
| 40 | LSO | Lesotho | 1.0075 | |
| 41 | BWA | Botswana | 1.0141 | |
| 42 | CMR | Cameroon | 1.0146 | |
| 43 | TJK | Tajikistan | 1.0164 | |
| | BEN | Benin | 1.0164 | |

## Table 6. (Continued)

### OO BCC VRS*

| Rank | DMU | Country | Score | Category |
|---|---|---|---|---|
| 20 | SWZ | Swaziland | 1.0234 | |
| 21 | HND | Honduras | 1.0239 | |
| 22 | TJK | Tajikistan | 1.0256 | |
| 23 | BEN | Benin | 1.0259 | |
| 24 | KWT | Kuwait | 1.0319 | |
| 25 | GUY | Guyana | 1.0355 | |
| 26 | MDA | Moldova | 1.0408 | |
| 27 | BOL | Bolivia | 1.0462 | |
| 28 | NIC | Nicaragua | 1.0600 | |
| 29 | ZWE | Zimbabwe | 1.0725 | |
| 30 | GAB | Gabon | 1.0832 | |
| 31 | SUR | Suriname | 1.1426 | |

### OO APM VRS*

| Rank | DMU | Country | Score | Category |
|---|---|---|---|---|
| 44 | KWT | Kuwait | 1.0211 | |
| | SYC | Seychelles | 1.0211 | |
| 45 | GUY | Guyana | 1.0334 | |
| 46 | SLE | Sierra Leone | 1.0380 | |
| 47 | BOL | Bolivia | 1.0442 | |
| 48 | MDA | Moldova | 1.0449 | |
| 49 | NIC | Nicaragua | 1.0576 | |
| 50 | GAB | Gabon | 1.0832 | |
| 51 | ZWE | Zimbabwe | 1.1139 | |
| 52 | SUR | Suriname | 1.1426 | |
| / | TCD | Chad | infeasible | / |
| / | VEN | Venezuela | infeasible | / |

* Note: Scores based on a national average across years of reference period 2007–2017.
Source: Own elaboration based on the calculation in DEA Frontier, 2018.

## Table 7. OO BCC-APM VRS Scores, Ranks of WTO Members for 2nd Stage of Development
(45 Efficiency-Driven Countries)

### OO BCC VRS*

| Rank | DMU | Country | Score | Category |
|---|---|---|---|---|
| 1 | BRA | Brazil | 1.0000 | Efficient |
|  | CHN | China | 1.0000 |  |
|  | DOM | Dominican Republic | 1.0000 |  |
|  | EGY | Egypt | 1.0000 |  |
|  | GTM | Guatemala | 1.0000 |  |
|  | IDN | Indonesia | 1.0000 |  |
|  | JAM | Jamaica | 1.0000 |  |
|  | NAM | Namibia | 1.0000 |  |
|  | PRY | Paraguay | 1.0000 |  |
|  | PER | Peru | 1.0000 |  |
|  | ZAF | South Africa | 1.0000 |  |
|  | LKA | Sri Lanka | 1.0000 |  |
|  | THA | Thailand | 1.0000 |  |
|  | ARG | Argentina | 1.0000 |  |
|  | CHL | Chile | 1.0000 |  |
|  | CRI | Costa Rica | 1.0000 |  |
|  | MYS | Malaysia | 1.0000 |  |
|  | MEX | Mexico | 1.0000 |  |
| 2 | SLV | El Salvador | 1.0002 | Inefficient |
| 3 | BGR | Bulgaria | 1.0003 |  |
| 4 | GEO | Georgia | 1.0009 |  |
| 5 | ARM | Armenia | 1.0023 |  |

### OO APM VRS*

| Rank | DMU | Country | Score | Category |
|---|---|---|---|---|
| 1 | CHN | China | 0.7580 | Efficient |
| 2 | ARG | Argentina | 0.8081 |  |
| 3 | LKA | Sri Lanka | 0.8527 |  |
| 4 | BRA | Brazil | 0.8562 |  |
| 5 | MYS | Malaysia | 0.8700 |  |
| 6 | CHL | Chile | 0.8737 |  |
| 7 | GTM | Guatemala | 0.8756 |  |
| 8 | EGY | Egypt | 0.8805 |  |
| 9 | IDN | Indonesia | 0.8898 |  |
| 10 | GEO | Georgia | 0.9085 |  |
| 11 | PER | Peru | 0.9260 |  |
| 12 | MEX | Mexico | 0.9262 |  |
| 13 | DOM | Dominican Republic | 0.9376 |  |
| 14 | CRI | Costa Rica | 0.9407 |  |
| 15 | JAM | Jamaica | 0.9455 |  |
| 16 | ARM | Armenia | 0.9581 |  |
| 17 | SLV | El Salvador | 0.9586 |  |
| 18 | THA | Thailand | 0.9607 |  |
| 19 | ECU | Ecuador | 0.9639 |  |
| 20 | COL | Colombia | 0.9726 |  |
| 21 | BGR | Bulgaria | 0.9738 |  |
| 22 | BRB | Barbados | 0.9798 |  |

## Table 7. (Continued)

| OO BCC VRS* ||||| OO APM VRS* |||||
|---|---|---|---|---|---|---|---|---|---|
| Rank | DMU | Country | Score | Category | Rank | DMU | Country | Score | Category |
| 6 | PAN | Panama | 1.0038 | | 23 | PAN | Panama | 0.9813 | |
| 7 | ALB | Albania | 1.0039 | | 24 | SVK | Slovakia | 0.9846 | |
| 8 | SVK | Slovakia | 1.0040 | | 25 | ALB | Albania | 0.9868 | |
| 9 | MUS | Mauritius | 1.0059 | | 26 | JOR | Jordan | 0.9922 | |
| 10 | LVA | Latvia | 1.0079 | | 27 | LVA | Latvia | 0.9936 | |
| 11 | TUR | Turkey | 1.0086 | | 28 | MUS | Mauritius | 0.9943 | |
| 12 | COL | Colombia | 1.0089 | | 29 | POL | Poland | 0.9952 | |
| 13 | POL | Poland | 1.0098 | | 30 | ROU | Romania | 0.9981 | |
| 14 | HUN | Hungary | 1.0103 | | 31 | MNE | Montenegro | 0.9994 | |
| 15 | ROU | Romania | 1.0104 | | 32 | HUN | Hungary | 0.9995 | |
| 16 | MNE | Montenegro | 1.0153 | | 33 | TUR | Turkey | 1.0012 | Inefficient |
| 17 | ECU | Ecuador | 1.0165 | | 34 | MAR | Morocco | 1.0126 | |
| 18 | MAR | Morocco | 1.0178 | | 35 | OMN | Oman | 1.0133 | |
| 19 | OMN | Oman | 1.0199 | | 36 | SAU | Saudi Arabia | 1.0144 | |
| 20 | BRB | Barbados | 1.0201 | | 37 | MKD | Macedonia, FYR | 1.0232 | |
| 21 | JOR | Jordan | 1.0261 | | 38 | LTU | Lithuania | 1.0313 | |
| 22 | SAU | Saudi Arabia | 1.0272 | | 39 | CPV | Cape Verde | 1.0390 | |
| 23 | MKD | Macedonia, FYR | 1.0279 | | 40 | TUN | Tunisia | 1.0522 | |
| 24 | CPV | Cape Verde | 1.0288 | | 41 | HRV | Croatia | 1.0803 | |
| 25 | LTU | Lithuania | 1.0313 | | 42 | URY | Uruguay | 1.1237 | |
| 26 | TUN | Lithuania | 1.0538 | | / | NAM | Namibia | infeasible | / |
| 27 | HRV | Croatia | 1.0803 | | / | PRY | Paraguay | infeasible | / |
| 28 | URY | Uruguay | 1.1237 | | / | ZAF | South Africa | infeasible | / |

* Note: Scores based on a national average across years of reference period 2007–2017.
Source: Own elaboration based on the calculation in DEA Frontier, 2018.

## Table 8. OO BCC-APM VRS Scores, Ranks of WTO Members for 3rd Stage of Development (36 Innovation-Driven Countries)

### OO BCC VRS*

| Rank | DMU | Country | Score | Category |
|---|---|---|---|---|
| 1 | BHR | Bahrain | 1.0000 | Efficient |
|  | CZE | Czech Republic | 1.0000 |  |
|  | FIN | Finland | 1.0000 |  |
|  | GRC | Greece | 1.0000 |  |
|  | HKG | Hong Kong SAR | 1.0000 |  |
|  | CHE | Switzerland | 1.0000 |  |
|  | IRL | Ireland | 1.0000 |  |
|  | ISR | Israel | 1.0000 |  |
|  | ITA | Italy | 1.0000 |  |
|  | JPN | Japan | 1.0000 |  |
|  | LUX | Luxembourg | 1.0000 |  |
|  | NZL | New Zealand | 1.0000 |  |
|  | SGP | Singapore | 1.0000 |  |
|  | SWE | Sweden | 1.0000 |  |
|  | TTO | Trinidad and Tobago | 1.0000 |  |
|  | USA | United States | 1.0000 |  |
| 2 | CYP | Cyprus | 1.0001 | Inefficient |
| 3 | DEU | Germany | 1.0011 |  |
| 4 | DNK | Denmark | 1.0013 |  |
| 5 | QAT | Qatar | 1.0024 |  |
| 6 | MLT | Malta | 1.0025 |  |

### OO APM VRS*

| Rank | DMU | Country | Score | Category |
|---|---|---|---|---|
| 1 | ITA | Italy | 0.7094 | Efficient |
| 2 | USA | United States | 0.7346 |  |
| 3 | ISR | Israel | 0.7758 |  |
| 4 | CZE | Czech Republic | 0.8495 |  |
| 5 | JPN | Japan | 0.8681 |  |
| 6 | DNK | Denmark | 0.8762 |  |
| 7 | HKG | Hong Kong SAR | 0.9060 |  |
| 8 | LUX | Luxembourg | 0.9061 |  |
| 9 | IRL | Ireland | 0.9081 |  |
| 10 | FIN | Finland | 0.9168 |  |
| 11 | BHR | Bahrain | 0.9202 |  |
| 12 | CYP | Cyprus | 0.9217 |  |
| 13 | GRC | Greece | 0.9260 |  |
| 14 | KOR | Korea, Rep. | 0.9363 |  |
| 15 | NZL | New Zealand | 0.9405 |  |
| 16 | QAT | Qatar | 0.9415 |  |
| 17 | ARE | United Arab Emirates | 0.9531 |  |
| 18 | EST | Estonia | 0.9558 |  |
| 19 | SGP | Singapore | 0.9571 |  |
| 20 | CHE | Switzerland | 0.9579 |  |
| 21 | NOR | Norway | 0.9662 |  |

| OO BCC VRS* | | | | | OO APM VRS* | | | | |
|---|---|---|---|---|---|---|---|---|---|
| DMU | Country | Score | Category | Rank | DMU | Country | Score | Category | |
| 7 | BEL | Belgium | 1.0032 | | 22 | FRA | France | 0.9727 | |
| | ARE | United Arab Emirates | 1.0032 | | 23 | MLT | Malta | 0.9736 | |
| 8 | AUS | Australia | 1.0034 | | 24 | ESP | Spain | 0.9750 | |
| 9 | EST | Estonia | 1.0041 | | 25 | DEU | Germany | 0.9771 | |
| 10 | GBR | United Kingdom | 1.0044 | | 26 | GBR | United Kingdom | 0.9795 | |
| 11 | KOR | Korea, Rep. | 1.0054 | | 27 | AUS | Australia | 0.9838 | |
| 12 | NOR | Norway | 1.0061 | | 28 | SWE | Sweden | 0.9882 | |
| 13 | ESP | Spain | 1.0067 | | 29 | BEL | Belgium | 0.9983 | |
| 14 | NLD | Netherlands | 1.0069 | | 30 | NLD | Netherlands | 1.0061 | Inefficient |
| 15 | FRA | France | 1.0107 | | 31 | AUT | Austria | 1.0070 | |
| | AUT | Austria | 1.0107 | | 32 | CAN | Canada | 1.0079 | |
| 16 | CAN | Canada | 1.0163 | | 33 | ISL | Iceland | 1.0200 | |
| 17 | PRT | Portugal | 1.0270 | | 34 | PRT | Portugal | 1.0248 | |
| 18 | SVN | Slovenia | 1.0285 | | 35 | SVN | Slovenia | 1.0276 | |
| 19 | ISL | Iceland | 1.0307 | | 36 | TTO | Trinidad and Tobago | 1.0370 | |

* Note: Scores based on a national average across years of reference period 2007–2017.

Source: Own elaboration based on the calculation in DEA Frontier, 2018.

Based OO BCC VRS scores for group of 56 countries within the 1st stage of development, overall 2007–2017 efficiency ranges from 1.0000 – the 1st position (for 26 countries, i.e., Angola, Burkina Faso, Guinea, Myanmar, Bangladesh, Burundi, Kyrgyzstan, Chad, Gambia, Ghana, India, Kyrgyzstan, Liberia, Madagascar, Malawi, Nepal, Rwanda, Uganda, Yemen, Zambia, Kazakhstan, Nigeria, Russian Federation, Ukraine, Venezuela and Mali) to 1.1426 – the last 31st position (Suriname), i.e., totally 30 countries recorded inefficient position (behind Suriname, Philippines, Tanzania, Haiti, Kenya, Lao PDR, Mauritania, Vietnam, Senegal, Pakistan, Côte d'Ivoire, Sierra Leone, Mozambique, Mongolia, Brunei Darussalam, Lesotho, Botswana, Seychelles, Cameroon, Swaziland, Honduras, Tajikistan, Benin, Kuwait, Guyana, Moldova, Bolivia, Nicaragua, Zimbabwe and Gabon placed). In the second step, a model of super-efficiency was calculated. Based OO APM VRS scores for a group of 56 countries within the 1st stage of development, overall 2007–2017 efficiency ranges from 0.6259 – the 1st position (Angola) to 1.1426 – the last 52nd position (Suriname). Totally 37 countries recorded efficient position, i.e., behind Angola, Myanmar, Nigeria, India, Yemen, Malawi, Pakistan, Liberia, Nepal, Kenya, Bangladesh, Guinea, Russian Federation, Rwanda, Uganda, Madagascar, Gambia, Ukraine, Ghana, Zambia, Tanzania, Burkina Faso, Mauritania, Burundi, Kazakhstan, Kyrgyzstan, Cambodia, Haiti, Mali, Côte d'Ivoire, Mozambique, Philippines, Senegal, Mongolia, Lao PDR, Vietnam and Brunei Darussalam placed. Within the whole sample of 56 countries, only 17 countries placed at inefficient positions (behind Suriname, Swaziland, Honduras, Lesotho, Botswana, Cameroon, Tajikistan, Benin, Kuwait, Seychelles, Guyana, Sierra Leone, Bolivia, Moldova, Nicaragua, Gabon and Zimbabwe). Only two countries, Chad and Venezuela, were identified as outliers in infeasible coefficient of super-efficiency in relation to production possibility frontier.

Based OO BCC VRS scores for group of 45 countries within the 2nd stage of development, overall 2007–2017 efficiency ranges from 1.0000 – the 1st position (for 18 countries, i.e., Brazil, China, Dominican Republic, Egypt, Guatemala, Indonesia, Jamaica, Namibia, Paraguay, Peru, South Africa, Sri Lanka, Thailand, Argentina, Chile, Costa Rica, Malaysia and

Mexico) to 1.1237 – the last 28th position (Uruguay), i.e., totally 27 countries recorded inefficient position (behind Uruguay, El Salvador, Bulgaria, Georgia, Armenia, Panama, Albania, Slovakia, Mauritius, Latvia, Turkey, Colombia, Poland, Hungary, Romania, Montenegro, Ecuador, Morocco, Oman, Barbados, Jordan, Saudi Arabia, Macedonia FYR, Cape Verde, Lithuania, Lithuania and Croatia placed). In the second step, a model of super-efficiency was calculated. Based OO APM VRS scores for a group of 45 countries within the 2nd stage of development, overall 2007–2017 efficiency ranges from 0.7580 – the 1st position (China) to 1.1426 – the last 42nd position (Uruguay). Totally 32 countries recorded efficient position, i.e., behind China, Argentina, Sri Lanka, Brazil, Malaysia, Chile, Guatemala, Egypt, Indonesia, Georgia, Peru, Mexico, Dominican Republic, Costa Rica, Jamaica, Armenia, El Salvador, Thailand, Ecuador, Colombia, Bulgaria, Barbados, Panama, Slovakia, Albania, Jordan, Latvia, Mauritius, Poland, Romania, Montenegro and Hungary placed. Within the whole sample of 45 countries, only 10 countries placed at inefficient positions (behind Uruguay, Turkey, Morocco, Oman, Saudi Arabia, Macedonia FYR, Lithuania, Cape Verde, Tunisia and Croatia). Only three countries, Namibia, Paraguay and South Africa, were identified as outliers in infeasible coefficient of super-efficiency in relation to production possibility frontier.

Based OO BCC VRS scores for group of 36 countries within the 3rd stage of development, overall 2007–2017 efficiency ranges from 1.0000 – the 1st position (for 16 countries, i.e., Bahrain, Czech Republic, Finland, Greece, Hong Kong SAR, Switzerland, Ireland, Israel, Italy, Japan, Luxembourg, New Zealand, Singapore, Sweden, Trinidad and Tobago, United States) to 1.0307 – the last 29th position (Iceland), i.e., totally 20 countries recorded inefficient position (behind Iceland, Cyprus, Germany, Denmark, Qatar, Malta, Belgium, United Arab Emirates, Australia, Estonia, United Kingdom, Korea Rep., Norway, Spain, Netherlands, France, Austria, Canada, Portugal and Slovenia placed). In the second step, a model of super-efficiency was calculated. Based OO APM VRS scores for a group of 36 countries within the 3rd stage of development, overall 2007–2017 efficiency ranges from 0.7094 – the 1st position (Italy) to 1.0370 – the last 36th position (Trinidad and Tobago). Totally 29 countries recorded efficient position, i.e., behind Italy, United States, Israel, Czech Republic, Japan, Denmark, Hong Kong SAR, Luxembourg, Ireland, Finland, Bahrain, Cyprus, Greece, Korea Rep., New Zealand, Qatar, United Arab Emirates, Estonia, Singapore, Switzerland, Norway, France, Malta, Spain, Germany, United Kingdom, Australia, Sweden and Belgium placed. Within the whole sample of 36 countries, only seven countries placed at inefficient positions (behind Trinidad and Tobago, Netherlands, Austria, Canada, Iceland, Portugal and Slovenia).

## Chinese Interaction

The rapid emergence of China as a world trade power has raised concerns in developed and developing economies alike over its potential impact on the world market. China's increasing integration with the global economy has contributed to sustained growth in international trade. Its exports have become more diversified, and greater penetration of industrial country markets has been accompanied by a surge in China's imports from all regions – especially Asia, where China plays an increasingly central role in regional specialization. Tariff reforms have been implemented in China since the 1980s; and, with its WTO accession, China has committed itself to additional reforms that are farreaching and challenging. Sustained implementation of these commitments would further deepen China's international integration and generate benefits for most partner countries. To fulfil membership requirements at the WTO, China has to implement its commitment to adopt broad and deep trade liberalization measures to bring its trade regime consistent with the WTO rules. Implementation of these liberalization measures implies a substantial reduction in tariffs and non-tariff barriers across all economic sectors in one of the world's largest and most rapidly expanding markets. Obviously, it will not only change China's resource allocation among its domestic production and export sectors but will also affect the structure of China's and trade with its trade partners. World trade patterns and production in other countries will have to adjust to accommodate such changes.

So, what are the implications of China's incorporation into the world market as well as global trade for the competitiveness of the other WTO members? China's integration with the global economy has contributed to sustained growth in international trade. Both its exports and imports have grown faster than world trade for more than twenty years. Although dramatic, these growth rates are not unprecedented and are similar to those seen earlier during the integration of other rapidly developing economies into the global trading system. As China's trade with the rest of the world has deepened, its composition and geographical pattern have also shifted. Its overall share of exports to industrial economies has increased and become more diversified. China has also become increasingly important within the Asian regional economy. Vertical specialization of production within Asia has led to an increasing share of China's imports coming from within the region, and China is now among the most important export destinations for other Asian countries. Trade reforms and commitments made as part of China's accession to the WTO have been crucial in promoting its integration with the global trading system. These reforms have included substantial tariff reductions and the dismantling of most nontariff barriers (NTBs). Improved market access following WTO accession has also been important. Continued implementation of WTO commitments in the coming years will further facilitate China's ongoing integration with the global economy and generate benefits for most partner countries. However, it may also pose significant challenges for the authorities; and the extensive safeguard provisions under the WTO agreement represent a downside risk that could constrain China's export growth in the future.

In the past decade, the WTO has adjudicated over forty disputes between China and other powerful economies. These cases are often trumpeted as a sign of the enduring strength of the trade regime and the efficacy of international law in managing geopolitical tensions associated with China's rise. This positive assessment obfuscates dangers lurking on the horizon. Nowadays, China presents a major challenge to the multilateral trade regime. At the heart of this challenge is the fact that China's economic structure is sui generis, having evolved in a manner largely unforeseen by those negotiating WTO treaty law. As a result, the WTO can deal effectively with only a limited range of disputes – those in which Chinese policies largely resemble elements of other alternative economic structures. Outside of this set of issues, the WTO faces two very different but equally serious challenges. The first is reinterpreting certain legal concepts to adapt and fit an unforeseen Chinese context. The second is deciding whether to expand the scope of its legal rules to accommodate issues that currently fall outside of its jurisdiction. The most likely outcome is one in which China's rise will exacerbate the diminishing centrality of the WTO law for global trade governance.

## International Comparison of Chinese Economy

Evaluation of WTO competitiveness was processed in the previous part, however, what are the impacts on the Chinese economy? Based on the empirical results above, at low levels of development, economic growth is determined primarily by the mobilization of primary factors of production: land, primary commodities, and unskilled labour. As economies move from low- to middle-income status, global competitiveness becomes Investment-driven (instead of Factor-driven), as economic growth is increasingly achieved by harnessing global technologies to local production. Foreign direct investment, joint ventures, and outsourcing arrangements help to integrate the national economy into international production systems, thereby facilitating the improvement of technologies and the inflows of foreign capital and technologies that support economic growth. In most economies, the evolution from middle-income to high-income status involves the transition from a technology-importing economy to a technology-generating economy, one that innovates in at least some sectors at the global technological frontier. For high-income economies at this Innovation-driven stage of economic development, global competitiveness is critically linked to high rates of social learning (especially science-based learning) and the rapid ability to shift to new technologies. The principal factors that contribute to competitiveness, and thereby improve living standards, will, therefore, differ for economies at different levels of development. For some low-income economies, the main challenge is to get the basic factor markets – for land, labour, and capital – working properly. As countries advance, the basic challenge is to make connections with international production systems by attracting sufficient flows of Foreign Direct Investment (FDI). Once reaching high-income status, the basic challenge facing countries is to generate high rates of innovation and commercialization of new technologies. Critical institutions in the country, and its barriers to continued growth will differ depending on the country's current position.

Related to the analysis of countries based on their stage of development, China belongs to the 2$^{nd}$ group of countries, i.e., Investment-driven stage of economic development relevant for efficiency-driven economies. In this stage, efficiency in producing standard products and services becomes the dominant source of competitive advantage. Economies at this stage concentrate on manufacturing and on outsourced service exports. They achieve higher wages but are susceptible to financial crises' and external, sector-specific demand shocks. This stage implies efforts of upgrading of the nation's industry as companies invest in modern technology and more efficient facilities. Therefore, these aspects are also important for orientation of the Chinese economy. In China, since the reform process started and an opening-up policy was adopted, the country has experienced a sharp increase in its growth rate and also its trade with the rest of the world: it has successfully converted itself from a country with protectionist trade policies to an outward-oriented one with an open economy. During this transition, its trade relations with the rest of the world went through various stages, from isolation and dependence on the Soviet economy to openness. Its accession to the WTO was a key step giving China the opportunity to participate in world trade within a multilateral trade system. It's 17 years since China's full opening up was marked by its accession to the WTO in 2001. With tough transitional challenges ahead and painstaking adjustments behind, China has risen to become a bellwether of global free trade and an advocate of globalization as a whole. As with virtually everything to do with contemporary China, things have changed so much and so quickly since 1978 that it is almost as if we are talking about two different places. And indeed, it is probably fair to say that we are dealing with two entirely different economies in that the 1978 version had little that we would recognize in the 2008 incarnation, the milestone year for changes in the world economy due to the economic crises. Whilst change in the domestic arena has done much to generate this change, engaging the global economy has also played its part in changing China – and in the process also changing the global economy. China's economic rise presages a fundamental change in the global economic and political system. China's integration into the global economy has been one of the main drivers of its economic growth. A particularly important contribution to GDP and employment growth has been made by some of its industries with comparative advantages and an increasing specialisation level. China has pursued in recent years export-oriented economic policies and becomes a big trader in world markets and the biggest economy after the United States and Japan. International trade has also helped improve the productivity of some domestic industries and led to faster technological progress. In particular, large imports of capital and intermediate goods have had an important effect on productivity through the technology incorporated in them; 'learning by doing' has also played a key role. An increase in trade of machinery parts and components (both exports and imports) and the convergence of the commodity composition of exports and imports have made intra-industry trade more important than before in East Asia (Ando, 2006). China's partners in the world economy are already benefiting, and stand to benefit more over the coming decades, from the economic impact of growth on a scale unprecedented in history.

Both the scale and the character of China's economic and social development mean that there will be powerful feedback effects as the rest of the world adjusts to China's presence in all aspects of global economic and political life. These will affect Chinese policies and systems, as well as behaviour in other countries towards China. Larger countries are likely to take an active position in managing both their economic and political interests as they are affected by the impact of developments in China on the structure of international markets for goods, services, capital and investment. This is not just a matter of the scale of China's growth and its role in the world, although certainly scale is one dimension. Within less than a few decades, China has transformed itself from being a 'small' economy to being a 'big' economy in terms of its impact on world trade and output, world prices, its role in international capital flows and financial markets, its impact on the global commons (including the environment and climate) and its stake in managing the international economic and political system. These changes have seen China seek to conform to established international norms and institutions (for example, through accession to the WTO), exercise responsibility within the G20 process in managing the global economic system and to play an increasingly active and constructive role in international diplomacy (for example, in the United Nations and through the Six-Party Talks on North Korea).

China's emergence as the world's second largest single trader in the world economy has been managed successfully within the global system of trade rules and institutions. As Chinese business goes abroad, there are more complex interactions between the market and the state. At home in China as well as abroad, and there are no international institutions, like the WTO for trade, within which to manage these dealings. Despite the scale of these changes and China's increasingly important role in the world, China's economy is still an economy in transition, with wide-ranging reforms still in progress. This affects the way in which the market operates across all sectors of the economy. China also has a political system that is different from the broadly representative political systems that typify the established international powers. Yet economic transition in China has clearly had and is continuing to have, an important impact on the political system and the way in which the political system operates within China. There is a question of whether continuing economic reform might lead inevitably to a trend towards further political system change because of the need for a separation of the state from the economic enterprise, to facilitate the governance and transparency necessary to achieve very high levels of prosperity. The relationship between the efficiency of economic institutions and the nature of the political institutions in which they are nested is one important question. Of more immediate interest and practical importance is development of an understanding of the way in which Chinese markets and business are affected by evolving economic and political institutions, how participants in these markets interact with the state in their dealings in international markets, and whether the relationship between the market and political system requires particular strategic policy responses from China's economic partners (Drysdale, 2010).

Related to China's economic partners, within the chapter, the country was compared with the other WTO members as a whole (see Table 9), as well as with countries in the same group of the $2^{nd}$ stage of development, i.e., Investment-driven economies (see Table 10), both in the reference period 2007–2017. Table 9 shows China results obtained in comparison with 137 countries, i.e., in the sample of all evaluated countries as a whole, both for efficiency and super-efficiency models in all individual years of reference period as well as for national average across all years of reference period 2007–2017. In a comparison of 137 countries, based on OO APM VRS model of super-efficiency, China get score 0.9032 overall efficiencies for 2007–2017 and placed $15^{th}$ position. In a comparison of all reference years, minimum super-efficiency score 0.8170 was recorded in 2007, i.e., the best result with respect to the orientation of OO APM VRS model of super-efficiency. On the contrary, maximum super-efficiency score 0.9676 was recorded in 2013, i.e., the worst result with respect to the orientation of OO APM VRS model of super-efficiency, for information about characteristics of model see Table 1.

Figure 6 shows the evolution of Chinese super-efficiency scores in all individual years within reference period 2007-2017, as well as increasing and decreasing trend scores over the entire period with maximum and minimum values, i.e., the best (0.8170 obtained in 2007) and worst (0.9676 obtained in 2013) scores.

## Table 9. OO BCC-APM VRS Scores of China (137 Countries)

| DMU | OO BCC VRS Model of Efficiency | | | | | | | | | | | Overall Efficiency* |
|---|---|---|---|---|---|---|---|---|---|---|---|---|
| | 2007 | 2008 | 2009 | 2010 | 2011 | 2012 | 2013 | 2014 | 2015 | 2016 | 2017 | OO BCC VRS |
| China | 1.0000 | 1.0000 | 1.0000 | 1.0000 | 1.0000 | 1.0000 | 1.0000 | 1.0000 | 1.0000 | 1.0000 | 1.0000 | 1.0000 |
| | OO APM VRS Model of Super-Efficiency | | | | | | | | | | | Overall Efficiency* |
| | 2007 | 2008 | 2009 | 2010 | 2011 | 2012 | 2013 | 2014 | 2015 | 2016 | 2017 | OO APM VRS |
| CHN | 0.8170 | 0.8839 | 0.8944 | 0.8543 | 0.9090 | 0.9201 | 0.9676 | 0.9268 | 0.9292 | 0.9162 | 0.9163 | 0.9032 (15th rank) |
| | Minimum (the best result) | | | | 0.8170 | | | | | 2007 | | |
| | Maximum (the worst results) | | | | 0.9676 | | | | | 2013 | | |

* Note: Scores based on a national average across years of reference period 2007-2017. Source: Own elaboration based on the calculation in DEA Frontier, 2018.

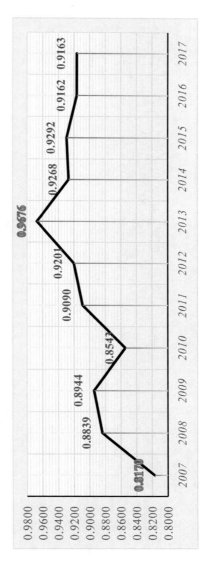

Source: Own elaboration based on the calculation in DEA Frontier, 2018.

Figure 6. Evolution of Chinese Super-Efficiency in 2007–2017 (137 Countries).

## Table 10. OO BCC-APM VRS Scores of China (45 Countries)

| DMU | OO BCC VRS Model of Efficiency | | | | | | | | | | | Overall Efficiency* |
|---|---|---|---|---|---|---|---|---|---|---|---|---|
| | 2007 | 2008 | 2009 | 2010 | 2011 | 2012 | 2013 | 2014 | 2015 | 2016 | 2017 | OO BCC VRS |
| China CHN | 1.0000 | 1.0000 | 1.0000 | 1.0000 | 1.0000 | 1.0000 | 1.0000 | 1.0000 | 1.0000 | 1.0000 | 1.0000 | 1.0000 |
| | OO APM VRS Model of Super-Efficiency | | | | | | | | | | | Overall Efficiency* |
| | 2007 | 2008 | 2009 | 2010 | 2011 | 2012 | 2013 | 2014 | 2015 | 2016 | 2017 | OO APM VRS |
| | 0.7141 | 0.8009 | 0.7581 | 0.7611 | 0.6839 | 0.7350 | 0.7579 | 0.7342 | 0.7600 | 0.8145 | 0.8182 | 0.7580 (1st rank) |
| Minimum (the best result) | | | | | 0.6839 | | | | | | 2011 | |
| Maximum (the worst result) | | | | | | | | | | | 0.8182 | 2017 |

* Note: Scores based on a national average across years of reference period 2007-2017. Source: Own elaboration based on the calculation in DEA Frontier, 2018.

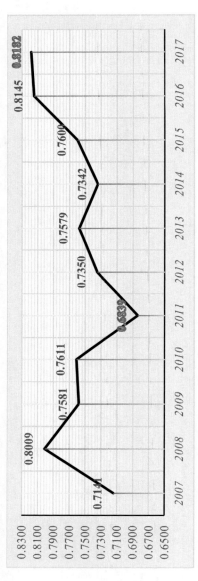

Source: Own elaboration based on the calculation in DEA Frontier, 2018.

Figure 7. Evolution of Chinese Super-Efficiency in 2007–2017 (45 Countries).

Figure 6 shows the evolution of Chinese super-efficiency scores in all individual years within reference period 2007–2017, as well as increasing and decreasing trend scores over the entire period with maximum and minimum values, i.e., the best (0.6839 obtained in 2011) and worst (0.8182 obtained in 2017) scores.

Table 10 shows China results obtained in the comparison of countries within the 2nd stage of development, i.e., Investment-driven economies, both for efficiency and super-efficiency models in all individual years of reference period as well as for national average across all years of reference period 2007–2017. In a comparison of 45 countries, based on OO APM VRS model of super-efficiency, China get score 0.7580 overall efficiencies for 2007–2017 and placed 1st position. In a comparison of all reference years, minimum super-efficiency score 0.6839 was recorded in 2011, i.e., the best result with respect to the orientation of OO APM VRS model of super-efficiency. On the contrary, maximum super-efficiency score 0.8182 was recorded in 2017, i.e., the worst result with respect to the orientation of OO APM VRS model of super-efficiency, for information about characteristics of model see Table 1.

## Pros and Cons of Chinese Economy

Ten years ago, the global financial crisis interrupted a period of sustained economic growth dating back to the 1960s. Since then, despite unorthodox monetary policy and fiscal stimulus packages, advanced economies have experienced prolonged comparatively sluggish growth. In emerging markets, the impact of the global financial crisis was lessened in part by interest rate differentials, with advanced economies fuelling capital inflows in the form of foreign direct investment, the commodity super boom, and – related to this – the rapid growth of China. China has come a long way since the 1978 election of President Deng Xiaoping heralded a new era of market-oriented reforms. In 1978, China started the historic process of reform and opening-up. This is a glorious chapter in the development epic of the country and the nation composed by the Chinese people, recording the great journey of the common progress of China and the rest of the world. It has not only profoundly changed the country, but also greatly influenced the whole world. From 1980 to 2010, its economy grew 18-fold, averaging 10 percent a year. It progressed from low-income to upper-middle income country status, lifting hundreds of millions out of poverty: by 2011 just 6 percent of people were in extreme poverty, compared with 61 percent in 1990 (World Bank Group and World Trade Organization, 2015). Opening-up was key to China's economic growth over the past 40 years. In the same vein, high-quality development of China's economy in the future can only be achieved with greater openness.

Recent developments – including the weakening of the yuan, the stock market crash, rapid credit growth, and a stalling property market – have cast some doubt on China's economic prospects. Yet a hard landing of the Chinese economy still seems unlikely, for three reasons. First, as the Global Competitiveness Index (GCI) shows, China possesses strong economic foundations. The country ranks 27th out of 137 economies in the 2017–2018 edition (WEF, 2017). China has achieved near universal primary education and high levels of public health, invested massively in transport and energy infrastructure and ensured a relatively stable macroeconomic environment. These successes not only have contributed to China's emergence as a manufacturing hub, they also represent assets on which to build. China's advantages are not shared by many neighbouring economies at a similar stage of development, as shown in Figure 8.

China (27th position) has gained one place as a result of steady, albeit incremental, improvements to its overall competitiveness score. Since last year, China has made progress in all pillars except its macroeconomic environment and infrastructure. A decline in the former is explained by a worsening of the government budget deficit, which has been slightly higher than the expected target for 2016. The score for the infrastructure pillar decreases for the second year in a row, the result in part of a decline in the quality of port infrastructure and the reliability of electricity supply as perceived by the business community. The largest gains are observed in technological readiness, owing to higher ICT penetration and the extent to which foreign direct investments have been bringing new technologies to

China. Despite the remarkable progress already made, further improvement on this front would foster the growth of emerging digital industries and create the conditions necessary to kick-start new ones. Other significant advances have been made in the goods market efficiency pillar as a result of a slight reduction in the number of procedures for starting a business compared to last year.

Second, an eventual slowdown was inevitable, predictable, and entirely normal, given China's impressive growth trajectory over the past two decades. WEF also compares China's annual real growth rate from 1980 to the GDP-weighted average growth rate of other countries in the income group to which it belonged in each year. Since 1991, China has grown faster than its peers every year. For several years in the 1990s, the differential was almost 10 percentage points. Since achieving upper-middle-income status in 2010, the differential has been around 5 percentage points.

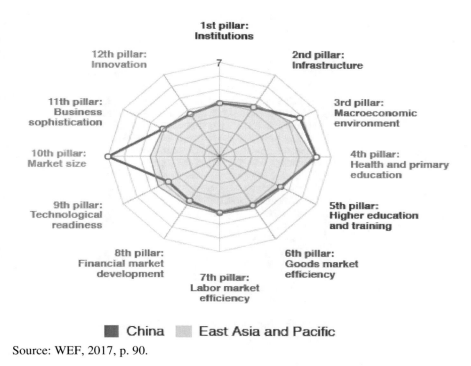

Source: WEF, 2017, p. 90.

Figure 8. China in 12 GCI Pillars (Score 1–7).

Third, even though it has not yet abandoned the official 7 percent target, there are signs that the government has been preparing for the economy's new phase and has been recalibrating its growth objectives from the quantitative to the qualitative. The 12th five-year plan, adopted in 2011 and covering 2010–2015, had called for a rebalancing of the economy; more recently, President Xi referred to a 'new normal' under which growth will be lower.

Even though the economy is unlikely to experience a hard landing, the challenges and downside risks are many. Under the new normal, productivity gains will be harder to achieve. This is reflected in China's stagnation in GCI rankings for the past four years. The drivers that fuelled China's growth – investment, low wages, urbanization – are yielding diminishing returns or even vanishing, as shown by the downward trend of overall productivity since 2007. Future gains will have to come through more market-oriented reforms that tackle remaining distortions, controls, and rigidities across the economy and that enable the more efficient use of factors of production.

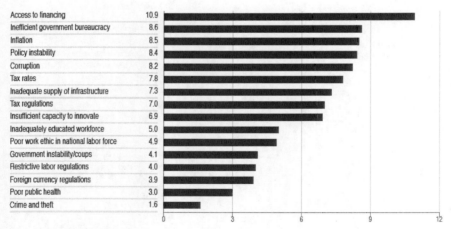

Source: WEF, 2017, p. 90.

Figure 9. The Most Problematic Factors for Doing Business in China.

GCI points to the structural weaknesses of China's financial sector: it ranks 78th for the soundness of its banks, which have accumulated many non-performing loans. The sector is dominated by large state-owned banks, and credit flows more to state-owned enterprises or large corporations with connections than too small- and medium-sized enterprises: access to finance is rated as the second most problematic factor for doing business in China (Figure 9). A rank of 46th on goods market efficiency highlights the need to create a level playing field in non-strategic economic sectors by reforming state-owned enterprises and subjecting them to fair domestic and foreign competition, and by tackling corruption and bureaucracy. Moving beyond market efficiency, the list of the most problematic factors for doing business in China is topped by its lack of capacity to innovate, which has become a growing concern in recent years (Figure 9). Evolving from a manufacturing-based economy to an innovation powerhouse for design and R&D requires a holistic approach to the innovation ecosystem, including nurturing talent (China ranks 47th in higher education and training) and technological readiness (ranking 73rd; technology is still far from universally available, let alone used).

The progress that China has already made in rebalancing its economy suggests its capacity to identify and rectify weaknesses in its growth model. Since 2005, the relative importance of manufacturing in China's economy has been declining steadily, and services now account for a bigger share of GDP. Meanwhile, a fledgeling social safety net consisting of a healthcare and pension system, along with rising incomes and lower exports, have initiated a rebalancing of demand toward domestic consumption. China's 'new normal' will bring further challenges in improving productivity, but its strong performance elsewhere in GCI indicates that the country is well positioned to meet them.

# CONCLUSION

Openness has non-economic benefits, too. Wider and deeper cross-border economic integration has contributed greatly to overall peace and stability since World War II. It has increased individuals' freedom to produce and consume in daily life, widening the life choices and chances of large numbers of ordinary people. However, openness and the links between trade and competitiveness have fallen off the agenda in recent years. Since the 2008–2009 crisis, policymakers have been in fire-fighting mode, focusing on fiscal and monetary macroeconomic stimulus and financial reregulation. This has arguably come at the expense of supply-side issues and structural reforms needed to address sluggish productivity growth. Supply-side constraints to growth – distortions in product and factor markets, education, skills, and infrastructure – have not been sufficiently addressed; if anything, market distortions have increased since the crisis, undermining competitiveness. And although protectionism has not surged, there is evidence of creeping protectionism, especially with increasing non-tariff barriers to trade. Global trade growth is weaker than at any time in the last two decades. Strengthening both global openness and domestic competitiveness has never been more important. To revive sluggish productivity and tap new sources of growth, innovation, job creation, and development, a trade-and-competitiveness agenda should be a priority for policymakers around the world.

The dynamics of economic, social, political and cultural change in the contemporary world are increasingly shaped by the pursuit and promotion of competitiveness. The economy's entry into globalization phase has radically altered the nature of competition. Numerous new actors from every market in the world are simultaneously in competition on every market. This new competition has accentuated the interdependence of the different levels of globalization. The world economy is changing in the face of growing competition as a consequence of globalization processes. These processes result in changing the position of global economic powers, the emergence of new powers, and thus in a new distribution of global forces. As WEF states (WEF, 2015, 5), these developments have also intensified competition in global markets, which, in turn, implies a greater need to be competitive to generate additional market opportunities and economic links in the presence of many more participants vying for the same space. The increasing spread of global value chains (GVCs) and skills present opportunities for countries to connect to high value-added parts of production processes without having to develop entire industries within their borders. GVCs have also brought into sharper focus the importance of trade facilitation, investment and 'behind-the-border' policies for competitiveness. GVCs are also called supply chains, multinational corporations, transnational corporations, etc. Their importance and at the same time the heterogeneity confirm Fojtíková and Vahalík (2016), and state that GVCs have a long tradition especially among developed countries. The international fragmentation of production brings through GVCs significant benefits also to developing countries which is a consequence of globalization processes in the world economy.

Globalization has obliged all countries to raise their standards of economic efficiency, hence the growing interest in and concern about competitiveness: nations, regions and cities have no option but to strive to be competitive in order to survive in the new global marketplace and the 'new competition' being forged by the new information or knowledge-driven economy. The evaluation of a country's performance is crucial to the country's efforts to improve its international competitiveness. Strengthening both global openness and domestic competitiveness has never been more important. Policy-makers at all levels have been swept up in this competitiveness fever too. This growing interest may perhaps be partly attributable to their awareness of the fact that all countries having to contend with raised standards of economic efficiency as a result of the globalization of goods and factor markets. The economy may be competitive but if the society and the environment suffer too much the country will face major difficulties and vice versa. Policies oriented to solve the main economic and social problems of their citizens may then not focus only on the improvement of indicators of competitiveness but also on the reduction of differences in competitiveness compared to other players in the world economy. Many of differences in economic growth and quality of life within a country may be explained by differences in competitiveness.

Methodological framework of the chapter measure macroeconomic competitiveness of WTO members based on GCI pillars, this chapter thus closely followed the methodology proposed by WEF. Determinants of competitiveness – pillars were distinguished into input and output size which measure different aspects of transformation processes of economic activities. Using efficiency analysis through DEA approach – the method aimed to identify the efficient and inefficient countries of the WTO and to estimate the relative efficiency of each country within the evaluated sample. Does it evolve the question: why measuring macroeconomic competitiveness is so important? Because 'if you cannot measure it, you cannot improve it' (Lord Kelvin, resp. an Irish mathematical physicist William Thomson). A quantitative score of competitiveness will facilitate WTO members in identifying possible weaknesses together with factors mainly driving these weaknesses. This, in turn, will assist countries in the catching up the process. In reality, every pillar may not play an equal role in the competitiveness of every country what is logical, and therefore the concept of different stages of economic development was applied. Therefore, follow-up research will thus orientate on regional relations and linkages across individual continents (based on driven forces of competitiveness relevant to each stage of development), and the added value of regions' links to the competitiveness of the WTO members, especially in the case of GVCs.

The world is undergoing a new round of major development, great change and profound readjustment. The mankind still faces growing uncertainties and destabilizing factors. Surging tides of anti-globalization in recent years, coupled with rising protectionism and unilateralism, have posed severe challenges to the multilateral trading system with the WTO at its core. Economic globalization has powered global growth and is an irreversible trend of our times. China and the multilateral trading system stand together through thick and thin. China will have important challenges in order to fulfil its commitments, comply with rules, actively participate in the improvement of the multilateral trading system, and give firm support to WTO in playing a greater role in global economic governance (China's State Council Information Office, 2018).

## ACKNOWLEDGMENTS

The chapter is supported by the Czech Scientific Foundation (Grant NO. 17-22426S), project Law Aspects of China´s Incorporation into the Global Trade System.

## REFERENCES

Andersen, Per, and Niels Christian Petersen. 1993. "A Procedure for Ranking Efficient Units In Data Envelopment Analysis." *Management Science* 3910):1261–1264.

Ando, Mitsuyo. 2006. "Fragmentation and vertical intra-industry trade in East Asia." *North American Journal of Economics and Finance* 17:257–281.

Annoni, Paola, and Kornelia Kozovska. 2010. *EU Regional Competitiveness Index 2010*. Luxembourg: Publication Office of the European Union, 2010.

Bagicha, Minhas S. 1962. "The Homohypallagic Production Function, Factor-Intensity Reversals, and the Heckscher-Ohlin Theorem." *Journal of Political Economy* 70:138–138.

Baldwin, Robert E. 1971. "Determinants of the Commodity Structure of U.S. Trade." *American Economic Review* 61:126–145.

Banker, Rajiv D., Charnes, Abraham, and William W. Cooper. 1984. "Some models for estimating technical and scale inefficiencies in data envelopment analysis." *Management Science* 30(9):1078–1092.

Barrell, Ray, Mason, Geoff, and Mary O´Mahony. 2010. *Productivity, Innovation and Economic Growth*. Cambridge: Cambridge University Press.

Brander, James A., and Barbara J. Spencer. 1981. "Export Subsidies and Market Share Rivalry." *Journal of International Economics* 18:83–100.

Charnes, Abraham, Cooper, William W., and Edward Rhodes. 1978. "Measuring the efficiency of decision making units." *European Journal of Operation Research* 2(6): 429–444.

China's State Council Information Office. 2018. *China and the World Trade Organization*. Last modified 2018. http://english.gov.cn/archive/white_paper/2018/06/28/content_281476201898696.htm.

Chipman, John S. 1966. "A Survey of the Theory of International Trade." *Econometrica* 34:18–76.

Cooper, William W., Li, Shanling, Seiford, Lawrence M., and Joe Zhu. 2004. "Sensitivity analysis in DEA." In *Handbook on Data Envelopment Analysis*, edited by William W. Cooper, Lawrence M. Seiford, and Joe Zhu, 71–92. Dordrecht: Kluwer Academic Publisher.

Cooper, William W., Seiford, Lawrence M., and Joe Zhu. 2004. "Data Envelopment Analysis: History, Models and Interpretaions." In *Handbook on Data Envelopment Analysis*, edited by William W. Cooper, Lawrence M. Seiford, and Joe Zhu, 1–40. Dordrecht: Kluwer Academic Publisher.

Cooper, William W., Seiford, Lawrence M., and Kaoru Tone. 2007. *Introduction to Data Envelopment Analysis and its Uses with DEA-solver Software and References*. New York: Springer.

Deprins, Dominique, Simar, Léopold, and Henry Tulkens. 1994. "Measuring Labor-Efficiency in Post Offices." In *The Performance of Public Enterprises: Concepts and Measurements*, edited by Maurice Marchand, Pierre Pestieau, and Henry Tulkens, 243–267. New York: North-Holland.

Drucker, Peter. 2001. *The Efficiency of the Decision Makers*. Bucharest: Editura Destin.

Drysdale, Peter. 2010. *Politics and Chinese integration into the global economy*. Last modified 2010. http://www.eastasiaforum.org/2010/04/04/politics-and-chinese-integration-into-the-global-economy/.

Eaton, Jonathan, and Gene M. Grossman. 1986. "Optimal Trade and Industrial Policy Under Oligopoly." *Quarterly Journal of Economics* 101:383–406.

Ethier, Wilfred J. 1982. "National and International Returns to Scale in the Modern Theory of International Trade." *American Economic Review* 72:389–405.

Ezeala-Harrison, Fidelis. 1999. *Theory and Policy of International Competitiveness.* Westport: Praeger.

Farrell, Michael J. 1957. "The Measurement of productivity efficiency." *Journal of the Royal Statistical Society* 120(3):253–290.

Feketekuty, Geza. 1966. "The Scope, Implication and Economic Rationale of a Competition-Oriented Approach to Future Multilateral Trade Negotiation." *The World Economy* 19(1):167–181.

Fojtíková, Lenka, and Michaela Staníčková. 2017. "The EU Member States Export Competitiveness and Productivity." *Politická ekonomie* 65(6): 669–689.

Fojtíková, Lenka, and Bohdan Vahalík. 2016. "Trade in Value Added and Its Impact on the Czech Foreign Trade." In *Proceedings of the 3rd International Conference on European Integration 2016*, edited *by* Eva Kovářová, Lukáš Melecký, and Michaela Staníčková, 229–238. Ostrava: VŠB - Technical University of Ostrava.

Grossman, Gene M., and Helpman, Elhanan. 1992. *Innovation and Growth: Technological Competition in the Global Economy.* Massachusetts: MIT Press.

Grossman, Gene M., and Horn, Henrik. 1987. "Infant Industry Protection Reconsidered: The Case of International Barriers to Entry." *Quarterly Journal of Economics* 53:767–787.

Hančlová, Jana, and Lukáš Melecký. 2016. "Application of the Nonparametric DEA Meta-frontier Approach with Undesirable Outputs in the Case of EU Regions." *Business Systems Research Journal* 7(2): 65–77.

Institute for Management Development. 2012. *IMD World Competitiveness Yearbook 2012.* Lausanne: IMD.

Jones, Ronald W. 1956. "Factor Proportions and the Heckscher-Ohlin theorem." *Review of Economic Studies* 24:1–10.

Kessing, Donald B. 1966. "Labour Skills and Comparative Advantage." *American Economic Review* 56:249–258.

Krugman, Paul. 1994. "Competitiveness: A Dangerous Obsession." *Foreign Affairs* 73(2):28–44.

Leamer, Edward E. 1984. *Sources of International Comparative Advantage*. Massachusetts: MIT Press.

Mandl, Ulrike, Dierx, Adrian, and Fabienne Ilzkovitz. 2008. *The effectiveness and efficiency of public spending*. Brussels: European Commission-Directorate General for Economic and Financial Affairs.

McKenzie, Lionel W. 1955. "Equality of Factor Prices in World Trade." *Econometrica* 23:239–257.

Melecký, Lukáš. 2018. "The main achievements of the EU structural funds 2007–2013 in the EU member states: efficiency analysis of transport sector." *Equilibrium. Quarterly Journal of Economics and Economic Policy* 13(2):285–306.

Melitz, Marc J. 2003. "The Impact of Trade on Intra-Industry Reallocations and Aggregate Industry Productivity." *Econometrica* 71:1695–1725.

Metzler, Lloyd. 1949. "International Demand and Domestic Prices." *Journal of Political Economy* 57:345–351.

Mihaiu, Diana Marieta, Opreana, Alin, and Marian Pompiliu Cristescu. 2010. "Efficiency, effectiveness and performance of the public sector." *Romanian Journal of Economic Forecasting* 1(4): 132–147.

Porter, Michael Eugene. 1990. *The Competitive Advantage of Nations*. New York: The Free Press.

President's Commission on Industrial Competitiveness. 1985. *Global Competition: The New Reality*. Washington: U.S. Government Printing Office.

Rybczynski, Tadeusz M. 1955. "Factor Endowment and Relative Commodity Prices." *Economica* 22:336–341.

Scott, Bruce R., and George C. Lodge. 1985. *US Competitiveness in the World Economy*. Boston: Harvard Business School Press.

Staníčková, Michaela. 2017. "Can the implementation of the Europe 2020 Strategy goals be efficient? The challenge for achieving social equality in the European Union." *Equilibrium. Quarterly Journal of Economics and Economic Policy* 12(3):383–398.

Starr, Martin K., and Jonathan Ullman. 1988. *The Myth of Industrial Supremacy. Global Competitiveness*. New York: W. W. Norton & Company.

Stolper, Wolfgang F., and Paul A. Samuelson. 1941. "Protection and Real Wages." *Review of Economic Studies* 9:58–73.

Tone, Kaoru. 2002. "A slacks-based measure of super-efficiency in data envelopment analysis." *European Journal of Operational Research* 143(1):32–41.

Trefler, Daniel. 1995. "The Case of the Missing Trade and Other Mysteries." *American Economic Review* 85:1029–1046.

Tyson, Laura. 1988. *Competitiveness: An Analysis of the Problem and Perspective on Future Policy. Global Competitiveness*. New York: W. W. Norton & Company.

Vanek, Jaroslav. 1963. *The Natural Resource Content of United States Foreign Trade 1870–1955*. Massachusetts: MIT Press.

World Bank Group, World Trade Organization. 2015. *The Role of Trade in Ending Poverty*. Last modified 2015. http://www.worldbank.org/en/topic/trade/publication/the-role-of-tradein-ending-poverty.

World Economic Forum. 2001. *Global Competitiveness Report 2001-2002*. Geneva: WEF.

World Economic Forum. 2015. *The Case for Trade and Competitiveness*. Geneva: WEF.

World Economic Forum. 2016. *Global Competitiveness Report 2016-2017*. Geneva: WEF.

World Economic Forum. 2017. *The Global Competitiveness Report 2017–2018*.

World Economic Forum. 2018a. *Global Competitiveness Index – Competitiveness Rankings*. Last modified 2018. http://reports.weforum.org/global-competitiveness-index/competitiveness-rankings/

World Economic Forum. 2018b. *Reports*. Last modified 2018. http://reports.weforum.org/global-competitiveness-report-2015-2016/downloads/?doing_wp_cron=1513437847.2438359260559082031250

World Trade Organization. 2016. *Members and Observers.* Last modified 2016. https://www.wto.org/english/thewto_e/whatis_e/tif_e/org6_e.htm.

*Chapter 3*

# A REVIEW OF THE CHALLENGES TO POLITICAL AND SOCIO-ECONOMIC DEVELOPMENT IN KENYA

### *Daniel N. Sifuna[1] and Ibrahim Oanda[2]*
[1]Department of Educational Foundations,
Kenyatta University, Nairobi, Kenya
[2]Council for the Development of Social Science Research in Africa,
CODESRIA, Dakar, Senegal

### ABSTRACT

Development policy in Kenya after independence sought to improve the socio-economic conditions of citizens. The leadership of the nationalist movement aimed to redress the racial, ethnic and gender inequalities that characterized society during the colonial period. The government has since independence in 1963, engaged different approaches to achieve these objectives through periodic national development plans. The emphasis and focus of the development policy have shifted over time due to persistent internal challenges and the exigencies of the external environment. The shifts in policy planning, however, have not redressed socio-economic challenges. Instead, each subsequent policy has produced contradictions, causing a small percentage of growth sectors and wealthy individuals, while informalizing production processes in many sectors of the economy and widening socio-economic marginalization of most of the population. In terms of political approaches to economic planning, Kenya has moved from the centralized statist approach in 1963 to an experimentation with a 'district focus' strategy in the 1980s; an era of devolved funding from the 1990s and, since 2010, a devolved governance structure. Shifts in approaches to socio-economic development and political organization have only exacerbated the problem of socio-economic inequalities. This chapter seeks to examine the dynamics behind these persistent challenges. The chapter is based on a re-interpretation of already published works and existing data. Data from social sectors that most manifest socio-economic inequalities will be highlighted to illustrate the trends.

## INTRODUCTION

Sessional Paper No. 10 of 1965 on *African Socialism and Its Application to Planning in Kenya*, was the first policy that articulated the Kenya government's development orientation and its contradictions (Republic of Kenya, 1965). According to this policy, Kenya was to develop a mixed economy with both state and private sector participation as a strategy for sustained economic growth. The policy identified areas that presented future problems to economic growth, including the need for rapid development of agricultural lands; accelerated industrial growth; attracting domestic and foreign capital, pursuing monetary policies that would promote the interests of equity and larger revenues; guarding foreign exchange reserves; providing for participation by Africans in the economy; relieving unemployment; removing idleness; reconciling pressures for expanding welfare schemes with the need for rapid economic growth and conserving natural resources (Republic of Kenya, 1965). The policy indicated the country's development choice as one that favored economic growth as opposed to social development (redistribution). Accordingly, the policy encouraged approaches to economic planning that favored public investments in already developed and high potential areas. It was argued that this approach was likely to yield faster returns due to an abundance of natural resources, fertile land and rainfall, transport and power facilities, and people already receptive to and active in development (Republic of Kenya, 1965). Policy makers then seemed to think that the problem of less developed areas accrued from citizens' resistance to new ways of doing things and their lack of the necessary discipline of planned and coordinated development (Ibid). Solving the problem of development in the less developed regions was expected to be a long-term problem, requiring concerted and prolonged effort to overcome. Prejudices and suspicions from these inhabitants had to be mitigated before it was possible for government to invest any resources. In other words, the lack of socio-economic development in these areas was blamed on the people residing there not lack of government strategy.

It is the contention of this chapter that Kenya has never gotten to deconstruct this initial exclusionist approach to policy planning, which explains divergencies in the country's socio-economic development to-date. The 1965 sessional paper promised equity and equal access to the benefits of development for every citizen, yet deferred government intervention in less developed areas, while blaming citizens for the levels of underdevelopment. Most of the undeveloped regions are in the arid and semi-arid regions (ASAL), which constitute approximately 70 per cent of Kenya's land area. The populations in these regions have been marginalized as far as reaping benefits of government policy interventions is concerned. This is one of the challenges that continue to compound Kenya's economic development. As we shall argue in the next section, while the challenges in these regions are ecological, government planning perceives the ecological challenge in terms of people's resistance to change.

## ECOLOGICAL AND DEMOGRAPHIC DIVERSITY AND SOCIO-ECONOMIC DEVELOPMENT

Over the years, Kenya's approach to development planning has been influenced by the country's varied agro-ecological and climatic zones. This has, in turn, influenced demographic dynamics to the extent that there seems to be a natural confluence between a people's capacity to manipulate nature and benefit from its agro-ecosystems, and current levels of socio-economic and political development of the various regions. The mediating factor determining current socio-economic conditions, however, has much to do with government planning policy for the various agro-climatic zones.

Kenya has a total area of 580,370 square kilometers (kms). Topographically, the altitude varies from sea level to the peak of Mt. Kenya, situated north of the capital Nairobi, which is 5,199 meters (m) above sea level. In terms of socio-economic profiles and economic potential of the different regions, the agro-climatic zone map of Kenya divides Kenya into seven (7) zones based on rainfall patterns and the potential for agriculture. In this context, agriculture is largely defined as cash and food-crops, to the exclusion of other agricultural practices such as pastoralism (Republic of Kenya, 1980). The zone is important as a source of rain and rivers. Zone one (I), according to the classification, has no direct bearing on agricultural production as it is confined to mountains and surrounding areas. Zone two (II) is the high agricultural productivity regions of central and Eastern Kenya (areas surrounding Mt. Kenya), areas in the Rift Valley region (Mau and Aberdare, including Kericho and Nyahururu) and the areas surrounding mount Elgon (Kitale and Webuye). Most of these areas were referred to as the white highlands, where colonial settler agriculture flourished during the colonial period. They are the areas that were earmarked by the 1965 session paper for government investments to sustain economic growth.

Zone three (III) comprises areas receiving annual rainfall of between 950 and 1500 mm. This zone is characterized by medium to small-scale agricultural cultivation and high population densities. It covers most parts of the Nyanza region (especially the highlands), Western and Central provinces, a good proportion of Central Rift-Valley (Nandi, Nakuru, Bomet, Eldoret, Kitale) and a small strip at the Coast province. Zone four (IV) receives lower rainfall of between 500-1000 mm. This is typically represented in regions surrounding Naivasha, vast parts of the Laikipia and Machakos districts and vast parts of the central and southern Coast Province. Zone five (V) is much drier compared to zone four's regions. This zone receives annual rainfall of between 300-600. It is prevalent in northern Baringo, Turkana, lower Makueni and vast parts of the North Eastern region of the country. In Kenya's socio-economic classification, some areas in zone IV and all areas in zone V are classified as semi-arid regions as they receive between 500 and 850mm of rainfall annually. These areas are further subdivided into four categories based on agricultural potential. These are a) semi-arid areas with mixed rain-fed and irrigation agriculture and high economic and political disparities; b) semi-arid areas with encroaching agro-pastoral use by marginalized smallholders; c) semi-arid areas with predominantly pastoralist use in the economic and political periphery; and, d) semi-arid areas that include protected areas and their surroundings. Kajiado, Narok, Mbeere, Mwingi, Kitui, Machakos and Makueni are considered semi-arid. Also covered under this category is the entire coast, except the Tana River district and some small part of central Kenya.

Zones six (VI) and seven (VII) constitute a few areas that are classified as semi-arid and a large part that is classified as arid, with desert-like conditions. Zone VI areas receive annual rainfall of between 200 to 400 mm and is erratic. The zone is found in the Marsabit, Turkana, Mandera and Wajir Districts. The pure arid, Zone VII, includes the Chalbi desert in the Marsabit district with sparse vegetation and pastoralism as the core economic activity. The arid regions are characterized by high temperatures with evapotranspiration rates more than twice the annual rainfall. In most cases, when it rains in these regions, it is in the form of short but high intensity storms that produce considerable run off and soil erosion. In these circumstances, average rainfall figures are deceptive because there tends to be a few years of rainfall well above average whilst the probability of occurrence is low. Approximate rainfall expectancy in the arid districts ranges from 150-450 mm in a year. Few areas have volcanic soils and alluvial deposits which are suitable for crop production. Water availability and accessibility is highly variable and is a considerable constraint to production.

This detailed description of the agro-ecological zones has been presented here as a prelude to explaining how ecological conditions have influenced socio-economic and political developments in the country. While the distribution of agro-eco-ecosystems is naturally determined, their productivity is determined by deliberate manipulation by human beings primarily for production and reproduction. Over the years, the natural occurrence and spread of the different ecological zones has been associated with a political process of naming and associating the economic potential of a region with its eco-system characteristics. This began with the onset of colonialism and was accentuated during the post-colonial period. The various agro-climatic zones, for example, are based on the rainfall potential of the region and its capacity for plantation agriculture. The zones that can support this notion of agricultural productivity account for approximately 20 per cent of the country but support roughly 80 per cent of the population. The semi-arid zones cover approximately 20 per cent of the entire land area while the arid zones, characterized by desert conditions, covers 60 per cent of the total landmass. What this means is that over time, conscious government planning has largely benefited regions in the 20 per cent agricultural zone in line with the economic development orientation of Session Paper No 10 of 1965. This is despite the fact that though the arid and semi-arid zones cannot support agricultural production, they are endowed with other resources such as extractives which, if developed, would improve the socio-economic profiles of the regions. Mineral resources currently exploited are gold, limestone, soda ash, salt, rubies, fluorspar, and garnets. By 2014, forested land in Kenya was less than ten per cent, which means that Kenya is a low cover forest country by United Nations standards (Republic of Kenya, 2014). The United Nations also classifies Kenya as a chronically water-scarce country with a renewable freshwater supply of about 647 cubic meters per capita, falling below the set marker for water scarcity of 1,000 m$^3$ per capita (World Bank, 2006).

In terms of demographic dynamics, Kenya comprises 42 ethnic groups, the Kikuyu, Luo, Kalenjin, Luhya, Kamba, Kisii, Mijikenda, Somalia and Meru being the largest in numerical strength, respectively (Republic of Kenya 2013). Christianity and Islam remain the main religions in the country. English is the official language while Kiswahili is the national language. The country's population has more than quadrupled since 1963, growing from around 8.1 million in 1963 to an estimated 48.462 million people in 2017 (Republic of Kenya 2018). Kenya has the sixth highest population in sub-Saharan Africa, behind Tanzania, South Africa, the

Democratic Republic of the Congo (DRC), Ethiopia and Nigeria. The total fertility rates per woman (henceforth, TFR) has, however, fluctuated from 4.9 in 2003, to 4.4 in 2009 and was at 4.6 in 2013 (KDHS 2010, Republic of Kenya 2009; Republic of Kenya 2013). Data on TFR is important as the poor regions of the country (Arid and semi-Arid areas), where less public resources have been invested over the years, have corresponding low levels of female schooling and high TFR. For example, by 2014, the arid and semi-arid counties of northeastern Kenya registered an average of 7.8 children per woman compared to a national average 3.9 children per woman (Republic of Kenya, 2014).

In terms of growth rates and composition of the age structure of the population, studies point to a trend where rates of population growth outpace rates of economic growth, therefore complicating the problem of socio-economic development. In 2008, Kenya's population was estimated at 34 million up from 28.7 million reported in the 1999 national census and from 15.3 million in the 1979 census. In 2006, the annual population growth rate was estimated at approximately 2.8 per cent, a rate substantially below that of the early 1980s when Kenya's growth reached four per cent (Republic of Kenya 2009). The 2009 national census established the proportion of the youth population as a share of the adult population to be 66 per cent. Government policy going forward was to stabilize the rates of population growth to 1.5 per cent per annum and reduce TFR per woman to 2.2 children (Republic of Kenya 2013).

In terms of age structure, data for 2018 shows the structure of Kenya's population as follows; children, 0-4 years (42.3 per cent); working population aged 15-64 years (55.1 per cent) and the aged population, 65+ years (2.7 per cent) (Republic of Kenya 2018). Of the population group aged 15-64, 36 percent constituted a population of youth aged 15-34 years (African Institute for Development Policy, AFIDEP et al. 2018). This is an age structure associated with a youth bulge, which if the country plans well, would benefit from the demographic divided. The likelihood of turning the youth dividend into a demographic dividend is, however, eroded by other socio-economic circumstances that the youth face. By 2014, approximately 67 per cent of Kenya's unemployed were youth aged between 15 and 34 years of age, while 3 per cent were enrolled in Technical and vocational Education and Training (TIVET) or university level institutions (Republic of Kenya 2014). However, due to government underfunding of institutions, the quality of education in universities has increasingly come under scrutiny. The labor markets have raised concerns over the years that poor-quality training in the institutions predisposes the youth to long periods of unemployment (AFIDEP et al. 2018, British Council, 2016).

But, even the best intentions of government policy to match population growth rates with economic growth rates continues to face hurdles around equating high populations numbers with control of political power and resources. While Session Paper No. 10 of 1965 might not have been intended in the current manner that its logic is applied in Kenya, high population numbers signify control of political and economic largesse. Kenyan politics is principally organized around ethnic groups and since the large ethnic groups have controlled political power since its independence, their areas have received a large share of public resources and are, therefore, more developed. As we shall see in the discussion on economic development, the large communities have also used their control of public resources to move to areas previously defined as 'underdeveloped' (areas Zones IV-VI). Using these resources and networks has transformed the economic fortunes of the regions where they have settled. This has created a dichotomy that has fueled the politicization of demographic planning in the country. The 'indigenous' inhabitants of these regions have not benefited from such resources and, therefore, think their socio-economic fortunes will also change if they grow their population and win political power. The ethnic groups with large populations see this as a strength to continue holding on to privilege. Politicians from both sides, therefore, approve population planning polices in their official capacities but in informal gathering continues to urge their constituents to increase their population numbers.

Government policy over the last two decades has not helped to diffuse these pressures. The allocation of devolved funds for constituencies and the development of social sectors (education, health) has been largely based on population numbers prior to considering a region's level of socio-economic development. Schools with high enrollments receive more public funding, even when located in high potential regions with wealthy household members compared to those schools in low density regions. This has maintained a general feeling that the policy rewards high population areas and those that are well-off compared to levels of socio-economic need. The Commission for Revenue Allocation (henceforth, CRA), a body established after the 2010 constitution, confronted this problem by crafting a formula that would be used to distribute national revenues to the counties. After much haggling, political pressure to adopt population numbers and density as basic criteria over poverty index and land area prevailed. The formula used to allocate funds to the constituencies is now 45 per cent allocation based on a country's population, 20 per cent poverty index and 8 per cent based on land area (Kaimenyi, 2013). This is problematic as it means that 73 per cent of the allocation is based on factors that disadvantage regions with low populations, high poverty index and a history of exclusion. These regions are not benefiting from public resources.

The contradictory policies, therefore, continue to influence household and community responses to government policies, including family planning policies and settlement patterns, with more people migrating to places they perceive they are likely to benefit from public services. By 2013, about 26 per cent of the population lived in urban areas, 61 per cent of whom were poor urban(slum) settlements (Republic of Kenya, 2013). The country's major cities (Nairobi, Mombasa, Kisumu, Nakuru, and Eldoret) have received much of these populations. According to the 2009 population census, Nairobi had the largest share of Kenya's urban population at 3.1 Million (25.9 per cent) followed by Mombasa at 925,000 (7.7 per cent); Kisumu, 383,00 (3.2 per cent); Nakuru, 367,000 (3.1 per cent); and Eldoret, 312 (2.6 per cent) (Central Bureau of Statistics, 2009). None of these cities are in the heartlands of the regions in Zones IV-VII.

## SOCIAL-CULTURAL SETTINGS, EDUCATION AND HEALTH INDICATORS

Cultural predispositions have been shown to be powerful determinants of a population's responses to processes of change and development (Holsinger 1977). In the case of Kenya, the link between these variables and how they relate to the uptake of modern schooling and public health practices have been controversial. From the onset of colonialism, the introduction of Christian missionary activities and colonial settler agriculture were met with varying degrees of acceptance. Regions that were particularly unreceptive to these new activities were accused of rejecting modernity. This theory was later reinforced by colonial anthropology and accentuated by approaches to economic planning in the post-colonial period (Goldsmith, 2011). It is interesting to note how the areas and regions so labelled during the colonial period continue to have the lowest levels of development interventions from public resources.

To be sure, aspects of tradition and customary practices have been maintained by all Kenyan communities and regions. There are, of course, differences in the extent of the community's recourse to traditional culture as part of their social economic practices. Communities in regions with high levels of socio-economic development do not encounter this contradiction of practicing aspects of traditional culture alongside modern ones or even within modern institutions like Christian churches. Culture and tradition in Kenya have become issues when government wants to explain failure to develop certain regions of the country or private individuals with political support want to alienate available resources in lands inhabited by the, so labelled, 'traditional communities' or both. Similar approaches to resource alienation and underdevelopment of some regions happened during the colonial period when the British administrators described the attachment of coastal and pastoralist communities to tradition as 'indolence' (Goldsmith, 2011). Such negative attitudes from British colonial administrators to local communities were accompanied with conquest and benign neglect resulting to the economic stagnation of formerly dynamic and wealthy communities (Goldsmith, 2011).

In the face of economic marginalization, blaming communities' attachment to tradition as their cause of economic underdevelopment continues, often justified by rebranded notions and labels on marginalized communities borrowed from colonial anthropology. This trend has been exacerbated by population growth and land pressure in the developed regions of the country, forcing people to move out to less denser areas, most of which are formerly neglected regions (Klopp and Lumumba, 2016). A common description of communities in coastal regions of Kenya is that they are 'lazy and bid their time sleeping under mango trees waiting for the fruits to fall and eat'. Mango trees grow naturally in most parts of the coastal region of Kenya. This description has been used to justify the alienation of land from coastal communities and its allocation to people migrating from up-country regions. For example, in Lamu, 95 per cent of inhabitants in the Mpeketoni and Mkunumbi settlements schemes are migrants from up-country and have title deeds to their land. The indigenous population, however, have no title deeds and cannot use their land as collateral (Commission for Revenue Allocation, 2012). The settlement schemes are served with modern infrastructure like water projects and roads; both facilities that are absent in lands settled by the indigenous peoples, who continue to be labelled 'traditional and conservative' while being denied the benefits of public provision. This is the fate of most communities inhabiting the semi-arid and arid ecological Zones IV-VII. Within these zones, political support and private capital have witnessed enclaves of wealth and well-being which mostly benefit the new settlers and marginalize further indigenous populations, pushing them away from public infrastructures such as schools and health centers. (Klopp and Lumumba, 2006)

The link between culture, ecology and socio-economic well-being in Kenya, therefore, remain contentious. Since levels of political support mediate this process, the roles individuals play in the society and the process and rewards that they reap, tend to differ depending on their age, gender, power, influence and abilities. At the same time, how others perceive them, and how they perceive themselves are largely a function of those roles and rewards. In effect, the process creates and sustains a human-made environment in a social sphere. In this regard, the physical and social environments that people inhabit determine their relationship to government and the attitudes and perception of what socio-economic development entails.

In terms of socio-cultural organization, some communities largely abandoned traditional practices, especially those related to social structure and kinship relations. Even within individual communities, social differentiation is widespread and is tied to property ownership and inheritance. Since Kenya is a predominantly agricultural country, land is a principal factor in production. Hence, access to and control over land has a critical impact on a family's socio-economic status, especially in the rural areas where approximately 80 per cent of the population lives. Most ethnic groups still use the traditional land tenure system. Traditional tenure practices provide land access to all members of the family lineage, while control over land use was vested in the clan or in the community. By the dictates of custom, women inherited property through their husbands while men's entitlement to land was cemented through marriage. In this regard, in the registration of traditional land holdings, husbands were the legally acknowledged title deed holders. Until recent changes in the legal provision and the 2010 Constitution, husbands could dispose of land without their wives' consent. The constitution and dispensation in new laws, protects wives' interests in the event of sale by requiring the consent of all family members before land and any other family property is sold. Additionally, the Law of Succession and the constitution entitles wives and daughters to a share in the estate, including real property of their husbands or fathers. With the completion of land registration in many parts of the country, real property can freely change hands solely on a "willing buyer and willing seller" basis. In this case, women, even when married can buy and sell land under their own names. However, despite coming into force with this legislation, discrimination against women is still common. Many people, especially men, consider sons as the proper heirs of the family name and property. This is because sons are thought to be essential to the continuation of the family lineage. There is, then, a strong preference for male children to inherit property. Such preference often encourages the continuation of reproduction beyond medically, socially and economically reasonable limits where the male child, or the desired number of male children, proves difficult to reach. This same desire for male children also helps perpetuate polygamy in some communities (Government of Kenya and UNICEF, 1992; Government of Kenya and National Environment Authority, 2009).

Gender differentiation also extends to decision-making and the division of labor. While there are increasing concerns for gender equity in the socio-economic sphere, patriarchy in most households and in the modern workplace is still practiced. Although patriarchy has its origin in the Western world, especially Europe, it has been subtly and crudely justified under the umbrella of the "traditional African society." The result is that there are some jobs which are considered to be exclusively within the male or female domain. This is reinforced by the traditional division of labor in many Kenyan households, which is far from being equitable as it burdens women much more than men. Although some changes have begun to occur, especially in the upper strata of urban Kenya, nearly all the household duties still fall on the female members. This system has been continued from the communal mode of production in the patriarchal form. Patterns of household decision-making by women as a group, particularly in rural areas have not changed significantly. In the male-headed households, especially when the man is the only bread winner, he makes the final decision on crucial household expenditures, though he might be prompted in the decision by his wife or children. However, it is also important to mention that as women achieved high levels of education, gained more knowledge of the world, and increased their visibility and importance as co-breadwinners in the economy, they have frequently exerted pressure on men, particularly in the urban areas to allow them a greater role in decision-making than they would have enjoyed in the past (Government of Kenya and UNICEF, 1990; Government of Kenya and UNICEF, 1991).

It is also important to note that the extended family obligations (helping blood relatives beyond one's children), which still persists, seems to play an enduring role on the national socio-cultural scene. The extended family tends to bear the burdens of the rampant dependency syndrome. It generally functions as an informal social insurance system or mutual support mechanism, whereby members of a family lineage tend to feel strongly obliged to care for one another. However, such obligations have evolved in response to changes in residential patterns and the stresses and strains emanating from the economic sphere. On the other hand, economic constraints and rural urban-migrations have occasionally spread members of the extended family over large distances. Under these circumstances, lack of frequent contact tends to weaken the rights and obligations within the family. Members of the extended family who are employed or generally well off, however, are expected to, and usually do, give material assistance to those who need help. Such assistance normally reinforces the perception of belonging together, even if it strains the resources of the giver. However, in the context of the modern cash economy, the extended family is often perceived as a burden and not an economic resource to some members, as income-earning opportunities are not widely accessible. The challenge for the individual families is to raise all family members to a higher level of well-being without doing irreparable damage to those family members who bear the productive burdens (Silberschmidt, 1991).

The uptake of formal schooling and modern public health practices, among the different regions and communities, has also been affected by the contradictions between availability and the influence of a community's culture and attachment to traditional practices. As stated earlier, the persisting contradiction in Kenya's approach to development has been to concentrate public resources in high density productivity regions. Less dense regions are rarely served by public utilities such as schools, which means the uptake of formal schooling is low. Health centers also do not exist, are too far or are not stocked. In the case of pastoralists, the same applies with respect to provision of modern veterinary services. Most of these communities are bound to seek recourse for sustainability in traditional systems of knowledge transmission and healing practices, including for their animals. This situation also affects communities living within the Lake Victoria basin. Though of medium density, served by modern institutions such as schools, the region suffers from high levels of disease prevalence, exacerbated by climatic conditions whose extremes overwhelm the community's coping capability. So, the attribution of tradition and conservatism to communities' failure to take up schooling and modern health practices, even when physical provision is unavailable, is one of the contradictions of development policy in Kenya.

For example, by 2016, the year for which the latest household budget survey data is available, the percentage of population that had attended three years or more of schooling was 89.4 per cent (KNBS 2018). But, this was below 50 per cent for the ASAL counties of Garissa, Marsabit, Mandera, Wajir, Turkana, and Samburu. At the same time the ASAL counties recorded higher than national average family household sizes (number of family members), Wajir (6.6), Garissa (5.5) and Mandera (6.4) compared to counties from high density regions that recorded smaller family household sizes such as Nyeri (2.9), Nairobi City (3.0) and Mombasa (3.0) (KNBS 2018: 70). School attendance followed the same pattern. The National Net Attendance Ratio (henceforth, NAR) for pre-primary, primary and secondary school was 63.5, 82.4 and 37.5 per cent, respectively. But the ASAL counties registered the lowest NAR, with Garissa County having the lowest NAR for pre-primary and primary school at 4.4 per cent and 37.8 per cent, and Turkana the lowest NAR for secondary school at 9.3 per cent (KNBS 2018: 72).

The same pattern was repeated regarding health indicators. Nationally, the proportion of children born in health facilities (hospitals, health centers, dispensary/clinics) improved significantly to 65.3 per cent in 2015/16 Kenya Integrated Health Baseline Survey (KIHBS) compared to 39.1 per cent reported in the 2005/06 KIHBS. However, the ASAL counties of Wajir, Mandera, Samburu and Marsabit had over 70 per cent of children born at home, while Kirinyaga, Nyeri and Kisii Counties recorded over 90 per cent of children born in a heath facility (KNBS 2018:106). These patterns do not reflect persistence of culture and traditions, but rather the lack of public provision. Kenyan society continuous to be fractured by entrenched vertical and horizontal inequalities, that have been perpetuated and reinforced over time by public spending patterns that systematically disadvantaged some groups and areas. Of the 47 new counties created through devolution, 23 are categorized as ASAL areas. These areas have, since the colonial period, been categorized as disadvantaged and allocated a lower share of public funds for years.

These indicators are partly explained by the fact that government spending per capita on these services is considerably less in these less developed areas. There are fewer school and health facilities and less teachers and health staff compared to high density areas. Non-governmental organizations (NGOs) also often place a higher priority on service delivery to settled agricultural communities. The reasons for low school attendance, especially among pastoral communities and indigenous communities in the coast region remain complex. Foremost, low school enrolment may also be due to a perception among pastoralists that formal education, as currently provided, undermines the principles on which pastoral livelihoods are based. Formal education places no value on the local practices and institutions of pastoral communities. In this way, it may introduce new divides into households and communities and undermine customary institutions.

## POLITICAL STRUCTURES, LEGAL AND RIGHTS FRAMEWORK

Kenya's political system is organized around ethnic mobilization rather than political ideologies. Control of executive political institutions (presidency, security agencies and some cabinet portfolios) has often meant control of economic resources which are distributed along ethnic lines to the exclusion of members of other ethnicities. Using ethnicity as the basis for political mobilization continues to predispose the country to challenges with regard to the rule of law as political actors escape accountability by invoking affinity to politically powerful ethnic patronage systems. Human rights violations occur frequently and equality is not put into practice. Impunity for serious crimes, notably human rights violations and corruption, remains a formidable challenge. The broad challenge that the system has faced over the years is lack of enforcement of accountability in the management of public affairs. The new constitution promulgated in 2010 was supposed to address these shortcomings. However, its full implementation ran into headwinds due to political gerrymandering revolved around the need to keep a strong centralized authority with attendant control of public resources. Corruption, both in the political and economic sense, remains a major challenge. Corruption is a major impediment to doing business in Kenya with allegations of misappropriation of public funds on the rise. The 2016 Corruption Perception Index released by Transparency International (TI) ranked Kenya among the most corrupt countries at 145 out of 176 countries (Deloitte, 2017).

The 2010 constitution established a presidential republic in which sovereignty is exercised by the people through democratically elected representatives, but limited presidential power through a decentralized political system. The constitution created 47 counties and an upper house in the Parliament, the Senate, where county governments have equal representation. Certain powers were transferred from the central government to the 47 newly created counties, ranging from economic development to health care, education and infrastructure. The rationale for devolution involved several factors, but the two most important ones were empowerment of local government and reducing inequality between regions. The constitution also included a Bill of Rights that recognized the socio-economic needs of Kenyan citizens (Republic of Kenya, 2010).

Issues of equity are addressed through the Bill of Rights. The counties receive grants from Treasury based on the recommendations of the CRA. The Constitution also provides for an Equalization Fund, which is set aside to provide basic services including water, roads, health facilities and electricity to marginalized areas. The rationale for the equalization fund is that extra resource allocations are needed for the marginalized regions in order to bring the quality of basic services these areas to the level generally enjoyed by the rest of regions of the country. In addition, the Constitution provides for the representation of minorities and marginalized groups in governance, and has provisions on enhancing access to employment and special opportunities in educational and economic fields for these groups. Therefore, the Constitution provides impetus to diminish Kenya's regional inequalities, which continue to be a recipe for disharmony and dissatisfaction among citizens. This will be a long-term struggle for the constitution's full implementation (Republic of Kenya, 2010).

The government consists of three arms, namely: The Legislature, which enacts laws; the Executive; and the Judiciary, which acts as an arbitrator. With the new constitution and the 2013 national elections, the legislator comprises of 47 elected senators and several nominated ones; the national assembly with over 300 elected members of parliament and a number of nominated ones; and the Attorney General who is an ex-officio member. Within the judiciary, there is the Chief Justice and the Supreme Court and other organs, while the executive is led by the presidency. Additionally, there is universal suffrage for all citizens over eighteen years. Voting is done by secret ballot. The Kenyan Constitution guarantees freedom of political participation without discrimination on the basis of race, religion and gender. Elections are conducted by the Independent Electoral and Boundaries Commission (IEBC) (Republic of Kenya, 2010).

The administrative structure consists of centralized services from line ministries. Based on the new constitution, there are 20 ministries and several independent non-ministerial departments. The role of these bodies is to facilitate policy formulation and deliver public services, including the implementation and monitoring of programs and projects. Within the county administrative system, the president appoints County Commissioners of the 47 counties, district commissioners and district officers. Under this hierarchical structure, district officers, chiefs and assistant chiefs are in charge of administrative divisions, locations and sub-locations, respectively (Republic of Kenya, 2010).

Within the context of the outlined political structures, there is now a rights and legal-based approach to development, which demands the broadening of the scope for marginalized groups' survival, protection, and participation. Such an approach centers around the principles of indivisibility, universality, equity and the best interests of humanity. Indivisibility refers to the mutual exercising of all rights in a complimentary, inter-dependent and non-hierarchical manner, while universality means that all rights apply to every citizen. The principle of participation requires that the beneficiaries participate in determining the objectives, process and outcomes of the program. These rights include the right to survival, development and protection. Survival rights include the right to life, the right to the highest attainable standard of health and nutrition as well the right to nationality. Development rights include the right to education, the right to social security and the right to leisure recreation and cultural activities, while the right to protection includes the right for respect for every one's views, freedom of expression, access to appropriate information and freedom of thought, conscience and religion.

For example, Articles 20, 35, 42, 43 and 53 state, among other rights, that "every person has the right to education." This is reinforced by Articles 10(1) and 10(2) which states the national values and principles of governance that are binding to all state organs and institutions in the country including education. Articles 52, 53, 54, 55 and 56 of the Constitution have provisions on children's right to free and compulsory, quality basic education, and provisions regarding access to educational institutions and facilities for persons with disabilities in ways compatible with the interest of the disabled persons (Republic of Kenya, 2010: 31-33). There are also provisions targeting facilitating access of youth and marginalized minority to quality education and training, and access to employment (Republic of Kenya, 2010:31-33).

The Kenyan Government has ratified many of the United Nations (UN) conventions, especially those affecting women, children and marginalized groups, and transformed them into legal and policy frameworks. Enforcement of these groups' rights is part of the Bill of Rights which is enforced in Kenya through Kenyan law. The Kenyan legal system is composed of Acts of Parliament, principles of common law and equity and the African customary law. The hierarchy of laws and the choice of laws applicable in the High Courts is provided for by Section 3 (1) of the Judiciary Act. These laws are the Constitution and written laws and the substance of the common law, and doctrines of equity and statutes. Customary laws apply insofar as they are not repugnant to morality and justice and are not inconsistent with any written law. The Constitution, which is the supreme law of the country, enables the existence of a plurality of personal laws by recognizing the diverse and heterogeneous nature of the Kenyan society.

This allows for the application of customary personal laws in matters such as adoption, marriage, divorce and burial. The Constitution also recognizes the diversity in religious laws by, for instance, recognizing the application of Islamic personal laws in the Kadhi's Court, which has jurisdiction in matters relating to personal status, marriage, divorce or inheritance proceedings if all the parties are Muslims. This integration of personal religious laws in the Constitution is said to have created a multi-tiered and multi-sourced system of law (Government of Kenya and UNICEF, 1998; Government of Kenya and National Environment Authority, 2009).

The Kenyan Constitution outlaws discrimination on the basis of sex, race, tribe, place of origin or residence or other local connection, political opinions color or creed. Following the Convention on the Elimination of all Forms of Discrimination Against Women (CEDAW) a constitutional amendment (Section 82), added "sex" as a ground upon which discrimination is prohibited. Discrimination arises where certain persons are denied or restricted from enjoying privileges or advantages that are accorded to others by sections of the Constitution. Some sections further prohibit persons performing functions of a public office or public authority from discriminating against persons within this definition. The specific inclusion of the term "sex" in Section 82 of the Constitution was crucial to the attainment of full protection of women's human rights and attainment of gender equality. This was particularly important considering that it was in the realms of personal laws, where different forms of gender discrimination prevail, making them critical in the attainment of moral and actual equality. Outlawing discrimination against women enabled them to challenge discriminatory laws and policies in a court of law and call for automatic repeal (Government of Kenya and UNICEF, 1992; Government of Kenya and National Environment Authority, 2009).

It should, however, be acknowledged that despite the progressive nature of the new Constitution, its successful implementation has been hampered by numerous challenges, which among others include a political leadership that is anchored in the conservatism and repression of the previous regimes and lack of adequate resources. The leadership has struggled to introduce legislation that attempts to claw back many of the rights and freedom currently enjoyed by ordinary citizens.

## ECONOMIC ISSUES

Kenya's economic performance has had an important bearing on all citizens, especially marginalized groups. The performance is a function of the resources available, their rate of growth and distribution among the various communities and regions. A well-endowed resource country that distributes such resources equitably among its citizens provides them with the means to meet their basic needs and to pursue other activities, which would include investments. Conversely, a country that is resource-poor or abundant but distributes inequitably will inevitably have many pockets of poor and disadvantaged people who are vulnerable. In this regard a country's economic performance is a fundamental determinant of maternal and child mortalities.

Kenya's economy is largely dependent on agriculture and manufacturing. The first decade (1963-1973) following the achievement of independence in 1963 was characterized by rapid economic growth averaging seven percent per annum. The performance of the economy was based on the extension of agricultural acreage, introduction of hybrid maize, exotic cattle and export crops, rapid expansion of public services and import substitution-led industrialization. In this phase, which some economists describe as Kenya's "golden age," the country enjoyed low inflation employment creation, a relatively stable balance of payments position and gross domestic product (henceforth, GDP), growth rates (Republic of Kenya, 1964).

However, this rapid growth era was effectively checked by the first oil shock of the period 1973-74, which was associated with the Arab-Israel war of 1973. During this war, there was a sharp rise in oil prices creating considerable external and internal imbalances in Kenya. The situation was temporarily resurrected by the coffee boom of 1976-77, when Brazil's coffee crop was destroyed by frost. Kenya experienced a second economic shock with the rise in coffee prices, which suddenly improved the balance of payments, but subsequently created major internal imbalances as the government failed to respond creatively to the economic windfall gains. This was followed by further decline in the performance of the economy due to a drop in the world prices of coffee, the onset of the second oil shock of 1979-82 and an expansive fiscal policy. Despite these setbacks, Kenya enjoyed a GDP growth rate of approximately 5.2 per cent per annum, which indicated a modest reduction in the high momentum achieved in the first decade. (Government of Kenya and UNICEF, 1992; Government of Kenya and National Environment Authority, 2009).

The third phase, roughly 1980-85, witnessed a sharp decline that registered a low GDP growth averaging approximately 2.5 per cent per annum with some years experiencing negative growth. The economic decline was as a result of several factors that included the continued high cost of oil products, global recession of 1980-82, and poor internal economic management. In the fourth phase, 1986-89, Kenya, like many of the developing countries, entered a period of structural adjustment programs (henceforth, SAPs) in agriculture trade and industry, finance sector, education, and health parastatals. The need for SAPs was recognized by the government much earlier and led to the publication of the Sessional Paper No. 1 of 1986, *Economic Management for Economic Growth*. The programs, which were medium to long-term, aimed at the supply side of the economy and attempted to restructure the sectors such that they were responsive to prices and market signals and, therefore, more efficient (Republic of Kenya, 1986; Government of Kenya and UNICEF, 1992, Government of Kenya and National Environment Authority, 2009).

In addition to the SAPs, the government also began implementing short-term macroeconomic stabilization programs, aimed at the demand side of the economy with an objective to reduce imbalances in the form of high inflation, high unemployment, high budget deficits and balance of payments. Such deficits were considered particularly harmful and unsustainable. Hence, the purpose of the stabilization programs was an attempt to suppress demand by making commodities expensive through currency devaluation, decontrolling prices and removing government subsidies and cutting expenditure on social services which included, among others, health services, education and public sector employment. Both the SAPs and the stabilization programs were associated with the World Bank and International Monetary Fund (IMF). The SAPs were commonly advocated by the World Bank, who also provided the bulk of their financing, while macroeconomic stabilization programs were financed by the IMF through balance of payments support. The two programs were typically initiated by the government, with the Bank and the Fund invited to provide technical and financial support (World Bank, 1989).

From the early 1990s, the Kenyan economy appeared to enter a fifth phase that was characterized by the slow growth, reminiscent of the early 1980s with the GDP growth of 4.3 per cent. In 1991, it fell to 2.2 per cent and was projected to decline to 2 per cent in 1992. The declining trend developed due to a variety of factors, including a fall in external resource flow; the poor performance in international markets by Kenya's main exports; the inability of the economy to attain macroeconomic balance (especially in the areas of fiscal balance, inflation, unemployment and balance of trade); and poor internal management. A good example of the economic decline was the dramatic fall in agriculture that recorded a negative growth rate of 1.1 per cent, a trend that was quite alarming as agriculture contributed to 27 per cent of the GDP. Most people directly or indirectly depended to the sector for their livelihoods (Loubser, 1983).

In response to the deteriorating economic conditions, the period 1991 to the end of the 1990s represented a period of accelerated implementation of the most comprehensive economic reforms in Kenya's history. These reforms focused on reforming the micro-environment and restructuring the incentive system to be more outward and efficiently oriented. The core reform measures included full liberalization of the foreign exchange and import licensing regime, coupled with tariff rationalization and lowering of tariff levels. Interest rates were liberalized in 1991, leading to market-determined interest rates. The government also eliminated price control and relaxed monopoly marketing arrangements in agriculture. To ensure a sound macroeconomic base, the government also restructured the fiscal and monetary policy environment to limit budget deficits and the reduction of monetary expansion. The Central Bank of Kenya (CBK) Act was also amended to strengthen the oversight and supervisory role of this bank over the financial sector and limit the government's ability to borrow from it. These measures tended to reverse the economic decline with significant improvement in the GDP, per capita income and sectoral growth rates. The rapid money expansion and inflation rates were brought under control through a tight monetary policy, but at the expense of extremely high real interest rates. The unsustainable fiscal deficits were brought under control, even as social expenditures. The exchange rate depreciated in nominal terms. These did not, however, improve the trade balance nor the debt burden. These reforms continued through the turn of the century, with greater emphasis on privatization, civil service reform and the rehabilitation of the infrastructure with the election of a new government in 2002. It was expected that with the recovery of the economy would result to employment growth, efficiency and the eventual transformation of the Kenya into a Newly Industrialized Country (NIC). (Republic of Kenya, 1991; Government of Kenya and UNICEF, 1989; Government of Kenya and UNICEF, 1992; Government of Kenya and National Environment Authority, 2009).

The SAPs and the macroeconomic stabilization programs, as stated above, were expected to stabilize the economy, reverse the economic decline and renew economic growth. Unfortunately, the programs had far reaching effects on different groups of people; interrupted existing economic structures, hurting some people while benefiting others. Particularly, with macroeconomic stabilization programs, the most affected people were those employed by the government and those relying on government subsidies, such as free health and education, and people whose consumption sources depended on imports. As a result of the government heavy subsidy to health and education; and since many marketed household goods had high import duty, many Kenyans felt the adverse effects of the macroeconomic stabilization programs. Additionally, employees whose earnings were fixed in nominal terms lost heavily. However, the poor households were impacted more by the adverse effects of stabilization measures as basic services were no longer free and prices of basic commodities fluctuated upwards more frequently. In theory, the hardships associated with both SAPs and macroeconomic stabilization programs were expected to be short-term, while in the long-run, everyone was expected to benefit, though not necessarily in proportion to the amount of suffering experienced during the implementation process (Government of Kenya and UNICEF, 1998; Government of Kenya and National Environment Authority, 2009).).

Overall analysis of the effects of SAPs and macroeconomic stabilization programs show that the programs exacerbated the levels of poverty among most of the populations in Kenya (Bryceson, et al, 2010). The country never recovered fully from the adverse effects of SAPS. Echoes of the adverse effects continue to be felt especially among the poorest communities, including the pastoralists living in arid and semi-arid areas, small scale farmers in low potential food producing areas, landless and tiny acreage dwellers and low income and unemployed urban dwellers, usually living in slum environments. Pastoralists, in particular derive their livelihood from the care of livestock. It is estimated that over 85 per cent of the pastoralist household fall below the poverty line. Through the same application, roughly 30 per cent of the small-scale rural farmers, who are increasingly migrating into the semi-arid and arid zones with low potential for agriculture, constitute among the poorest of the poor. Increasingly, over 25 per cent of the rural households in Kenya are now landless or approaching landlessness, and among them over fifteen per cent are classified as destitute. Based on Global Poverty Index Scale, 48.8 per cent, 28.3 percent and 12.9 per cent of Kenyans were classified as being vulnerable to poverty, in severe poverty or destitute respectively by 2014(Oxford Poverty and Human Development Initiative, OPHI, (2017). But the severity of prevalence across the country seemed to follow patterns established earlier as a consequence of exclusionist post-independence development polices and later the adverse effects of SAPS. North Eastern, Western and Coast regions of the country recorded high destitution rates of 48.8 per cent, 17.1 per cent and 16.2 per cent compared to 0.0 per cent, 2.8 per cent and 10.1 per cent recorded for Nairobi, Central and Eastern regions of the country within the same period (OPHI 2017). Studies that surveyed the adverse effects of SAPS on the population across the country record similar patterns (Quick and Musau,

1994; Government of Kenya and UNICEF, 1992; Government of Kenya and UNICEF, 1998; Government of Kenya and National Environment Authority, 2009).

Kenya ranks among the least developed countries, where the poverty index shows more than 50 per cent of its population is below the global described poverty line (World Bank 2004). Since independence, one of the principal goals of Kenya's development effort has been to reduce poverty. Most of the poor people rely more heavily and directly on local natural resources for their livelihoods than other socio-economic groups due to lack of alternative livelihood options accessible to them (Rietbergen et al., 2002). Poverty is a major cause and consequence of the environmental degradation and resource depletion, where major environmental challenges include deforestation, soil degradation and desertification, declining biodiversity and marine resources (Okwi et al, 2005). Others include water scarcity and deterioration of water and air quality. Poverty hinders access to basic needs such as health care, nutrition and education.

Despite a new 2010 constitution and numerous policy interventions, including provision of development funds such as Free Primary Education (FPE), Secondary Schools Bursary Fund (SEBF), Constituency Development Fund (CDF), Local Authority Transfer Fund (LATF) or Rural Electrification Fund (REF), levels of deprivation remain high in some areas compared to others. A report by the Society for International Development and the Kenya National bureau of Statistics (KNBS/SID 2013), for example showed that one quarter of Kenya's population had no education in 2013. Slightly more than half of the population had primary education only, and 23 per cent of the population had secondary education and above. In the Loima Constituency of Turkana county, however, 93.0 per cent of the population had no education, compared with the Makadara Constituency in Nairobi County where only 8.2 per cent of the population had no education, a difference of 84.8 percentage points. Hence, like it was at independence, geographical location is still a major determinant of vulnerability, deprivation, and opportunity, all of which had been buttressed by government development policy over the decades (KNBS/SID 2013).

A 2017 report by British charity, Oxfam international, confirms these assertions. The report showed that the rich captured the larger share of the benefits of economic growth, essentially widening the gap between the rich and the poor. Less than 0.1per cent of the population in the country own more wealth than the bottom 99.9 per cent; the number of super-rich in Kenya is one of the fastest growing in the world, with the numbers expected to grow by 80 per cent over the next 10 years. At the same time, there is unequal access to education and health with nearly one million primary school-aged children still out-of-school – the ninth highest number of any country in the world. A quarter of the Kenyan population regularly lack access to healthcare and gender inequalities remain persistent because economic policy creates extreme inequality, and prevents women's economic empowerment. For example, only six per cent of the 96 per cent of Kenya's rural women population works on farms, having title deeds to land (OXFAM, 2017). Clearly, the promise made at independence to spread economic growth evenly across the population has not materialized.

Over the last two decades, the increasing ratio of public debt and the management of that debt has added to the challenges that Kenya faces in pursuance of economic development. The country has relied over the years on external borrowing to fund capital development. This, however, increased in the last two decades. This, coupled by weak economic governance institutions and corruption, has seen the debt and the cost of servicing it rises without commensurate developments on the ground. According to the 2018 Budget Policy Statement, Kenya's Public Debt to GDP ratio for the fiscal year 2017/18 was estimated at 53.0 per cent, while the IMF gave an estimate of 56.2 per cent for 2017 (rising from 44.0 per cent 5-years ago, and 38.4 per cent10-years ago) (Republic of Kenya, 2018). This means that Kenya will spend approximately 40.3 percent of tax revenues finance debt payments in the fiscal year 2017/18. Debt servicing is likely to limit the amount of funds being sent to the counties as a share of their development budgets and as part of the equalization fund that is meant to redress historical neglect.

## CONCLUSION

The question one is bound to reflect on is how much Kenya has changed in terms of its socio-economic development since independence. In terms of development logic, the country has kept along the path commenced roughly 50 years ago with minimal modifications in policy planning and implementation. For 50 years, centralized planning was pursued, which made individuals and regions with a head start in development indicators benefit more. Because control of political power has been central in mediating access to economic resources, political life and culture in Kenya, over the years, has become violent and insecure as regions and ethnicities work together to shore their numbers at the polls and get access to power and resources. The 2010 Constitution that resulted as a political settlement to cure long-term grievances of exclusion is still under implementation. The Constitution secured broad-based rights for marginalized groups, including their social rights. However, the full implementation of the constitution and enjoyment of these rights is dependent on the growth of the economy. Currently, such growth seems compromised by high population growth rates and government dependency on unsustainable external borrowing. If funding goes to the counties because of debt servicing, grievances from the periphery of marginalization are likely to emerge, in addition to another renegotiation of the regions and ethnic groups' relationship to the state.

## REFERENCES

Abagi, O. (2014). 'Overview of Political, Economic and Education Context in Kenya, 1963-2013'. In O. Abagi and I. O. Ogachi (Eds.) *Fifty Years of Education Development in Kenya: Mapping out the Gains, Challenges and Prospects for the Future,* Nairobi: The Jomo Kenyatta Foundation.

African Institute for Development Policy, AFIDEP. (2018). Regional Analysis of Youth Demographics; East African Community Countries.

*Briefing Note.* Available at: https://www.afidep.org/download/research-briefs/14.06.2018-ReAYD-Briefing-Note_EAC.pdf.

British Council. (2016). 'Universities, employability and inclusive development; Repositioning higher education in Ghana, Kenya, Nigeria and South Africa'. *Research Report.*

Bryceson, D., Sarkar, P., Fennell, S., & Ajit Singh, A. (2010). *Globalisation, structural adjustment and African agriculture: Analysis and evidence.* Centre for Business Research, University of Cambridge Working Paper No. 414

Commission for Revenue Allocation, Kenya. (2012). 'Historical Injustices: A complimentary Indicator for Distributing the Equalization fund'. *CRA Working Paper* No. 2012/2.

Deloitte (2017. )*Kenya Economic Outlook. 2017. Joining the Dots.* Deloitte and Touche.

Goldsmith Paul. (2011). 'The Mombasa Republican Council Conflict Assessment: Threats and Opportunities for Engagement' *A Report based on Research Commissioned by Kenya Civil Society Strengthening Programme.* USAID/PACT/ACT.

Government of Kenya and UNICEF. (1991). *Household Welfare Monitoring and Evaluation Survey, Kitui, Baring, Embu, and South Nyanza* Nairobi: Ministry of Planning and National Development and UNICEF Kenya Country Office.

Government of Kenya and UNICEF. (1992). *Children and Women in Kenya: A Situation Analysis 1992,* Nairobi: UNICEF Kenya Country Office.

Government of Kenya and UNICEF. (1998). *Children and Women in Kenya: A Situation Analysis,* Nairobi: UNICEF Kenya Country Office.

Government of Kenya/National Environmental Management Authority, NEMA, (2009). *National Environment Action Plan Framework 2009-2013.* National Environmental Management Authority, Government of Kenya.

Holsinger, Donald B. and Theisen Gary L.(1977). 'Education, Individual Modernity, and National Development: A Critical Appraisal'. *The Journal of Developing Areas, Vol. 11, No. 3 (April),* pp. 315-334.

Kaimenyi Mwangi. (2013). *Kenya Devolution and Resource Sharing Calculator*. The Brookings Institution. https://www.brookings.edu/opinions/devolution-and-resource-sharing-in-kenya/.Accessed 13th September 2018.

Kenya National Bureau of Statistics, KNBS. (2018). 'Kenya Integrated Household Budget Survey (KIHBS)' 2015/2016. *Basic Report*. KNBS, Nairobi.

Kenya National Bureau of Statistics, KNBS. (2010). *Kenya Demographic and Health Survey* 2008-09. Calverton, Maryland: KNBS and ICF Macro.

Kenya National Bureau of Statistics, KNBS. (2018). *Economic Survey*. KNBS Nairobi.

Klopp, Jacqueline and Odenda Lumumba. (2016). 'The State of Kenya's Land Policy and Land Reform: A Political Institutional Analysis,' *A paper presented at the Annual World Bank Conference on Land Governance*, Washington, DC, 14-18 March, 2016.

Loubser, J. J. (.1983). *Human Resource Development in Kenya: An Overview*, Ottawa: Canadian International Development Agency.

Ministry of Health. (1989). *Health Information Systems Annual Report*, Nairobi.

Ministry of Health. (1990). *Health Information Systems Annual Report*. Nairobi.

Ministry of Health. (1992). *Report of the National Control Program (NASP)*, Nairobi.

Okwi. P. O., Emwanu, T Begumana, J. Hoogeveen, J. G. (2005).'Welfare and Environment in Rural Uganda: Results from a Small-Area Estimation Approach'. *PREM Working Paper* 05-04.

Oxfam. (2017). 'Kenya: extreme inequality in numbers. *Oxfam*. https://www.oxfam.org/en/even-it/kenya-extreme-inequality-numbers, accessed 13 September 2018.

Oxford Poverty and Human Development Initiative, OPHI. (2017). *Kenya Country Briefing*, Multidimensional Poverty Index Data Bank, OPHI, University of Oxford. Available at: www.ophi.org.uk/multidimensional-poverty-index/mpi-country-briefings/.

Quick J. D. and N. S. Musau. (1994). *Impact of Cost Sharing in Kenya - 1989/93*. Kenya Health Care Financing Project. Nairobi: MOH Kenya.

Republic of Kenya.(1964). *Development Plan,* Nairobi: Government Printer.

Republic of Kenya. (1965). *Sessional Paper No. 10 of 1965. African Socialism and Its Application to Kenya.* Nairobi: Government Printer.

Republic of Kenya. (1980). *Exploratory Soil Map and Agro-Climatic Zone Map of Kenya.* National Agricultural Laboratories, Nairobi, Kenya. Ministry of Agriculture Kenya Soil Survey, Nairobi.

Republic of Kenya. (2009). *Population and Housing Census; Analytical Report.* Kenya National Bureau of Statistics. Nairobi.

Republic of Kenya. (2010). *Kenya Constitution 2010,* Nairobi: Government Printer.

Republic of Kenya. (2013). *Kenya Population Situation Analysis.* National Council for Population and Development. Nairobi.

Republic of Kenya. (2014). 'Kenya Country Report for the 2014 Ministerial Conference on Youth Employment'. *How to improve, through skills development and job creation, access of Africa's youth to the world of work'.* Abidjan, Côte D'Ivoire, 21–23 July.

Republic of Kenya. (2014). *National Forest Policy,* Ministry of Environment, Water and Natural Resources. Nairobi. Government printer.

Republic of Kenya. (2018). *Economic Survey.* Nairobi. Kenya National Bureau of Statistics/Government Printer.

Rietbergen Simon, Bishop Joshua and Mainka Sue. (2002). *Ecosystem Conservation - A neglected tool for Poverty Reduction.* International Institute for Environment and Development (IIED)/Regional International Networking Group (RING). Available at: http://pubs.iied.org/pdfs/11033IIED.pdf.

Silberschmidt, M. (1991). *Rethinking Men and Gender Relations: An investigation of Men and their Changing Roles within the Household and Implications for Gender Relations in Kisii, Kenya, Copenhagen*: Centre for Development Research.

UNESCO. (2000). *World Education Forum: Final Report,* Paris: UNESCO.

United Nations. (1979). *Convention on the Elimination of all Forms of Discrimination against Women,* New York: United Nations.

World Bank. (2006). *Republic of Kenya: Country Social Analysis,* Washington D. C. The World Bank.

## BIOGRAPHICAL SKETCHES

### *Daniel N. Sifuna*

**Affiliation:** Department of Educational Foundations, Kenyatta University, Nairobi, Kenya

**Education:** Bachelor of Education (BEd), Makerere University (Uganda); Master of Arts (Education) and Doctor of Philosophy, University of Nairobi (Kenya)

**Research and Professional Experience:** My professional career has largely been in teaching and research since appointment as a university teacher in the mid-1970s. I have also undertaken many consultancies with local and international organizations. A few examples illustrate this exercise: we completed a study on universities graduate employability in Kenya funded by the British Council in 2015; National Sector Skills Survey for the Government of Rwanda 2011-2013; Evaluation of the the Belgium Government Support Programme for Moi University 2011-2012; Stop Violence Against in School in Tana River County 2008-2011; Baseline Study on Early Childhood Education in ASAL Regions, Ministry of Education and UNICEF 2008; Tusome Vitabu, CARE Tanzania, 2006; Child Labour in Kenya, Ministry of Labour, 2000, among others.

**Professional Appointments:** Tutorial Fellow, 1973 and Lecturer 1975, University of Nairobi, 1975; Senior Lecturer 1979, Associate Professor 1984, Full Professor 1988, Kenyatta University.

**Honors:** JICA award for visiting professor, Hiroshima University, September 1999-April, 2000. US Information Service Textbook Research Award January to March 1992. DAAD award Heidelburg University, January-April, 1990. Council for International Cooperation in Higher Education Fellowship, university of London, January to April, 1983. Fulbright-Hayes Fellowship, January to May 1980.

**Publications from the Last 3 Years:**

*Books and Chapters*

[1] 2018: With I. O. Oanda, Non-Tenured Academics and the Dilemma of the Academic Profession in Kenyan Universities. In I. I Munene (Ed.) *Contextualizing and Organizing Contingent Faculty: Reclaiming Academic Labour in Universities*, Lenham: Lexington Books.

[2] 2017: With N. Wasike, *Changing trends in the Financing of Public Universities in Africa: Implications on Management and Quality Education,* Beau Basin, Mauritius: Lambert Academic Publishing

[3] 2017: University of Nairobi: Review of the Flagship Role in Higher Education in Kenya. In D. Teferra (Ed.) *Flagship Universities in Africa,* London: Palgrave Macmillan.

[4] 2016: *Universities, Employability and Inclusive Development: Repositioning Higher Education in Ghana, Kenya, Nigeria and South Africa,* London: British Council.

[5] 2016: Universal Primary Education and the Challenge of Quality in Sub-Saharan Africa. In I. I Munene (Ed.) *Achieving Education for All: Dilemmas in System-Wide Reforms and Learning Outcomes in Africa,* Lenham: Lexington Books.

*Articles in Refereed Journals*

[1] 2016: With O. Abagi and M. N. Wasike, "Female Genital Mutilation/Cutting among the Wardei of Kenya: Practice, Effects

and Prospects for Alternative Rites of Passage." *Journal of Anthropological Research,* Vol. 72 No.3.

## Ibrahim O. Oanda

**Affiliation:** Council for the Development of Social Science Research In Africa, CODESRIA.

**Education:** PhD, (Education) Kenyatta University, Kenya, 2002.

**Research and Professional Experience:** 18 Years Teaching undergraduate and Graduate level and rose from Rank of Assistant lecturer in 1996 to Associate Prof in 2015. Currently heads the Training, Grants and Fellowship program at CODESRIA. Before his current appointment, Oanda served the Council as program officer researcher (June 2015-June 2016), and as Coordinator of the Higher Education Leadership program, HELP, (June 2012-Auhust 2014). Oanda Joined CODESRIA from Kenyatta university Kenya where he taught as Associate Professor in the department of Educational Foundations. He has research interests in African higher education and has published Journal articles and book chapters, and co-authored one book on privatization of higher education in Africa.

**Publications from the Last 3 Years:**

[1] Tristan McCowan, Ibrahim Oanda and Moses Oketch (2017 March). "Towards National Graduate Destinations Survey in Kenya: An exploratory study of their Universities." *Higher Education Policy.* doi: 10.1057/s41307-017-0044-x\.

[2] Ibrahim Oanda and Sall Ebrima(2016). "From Peril to Promise: Repositioning Higher Education for the Reconstruction of Africa's Future" in Peril and Promise Fifteen Years On: Analysis and Critique. *International Journal of African Higher Education,* (Special Issue) 3 (1) 51-78. http://ejournals.bc.edu/ojs/index.

php/ijahe/index/.
[3] Ibrahim Oanda and Daniel Sifuna (2016); 'Divergent Narratives on Graduate Employability in Kenya; Dysfunctional institutions or Dysfunctional labour markets? in *Universities, Employability and Inclusive Development: Revitalizing Higher Education in Ghana, Kenya, Nigeria and South Africa*. Tristan MacCOwan et al. British Council Final project Report. International Higher Education. 39-56.
[4] Ibrahim Oanda (2016, April): 'The Evolving Nature of Student Participation in University Governance in Africa: An overview of policies, trends and emerging issues': in *Student politics in Africa: Representation and Activism*. African Minds, vol 2, *African Higher Education Dynamics Book series*.
[5] Ibrahim Oanda (2016). 'Engaging the African Academic Diaspora: How Ready Are Universities in Africa?' *International Journal of African Higher Education*, 25-26. http://ejournals.bc.edu/ojs/index.php/ijahe/

In: Progress in Economics Research
Editor: Albert Tavidze

ISBN: 978-1-53615-120-6
© 2019 Nova Science Publishers, Inc.

*Chapter 4*

# GROWING MARKET ECONOMY AND INSTITUTIONS: EVIDENCE FROM THE FORMER SOVIET REPUBLICS

*Enrico Ivaldi*[1,*], *Marta Santagata*[2]
*and Riccardo Soliani*[3]

[1] Department of Political Science, University of Genoa, Italy and Centro de Investigaciones en Econometrìa, Universidad de Buenos Aires
[2] PhD program in Economics; University of Genoa, Italy
[3] Department of Political Science; University of Genoa, Italy

## ABSTRACT

Twenty-five years ago, the Soviet Union broke up and its 15 Republics gained independence. The present paper analyses their respective levels of development and quality of governance. To assess the relation between development paths and institutions in the Republics of the former Soviet Union, we build an index of development, FSD, based on the World Bank

---

[*] Corresponding Author E-mail: enrico.ivaldi@unige.it.

data. Then we consider the impact of governance on economic growth through a new index, the FSG, elaborated from World Bank data as well. The two indices are highly correlated. Not unexpectedly, FSG shows a significant correlation also with the Adjusted Human Development Index (AHDI): human development can be encouraged by fair institutions. On the contrary, rate of growth and FSD have a weak correlation; apparently, the latter conveys more information than the mere growth of GDP.

# INTRODUCTION

This paper investigates the levels of development of the former soviet Republics with a focus on the differences between Russia and thirteen other countries that twenty-five years ago were part of the Soviet Union.

The countries of the former Soviet Union over the last 20 years have experienced an impressive transformation, and fundamental changes have occurred in almost all their political, economic and social aspects (Rechel, Richardson, & McKee, 2014).

The transformation from command to market-oriented economies and the emergence of multi-party political regimes in the former Soviet Union, against the background of the global processes of change, created an unstable political climate in North and Central Asia, with relevant elements of corruption. Slow economic recovery and social policy shortcomings launched numerous challenges for democracy and good governance in the rubble of the Soviet Empire (Petrovsky, 2004) (Bugnacki, 2015).

The market economy and new freedoms positively impacted citizens' lives, but the levels of development within the former soviet countries are still very different, as witnessed by life expectancy, which, among these countries, has a variation of seven years and half (Rechel, Richardson, & McKee, 2014).

For these reasons, the economic and social performance of former Soviet Union is a fascinating field of study.

In this paper, we analyse the development of the area from a more comprehensive point of view than the traditional GNP per-capita.

The concept of development is problematic and analysing development entails a difficult selection of which variables should be included in the study. In our analysis, we decide to adopt the concept of "human development," which finds its theoretical basis in Sen's capabilities approach that identifies welfare with "a person's capability to have various functioning vectors and to enjoy the corresponding well-being achievements" (Sen, 1985, UNDP 1996).

The first major attempt to translate the capabilities approach into a tractable ranking of nations came in the 1990 UNDP Human Development Report. The HDR's objective was to "capture better the complexity of human life" by providing a quantitative approach to combining various socio-economic indicators into a measure of human development (UNDP, 1990).

In fact, indicators of wealth, which reflect the quantity of resources available to a society, provide no information about the allocation of those resources and, thus, it is no wonder that countries with similar average incomes can differ substantially when it comes to people's quality of life. Recent United Nations documents emphasize "human development", measured by life expectancy, adult literacy, access to all three levels of education, as well as people's average income which is a necessary condition of their freedom of choice (Soubbotina & Sheram, 2000).

Indeed, as Smith points out, governance can be considered as an end in itself or as a mean to development and reduction of poverty (Smith, 2007). In particular, poor governance is among the most important causes of state failure and underdevelopment; therefore, reforms and innovation in administration are an important pre-requisite for development (Ciborra & Navarra, 2005).

In fact, cross-country regressions persistently demonstrate large and statistically significant correlations between institutional variables and growth (Shirley, 2005).

The importance of institution has been registered by different authors. In particular, Rodrik et al. found that the quality of institutions "trumps" everything else in determining development (Rodrik et al., 2004).

We analyse the relation between development and good governance using the Worldwide Governance Indicators (WGI) created by the World Bank (WB). The WGI are a long- standing research project to develop cross- country indicators of governance. They consist of six composite indicators: Voice and Accountability, Political Stability and Absence of Violence/Terrorism, Government Effectiveness, Regulatory Quality, Rule of Law, and Control of Corruption (Kaufmann et al. 2010).

In the former Soviet Union, the transition to market economies spurred legal reforms necessary for domestic and international markets. Formerly public assets where sold cheaply to insiders, often at low price. Unfair practices and asset grabbing emerged, long as the need of better laws and institutions. Correspondingly, in the push for financial liberalization, the inflows to emerging markets became volatile, precipitating the 1997 Asian financial crisis. However, Asia had sound fundamentals: budget surpluses, high savings, low inflation, stable currencies, free trade, and a vast private sector. Thus, the institutional framework, namely financial deregulation, was considered as the real weak point, and reforming it was the most urgent challenge. The necessity of understanding how governance is related to development in post-Soviet countries emerged and offered a major field of research (Rule of Law and Economic Development Research Group, 2012).

The aim of the present paper is twofold. First: after a brief discussion of the most common macroeconomic indicators in the country are examined, we propose an index of economic performance in 2015 (FSD), wider than the rate of growth of GDP. Secondly, we elaborate an index of governance (FSG) in 2015. The correlation between the two indexes, and between each of them and other indicators (GDP growth and IHDI), allow us to put forward some conclusions about growth and its economic and social sustainability in the Russian Federation as well as the other countries studied.

This paper is divided into four parts: in the first part we analyse some macroeconomic indicators in former soviet Republics, in the second part we illustrate the methodology used to construct the indices of development and governance. In the third part, we analyse our results and finally, we comment and discuss our main findings.

## MACROECONOMIC INDICATORS AND SOCIAL CONDITIONS

We take variables in pairs in order to analyse the position of each country with respect to both the mean and the other Republics.

Figure 1 represents Inflation and Unemployment in 2015 for the considered countries (see list in Appendix 1). The familiar Phillips relation holds also in this case.

We indicate in the graph the average values of inflation and unemployment, to grasp easily the situation of the countries.

Moldova presents a particular condition with a very low unemployment rate. It could be due to hidden unemployment in agriculture and conditioned by emigration. Inflation is quite high, in comparison with most Republics, but near the average and lower than in Russian Federation.

Armenia and Ukraine are eccentric. Ukraine has a high level of inflation, with unemployment around the average; the civil war could be considered the main cause of this performance. Armenia has very high unemployment, with low inflation. The political difficulties of Armenia and the legacy of its former conflict with Azerbaijan can explain this datum.

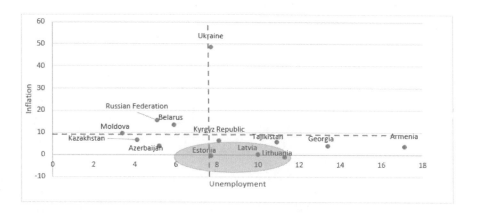

Figure 1. Inflation and Unemployment in 2015.

The Baltics register low or negative inflation. This suggests similarity to European economies. Such an affinity is reinforced by high levels in other indicators, i.e., exports, GDP per capita and HDI Adjusted. Finally, like

European countries, the Baltics are not best-performing when we analyse unemployment rates.

The Russian Federation, with respect to the Baltics, has lower levels of unemployment, by far below the average, and it could be due to the relevance of the public and military sectors as inheritance from the past, while these sectors in the more European Baltics have lost importance.

Figure 2 examines exports as a percentage of GDP and the GDP growth rate in 2015.

We observe four negative GDP growth rates, among which one, Moldova, is near to zero. It is interesting to observe the importance assumed by exports in the rate of growth for the Baltics; but this relation is not satisfied for other countries. If we analyse Belarus and Ukraine, we register the same export/GDP ratio than the Baltics but their GDP growth rates are negative and, partially, it is the same for the Russian Federation. This could be due to the respective composition of export: we will return on this point.

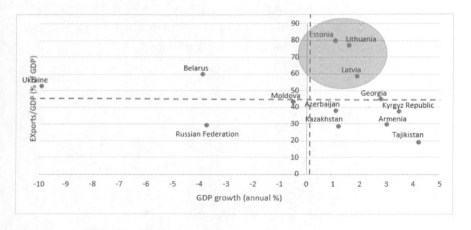

Figure 2. Exports and GDP growth rate in 2015.

Ukraine presents strongly negative GDP growth. This could be due to the civil war. Our hypothesis is confirmed by the analysis of the growth rate from January 20014 to January 2016, which has an extremely difficult trend in contrast with more positive values in the preceding years. The Export/GDP rate is still high in 2015 just because the denominator is low.

Figure 3 shows the composition of export, expressed as the ratio of agriculture products, fuels and mining products, and manufactures, on export. The three Baltic countries, which up to now seems the best-performing, export manufactures and only small amounts of fuels and mining products. This composition reveals a quite solid economic system, not harmed by the volatility of the prices of commodities and row materials, nor by the known "curse of natural resources".

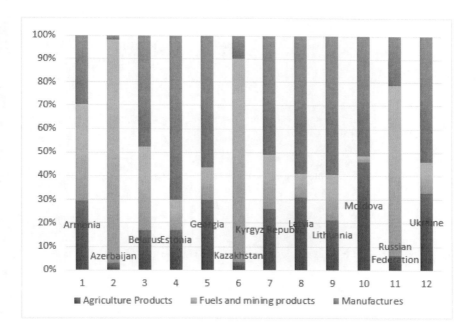

Figure 3. Exports (Agricultural Products, Fuels and mining products and Manufactures)[1].

Figure 4 analyses Central Government Debt. In this case, the situation in the Baltics is quite heterogeneous: Estonia has central government debt lower than Lithuania and Latvia, and slower growth. However, the Baltics present a situation better than most European Countries both in GDP growth

---

[1] Tajikistan data are not available in the WTO database.

rate and in Central Government Debt. Finally, also in this case, the Ukraine is an outlier: again, the civil war may be the cause.

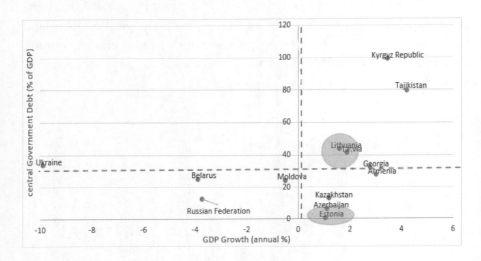

Figure 4. Central Government Debt and GDP growth in 2015.

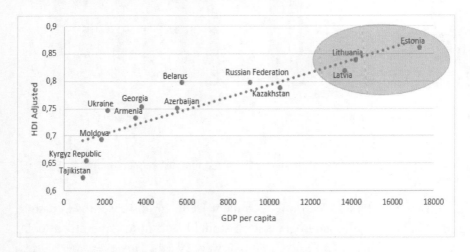

Figure 5. HDI Adjusted and GDP per capita in 2015.

Figure 5 shows levels in Human Development Index Adjusted and in GDP per capita. We remind that the IHDI combines country's average achievements in health, education, and income; besides, it takes into account how those achievements are distributed among population by "discounting" each dimension's average value according to the level of inequality (UNDP, 2015).

In this case, the regression line makes sense, because it helps understanding the relation between the variables. $R^2$ is satisfying (0,785): we can guess that GDP per capita explains slightly less than 80% of human development. In richer countries, high GDP per capita should accompany with high IHDI. If not, good economic performance does not give rise to good quality of life; namely, education, health and fair distribution.

It is relevant to observe that the Baltics are the better-performing countries also in this case, since they present highest level of both HDI Adjusted and GDP per capita. The Russian Federation has the highest level of HDI Adjusted among the other former soviet Republics, slightly more than Belarus, where the GDP per capita is by far lower. A couple of Asian republics show a bad performance, that is low IHDI, even in proportion with their low GDP per capita.

## METHODOLOGY

We decide to construct Former soviet Development Index (FSD) and Former soviet Governance Index (FSG) starting from two databases of the WB. The first one consists in the most popular indicators included in the big WB database "World Development Indicators" and the second one is the "Worldwide governance indicators" database.

We list in Table 1 the indicators we used for our FSD.

In the full database, the WB includes between the most popular development indicators the GDP growth that we have excluded since we will evaluate the similarity between the trend in our FSD and in GDP growth.

## Table 1. Variables selected from World Development Indicators (WB)

| Variable | Source | Description |
| --- | --- | --- |
| GDP per capita (current US$) | World Bank | GDP per capita is gross domestic product divided by midyear population. GDP is the sum of gross value added by all resident producers in the economy plus any product taxes and minus any subsidies not included in the value of the products. It is calculated without making deductions for depreciation of fabricated assets or for depletion and degradation of natural resources. Data are in current U.S. dollars. |
| Exports of goods and services (% of GDP) | World Bank | Exports of goods and services represent the value of all goods and other market services provided to the rest of the world. They include the value of merchandise, freight, insurance, transport, travel, royalties, license fees, and other services, such as communication, construction, financial, information, business, personal, and government services. They exclude compensation of employees and investment income (formerly called factor services) and transfer payments. |
| GNI per capita, PPP (current international $) | World Bank | GNI per capita based on purchasing power parity (PPP). PPP GNI is gross national income (GNI) converted to international dollars using purchasing power parity rates. An international dollar has the same purchasing power over GNI as a U.S. dollar has in the United States. GNI is the sum of value added by all resident producers plus any product taxes (less subsidies) not included in the valuation of output plus net receipts of primary income (compensation of employees and property income) from abroad. Data are in current international dollars based on the 2011 ICP round. |
| GINI index (World Bank estimate) | World Bank | Gini index measures the extent to which the distribution of income (or, in some cases, consumption expenditure) among individuals or households within an economy deviates from a perfectly equal distribution. A Lorenz curve plots the cumulative percentages of total income received against the cumulative number of recipients, starting with the poorest individual or household. The Gini index measures the area between the Lorenz curve and a hypothetical line of absolute equality, expressed as a percentage of the maximum area under the line. Thus a Gini index of 0 represents perfect equality, while an index of 100 implies perfect inequality. |
| Inflation, consumer prices (annual %) | World Bank | Inflation as measured by the consumer price index reflects the annual percentage change in the cost to the average consumer of acquiring a basket of goods and services that |

| Variable | Source | Description |
| --- | --- | --- |
| | | may be fixed or changed at specified intervals, such as yearly. The Laspeyres formula is generally used. |
| Internet users (per 100 people) | World Bank | Internet users are individuals who have used the Internet (from any location) in the last 12 months. Internet can be used via a computer, mobile phone, personal digital assistant, games machine, digital TV etc. |
| Imports of goods and services (% of GDP) | World Bank | Imports of goods and services represent the value of all goods and other market services received from the rest of the world. They include the value of merchandise, freight, insurance, transport, travel, royalties, license fees, and other services, such as communication, construction, financial, information, business, personal, and government services. They exclude compensation of employees and investment income (formerly called factor services) and transfer payments. |
| Life expectancy at birth, total (years) | World Bank | Life expectancy at birth indicates the number of years a new born infant would live if prevailing patterns of mortality at the time of its birth were to stay the same throughout its life. |
| Literacy rate, adult total (% of people ages 15 and above) | World Bank | Adult literacy rate is the percentage of people ages 15 and above who can both read and write with understanding a short simple statement about their everyday life. |
| Unemployment, total (% of total labor force) (modelled ILO estimate) | World Bank | Unemployment refers to the share of the labor force that is without work but available for and seeking employment. |
| Poverty headcount ratio at national poverty lines (% of population) | World Bank | National poverty headcount ratio is the percentage of the population living below the national poverty lines. National estimates are based on population-weighted subgroup estimates from household surveys. |
| Agriculture, value added (% of GDP) | World Bank | Agriculture corresponds to ISIC divisions 1-5 and includes forestry, hunting, and fishing, as well as cultivation of crops and livestock production. Value added is the net output of a sector after adding up all outputs and subtracting intermediate inputs. It is calculated without making deductions for depreciation of fabricated assets or depletion and degradation of natural resources. The origin of value added is determined by the International Standard Industrial Classification (ISIC), revision 3. Note: For VAB countries, gross value added at factor cost is used as the denominator. |
| $CO_2$ emissions (metric tons per capita) | World Bank | Carbon dioxide emissions are those stemming from the burning of fossil fuels and the manufacture of cement. They include carbon dioxide produced during consumption of solid, liquid, and gas fuels and gas flaring. |

## Table 1. (Continued)

| Variable | Source | Description |
|---|---|---|
| Central government debt, total (% of GDP) | World Bank | Debt is the entire stock of direct government fixed-term contractual obligations to others outstanding on a particular date. It includes domestic and foreign liabilities such as currency and money deposits, securities other than shares, and loans. It is the gross amount of government liabilities reduced by the amount of equity and financial derivatives held by the government. Because debt is a stock rather than a flow, it is measured as of a given date, usually the last day of the fiscal year. |

## Table 2. Variables from the Worldwide Governance Indicator database

| Variable | Source | Description |
|---|---|---|
| Control of Corruption: Estimate | World Bank | Control of Corruption captures perceptions of the extent to which public power is exercised for private gain, including both petty and grand forms of corruption, as well as "capture" of the state by elites and private interests. |
| Government Effectiveness: Estimate | World Bank | Government Effectiveness captures perceptions of the quality of public services, the quality of the civil service and the degree of its independence from political pressures, the quality of policy formulation and implementation, and the credibility of the government's commitment to such policies. |
| Political Stability and Absence of Violence/Terrorism: Estimate | World Bank | Political Stability and Absence of Violence/Terrorism measures perceptions of the likelihood of political instability and/or politically-motivated violence, including terrorism. |
| Regulatory Quality: Estimate | World Bank | Regulatory Quality captures perceptions of the ability of the government to formulate and implement sound policies and regulations that permit and promote private sector development. |
| Rule of Law: Estimate | World Bank | Rule of Law captures perceptions of the extent to which agents have confidence in and abide by the rules of society, and in particular the quality of contract enforcement, property rights, the police, and the courts, as well as the likelihood of crime and violence. |
| Voice and Accountability: Estimate | World Bank | Voice and Accountability captures perceptions of the extent to which a country's citizens are able to participate in selecting their government, as well as freedom of expression, freedom of association, and a free media. |

The table above shows the variables taken from the Worldwide Governance Indicators in order to construct FSG. All these variables constitute estimations by the WB: Estimate gives the country's score on the aggregate indicator, in units of a standard normal distribution, i.e., ranging from approximately -2.5 to 2.5.

To analyse development and governance we decide to construct two composite indicators.

A composite indicator is an aggregated index comprising individual indicators and weights that commonly represent the relative importance of each indicator and as Nardo et al. point out "they are increasingly recognized as a useful tool for policy making in conveying information on countries' performance and composite indicators are much easier to interpret than trying to find a common trend in many separate indicators".

To construct our multidimensional indices we follow three steps (Nardo, et al. 2005):

1) Choose indicators between the initial list (Table 1 and Table 2),
2) Assign weights to each indicator
3) Aggregate indicators to construct a multidimensional index

To select indicators, we apply a principal component analysis that is one of the methods of extraction of factors which factorial analysis makes use of: we opted for these methodology in order to decide which variables have to be used (Ivaldi et al., 2016a; 2016b)

In component analysis we simply transform the original variables into a new set of linear combinations (principal components). With principal component analysis we partition the total variance by first finding the linear combination of the variables that accounts for the maximum amount of variance:

$$y_1 = a_{11}x_1 + a_{12}x_2 + \cdots + a_{1p}p$$

where $y_1$ is the first principal component.

Then, the procedure finds a second linear combination, uncorrelated with the first components, such that it accounts for the next largest amount of variance (after the variance attributable to the first component has been removed) in the system. The equation of the second component is:

$$y_2 = a_{21}x_1 + a_{22}x_2 + \cdots + a_{2p}p$$

And the procedure goes on in this way. Thus the use of principal components allows to create a set of uncorrelated variables (the components) by transforming a set of correlated variables. It means that the Pearson correlation between components is equal to 0 (Pituch & Stevens, 2016).

In order to make factors more interpretable, a process of rotation is applied. In fact, as Pituch and Stevens point out: "The factors are derived not to provide interpretability but to maximize variance accounted for and a transformation of the factor (typically a rotation) often provides lot much improved interpretability" (Pituch & Stevens, 2016).

A number of analytic rotation methods have been developed and although these rotation methods differ in a number of respect, perhaps the most fundamental distinction that can be made is between orthogonal and oblique rotations (Fabrigar et al. 1999). Orthogonal rotations produce factors that are uncorrelated (i.e., maintain a 90° angle between axes); oblique methods allow the factors to correlate (i.e., allow the X and Y axes to assume a different angle than 90°). Traditionally, researchers have been guided to orthogonal rotation because (the argument went) uncorrelated factors are more easily interpretable (Osborne, 2015).

Gorsuch lists four different orthogonal methods (equamax, orthomax, quartimax, and varimax) and 15 different oblique methods. As he points out: "If the simple structure is clear, any of the more popular procedures can be expected to lead to the same interpretations." He then recommends rotating with varimax (orthogonal) or promax (oblique) (Gorsuch, 1983). The application of the varimax rotation was deemed appropriate as each factor has high correlations with a smaller number of variables and low correlations with the other variables and this generally makes interpretation of resulting factor easier (Kaiser, 1960).

Once extraction and rotation have been carried out, it is important to select which factors, i.e., variables, are to be used in the indicator.

This has been done taking simultaneously into consideration three selection criteria:

- Kaiser criterion: on the basis of which it is necessary to retain all factors extracted which have an eigenvalue greater than one because smaller values relate to factors which can explain less than what a single variable can explain; (Kaiser, 1960)
- Explained variance criterion: in this case the basis for the selection is the cumulative explained variance. A level of explained variance of 65% - 70% is considered significant (Stevens, 1986)
- *Scree test*: this method aims to give a graphical representation of the factors to be taken into consideration. The graph shows the value of the eigenvalue on the vertical axis and the number of eigenvalues on the horizontal axis. The eigenvalues are plotted as points connected by a single line. According to the Cattell method, the choice of factors should be limited to the point where there is a levelling in the slope of the line (Cattel, 1966).

Once chosen variables, we have opted for equal weighting. Indeed, even though it would be desirable to assign different weights to the various factors considered, there is no reliable basis for doing this (Myer & Jencks, 1989). However, this does not mean no weighting, because equal weighting does imply an implicit judgment on the weights being equal (Nardo et. al, 2005; Landi et al. 2017).

At this point the chosen methodology is to build the two indices, FSD and FSG, by applying factor analysis performed on the selected variables. In this case we can use as index values the factor scores, which represent the position of each observation in the space of representation identified from the extracted factors (Hogan & Tchernis, 2004).

While several different methods of estimating factor scores are available, as Pituch and Stevens point out, two are commonly used: 1) regression method and 2) sum/average scores.

In the regression method, regression weights are obtained and factor scores are created by multiplying each weight by respective observed variable, which is in z-score form. The second method, is simpler and it allows to sum or average scores across the observed variables that load highly on a given factor as observed in the pattern matrix. Nevertheless, in this case we opted for the regression method, which allows to estimate the score on the common factor as a linear combination of the original variables (Pituch & Stevens, 2016).

Once obtained factorial scores we have been able to rank countries in order to identify which countries are more developed and to observe if that countries with high scores in FSD are the same countries that have high scores in FSG.

To complete our analysis, we divide countries in classes in order to make the comparison between the two indices easier. To create classes, we apply a cluster analysis since it can be applied to group the information on constituencies (e.g., countries) (Nardo et al. 2005).

Clustering is a division of data into groups of similar objects; they are similar between themselves, but are dissimilar to the elements of other groups. Each group, called a cluster, consists of objects that are similar between themselves and dissimilar to objects of other groups (Berkhin 2006). Traditionally, clustering techniques are broadly divided in hierarchical and partitioning and in our work we decide to apply the first since our dataset is quite small, otherwise this technique would be very suboptimal. Hierarchical clustering builds a cluster hierarchy or, in other words, a tree of clusters, also known as a dendrogram. Hierarchical clustering methods are categorized into agglomerative (bottom-up) and divisive (top-down). To merge or split subsets of points rather than individual points, the distance between individual points has to be generalized to the distance between subsets. Such derived proximity measure is called a linkage metric. The type of the linkage metric used significantly affects hierarchical algorithms, since it reflects the particular concept of closeness and connectivity (Berkhin, 2006).

Major inter-cluster linkage metrics include single link, average link, and complete link. The underlying dissimilarity measure (usually, distance) is computed for every pair of points with one point in the first set and another point in the second set. A specific operation such as minimum (single link), average (average link), or maximum (complete link) is applied to pair-wise dissimilarity measures:

$$d(C_1, C_2) = operation\ \{d(x,y) | x \in C_1, y \in C_2\}$$

The methods using inter-cluster distances defined in terms of pairs with points in two respective clusters (subsets) are called graph methods". Such methods can be appended by so-called geometric methods in which a cluster is represented by its central point. It results in centroid, median, and minimum variance linkage metrics.

In our work we decide to use Ward's method that says that the distance between two clusters, A and B, is how much the sum of squares will increase when we merge them. With hierarchical clustering, the sum of squares starts out at zero (because every point is in its own cluster) and then grows as we merge clusters. Ward's method keeps this growth as small as possible (Ward, 1963).

# RESULTS

Our analysis takes into account 13 former soviet Republics since we eliminated from our database two countries, Uzbekistan and Turkmenistan, because of missing data. Full databases with countries and variables are presented in Appendix 1.

We first select variables to build the multidimensional index of development, FSD.

Starting from the variables listed in Table 1 we use principal component analysis to evaluate which variables should be left following the three criteria we already highlighted above: Kaiser's method, scree test and explained variance criterion.

Figure 6 shows scree plot and Table 3 shows values of explained variance. Since second component explains just 62% of the variance we decide to take into account all the three components and so we decide not to exclude any variable as suggested by the other two methods, too.

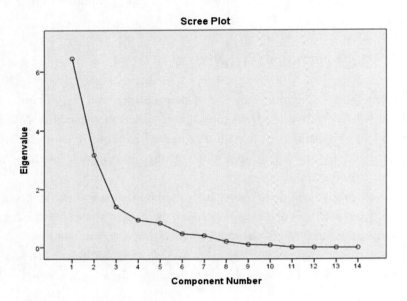

Figure 6. Scree Plot for FSD.

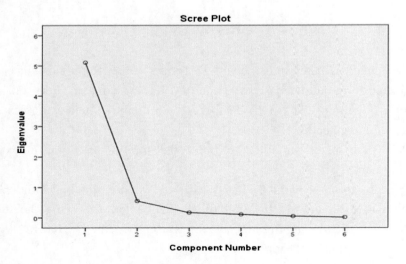

Figure 7. Scree Plot for FSG.

## Table 3. Total Variance Explained (Development Variables)

| Total Variance Explained | | | |
|---|---|---|---|
| Component | Rotation Sums of Squared Loadings | | |
| | Total | % of Variance | Cumulative % |
| 1 | 6.033 | 43.095 | 43.095 |
| 2 | 2.667 | 19.048 | 62.144 |
| 3 | 2.302 | 16.446 | 78.589 |

Extraction Method: Principal Component Analysis.

Then, we use principal component analysis to select variables in order to create FSG. As we can see from Figure 7, just the first component has an eigenvalue higher than 1. All variables are allocated on the first component and therefore, also in this case, we include all the indicators in the model.

Once decided the variables of our model we calculate factorial scores that represent the value of our multidimensional indices.

Values of FSD and FSG are shown in Table 3 and 4 where we have ranked the countries from the better-performing to the less-performing ones.

The final step is grouping the values of indexes into categories to identify the areas with similar socio-economic conditions. Applying cluster analysis to FSD and FSG we obtain four classes in which we can group the former soviet Republics and Figures 8 and 9 show the resulted dendrograms from this analysis.

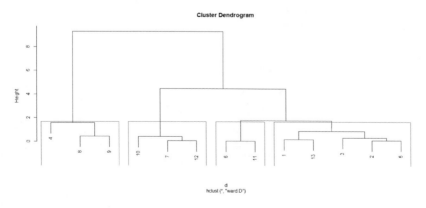

Figure 8. FSD Dendrogram.

## Table 4. FSD: Scores, rank and classes

| Rank | Country | FSD score | Class |
|---|---|---|---|
| 1 | Estonia | 2,10698 | 1 |
| 2 | Lithuania | 1,34468 | 1 |
| 3 | Latvia | 1,04231 | 1 |
| 4 | Russian Federation | 0,24995 | 2 |
| 5 | Kazakhstan | 0,2254 | 2 |
| 6 | Belarus | -0,04473 | 3 |
| 7 | Georgia | -0,20429 | 3 |
| 8 | Azerbaijan | -0,28261 | 3 |
| 9 | Armenia | -0,45316 | 3 |
| 10 | Ukraine | -0,58959 | 3 |
| 11 | Moldova | -0,9817 | 4 |
| 12 | Kyrgyz Republic | -1,18844 | 4 |
| 13 | Tajikistan | -1,22479 | 4 |

## Table 5. FSG: Scores, rank and classes

| Rank | Country | FSG score | Class |
|---|---|---|---|
| 1 | Estonia | 1,88166 | 1 |
| 2 | Lithuania | 1,4335 | 1 |
| 3 | Latvia | 1,30745 | 1 |
| 4 | Georgia | 0,774 | 2 |
| 5 | Armenia | -0,10656 | 3 |
| 6 | Moldova | -0,17363 | 3 |
| 7 | Kazakhstan | -0,3562 | 3 |
| 8 | Russian Federation | -0,63097 | 4 |
| 9 | Belarus | -0,66104 | 4 |
| 10 | Azerbaijan | -0,66994 | 4 |
| 11 | Kyrgyz Republic | -0,85756 | 4 |
| 12 | Ukraine | -0,85835 | 4 |
| 13 | Tajikistan | -1,08235 | 4 |

## Table 6. Spearman's Rho FSD – FSG

| Correlations | | | | FSD | FSG |
|---|---|---|---|---|---|
| Spearman's Rho | FSD | | Correlation Coefficient | 1,000 | ,758[**] |
| | | | Sig. (2-code) | . | ,003 |
| | | | N | 13 | 13 |
| | FSG | | Correlation Coefficient | ,758[**] | 1,000 |
| | | | Sig. (2-code) | ,003 | . |
| | | | N | 13 | 13 |

** Correlation is significant at the 0.01 Level (2-tailed).

## Table 7. Spearman's Rho FSD – GDP Growth

| Correlations | | | | FSD | GDP growth |
|---|---|---|---|---|---|
| Spearman's Rho | FSD | | Correlation Coefficient | 1,000 | -,297 |
| | | | Sig. (2-code) | . | ,325 |
| | | | N | 13 | 13 |
| | gdpgrowth | | Correlation Coefficient | -,297 | 1,000 |
| | | | Sig. (2-code) | ,325 | . |
| | | | N | 13 | 13 |

** Correlation is significant at the 0.01 Level (2-tailed).

## Table 8. Spearman's Rho FSG-HDI Adjusted

| Correlations | | | | FSG | IHDI |
|---|---|---|---|---|---|
| Spearman's Rho | FSG | | Correlation Coefficient | 1,000 | ,707** |
| | | | Sig. (2-code) | . | ,007 |
| | | | N | 13 | 13 |
| | IHDI | | Correlation Coefficient | ,707** | 1,000 |
| | | | Sig. (2-code) | ,007 | . |
| | | | N | 13 | 13 |

** Correlation is significant at the 0.01 Level (2-tailed).

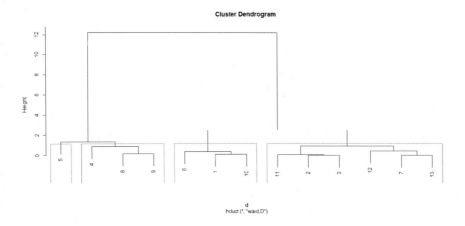

Figure 9. FSG Dendrogram.

Finally, to test our indices we calculate Spearman's Rho between our indices (Table 6), between FSD and GDP growth (Table 7) and between

FSG and HDI Adjusted (Table 8). We present data relative to GDP Growth and HDI Adjusted in Appendix 2.

We show all our results in Tables 3 and 4 where we report the rank of countries, respectively for FSD and FSG, and we present the values the two indices assume and the division in the four different classes obtained with cluster analysis.

## DISCUSSION

The Former soviet Republics Development Index take into account sustainability both economic and social. Indeed, it includes macroeconomic variables (inflation, import, export, public debt), which express the economic constraints and sustainability of growth, and socio-economic and social variables (unemployment, poverty ratio, relevance of agriculture interpreted as economic backwardness, internet users and variables included in the IHDI: literacy, life expectancy, GDP per capita, Gini coefficient). Considering the level of development of the former soviet Republics we have decided not to consider CO2 emissions in terms of environmental sustainability (Ivaldi & Soliani, 2014)

As we can see in Table 4, the Baltics are the best-performing. In the analysis of macroeconomic indicators, the three Republics show very similar characteristics (only with regard to the public debt, Estonia is better than the others, which however have a public debt / GDP ratio less than 50%), which apparently set them nearer EU countries, rather than the other Republics of the former Soviet Union. As to our indexes, Estonia, Latvia and Lithuania are at the top in both classifications. The high correlation between FSD and FSG confirm the key role of fair political institutions to obtain economic and social development; the "European" path of development of Baltic Republics appears also from this point of view. Their strength is especially highlighted by the following variables: low inflation, low added value of agriculture, high GDP per capita, good education, export and many internet users.

Estonia, the first of the Baltics, presents good performances in: public debt ratio (it has much better than in Lithuania and Latvia, which are, respectively, 10$^{th}$ and 11$^{th}$), GDP and GNI per capita, export, internet users and life expectancy, where it presents 3 years more than the other Baltics.

The Baltics' weak point is the value of Gini index, since they are just before the Russian Federation and Georgia that are second-to-last and last. This weakness is confirmed by the variable "Poverty headcount ratio" and by the unemployment quite high (Santagata et al. 2017). It seems that the market economy here is able to create good economic performance, with also some social satisfying results; but these countries, which express good governance, are not able yet to fight seriously and successfully against unemployment and inequality. According to our results, these issues should be at the first page of their political agenda.

The performance of Russia, as to FSD, is good. It is at fourth place, in the second class; but the distance from the first group, indicated by the FSD score, is high (Latvia: 1,04; Russia: 0,25). We conclude that, apart from the Baltics, the economic and social performance of the Russian economic system is better in comparison with the remaining countries of the former USSR. The Russian Federation follows the Baltics for number of internet users; this could be due to the big urban agglomerate with high density of population. On the other hand, Russia is bad-performing for what concern inflation, Gini index and life expectancy: it emerges a large country with advanced aspects, like internet diffusion, and black spots, like life expectancy. The turbulence of the unequal Russian society pushes inflation. The mix of inflation, inequality and development export-led, with export based on oil and natural gas, reveals the fragility of the country. The poor score obtained in FSG, where Russia belongs to the last lass, further witnesses the major difficulties of establishing a market economy with a fair and strong democratic regime. At present, the Russian Federation is oriented to Europe as exporter but it does not import the European models of development. Kazakhstan, which is in the second class as well, export great amount of fuels and mineral products; its good performance is probably due to it.

The last three positions in FSD rank are occupied by Moldova, Kyrgyz Republic and Tajikistan. They have almost the same position if we analyse GDP per capita and GNI per capita. They are very bad-performing in number of internet users, Tajikistan in the last country for life expectation and Kyrgyz is the third from the bottom. In general, Moldova is quite better than the other two former soviet Republics and in fact, even if they are on the same cluster, Moldova shows a higher factorial score that Tajikistan and Kyrgyz Republic.

We show in Figure 10 the map of the former soviet Republics analysed, divided for classes with respect to FSD score.

Figure 10. FSD map.

Analysing FSG rank (Table 5) we find that the first three countries are once again the Baltics. In particular, Estonia is the first of the rank. If we observe single variables ranks it is easy to notice that Estonia is the first in each one except for political stability.

Passing from FSD to FSG we observe an improvement in ranking for Moldova.

The Russian Federation belongs to the 4$^{th}$ cluster. However, we must note that this cluster is wider than the 4$^{th}$ class for FSD and that the Russian Federation is the first of his cluster. The former Soviet Union, as far as the thirteen Republics are concerned, and with regard to 2015, gives a quite large group of countries with poor administration and government, in comparison with the rest of Republics.

Tajikistan occupies the last position and it is always the last in each variable.

Ukraine is the second to last in FSG rank; this is due to a deep political instability, since the country has been interested by the known, and mentioned, political turmoil.

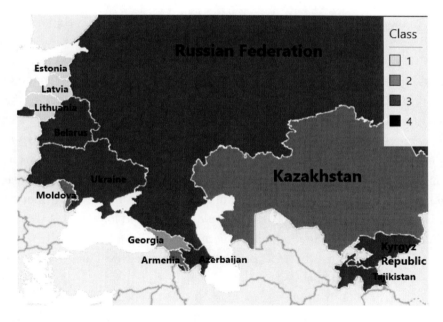

Figure 11. FSG map.

We underline that all variables part of FSG have similar trend and high correlation; therefore, we observe a homogeneity for each country, with reference to these variables. In Figure 11 we show the map of the former soviet Republics divided in the four different classes of FSG. Finally, about Spearman's Rho we analyse three different correlations.

First of all, the correlation between FSG and FSD (Table 6) has to be considered high since its value is almost 0.76. This confirms that governance and development are two sides of the same coin. If we remember that FSD is an index of economic performance that includes also socio-economic variables, we can say that good governance lead to higher development in broad sense. As UN General Assembly recognizes: "transparent, responsible, accountable, open and participatory government, responsive to the needs and aspirations of the people, is the foundation on which good governance rests, and that good governance at the national and international levels is essential for sustained economic growth, sustainable development and the eradication of poverty and hunger" (UN General Assembly, 2012). The blending of transparent, accountable and capable institutions of governance is essential for sustainable economic and social development.

Then, Table 7 shows results for Spearman's Rho calculated between GDP Growth and FSD. The value of Rho demonstrates that there is no relation between these two variables. The concept of socio-economic performance and development expressed by FSD cannot be reduced to the rate of growth. As Sobboutina and Sheram pointed out: although they reflect the average incomes in a country, GNP per capita and GDP per capita have numerous limitations when it comes to measuring people's actual well-being. Thus, to judge the relative quality of life in different countries, one should also take into account other indicators: for instance, the distribution of income and incidence of poverty, people's health and longevity, access to education, and more (Soubbotina & Sheram, 2000).

GDP growth is an imperfect proxy for more general welfare, or a means toward enhanced human development (Ranis, 2004).

While growth in domestic product (GDP) is necessary to meet all essential human objectives, it is important to study how this growth translates - or fails to translate - into human development in various societies (UNDP 1990). Finally, we analysed correlation between FSG and HDI Adjusted (Table 8): Spearman's Rho assumes a value of almost 0.71. Considering that FSG includes variables that represent human and civil development in a legal system that are not included in the IHDI, the former can be considered as a complementary index to the latter.

## Conclusion

The present paper proposes some considerations about the economic and social situation in the former USSR. We considered thirteen countries, for which we found comparable data, in 2015, bringing about a static analysis.

In the first part, we study a set of macroeconomic indicators that provide information about the sustainability of economic growth of the countries considered. Baltic Republics have a situation significantly better than the others, and comparable to the EU. Ukraine suffers for the consequence of the civil war, and also other countries are marked by political and military tension (Armenia and Azerbaijan). Russia and Kazakhstan base their export to fuels and mining products. Russia, in particular, has negative rate of growth, high inflation and unemployment quite low. We can understand these data as a situation where social tension, engendered by a model of growth led by the export of oil and gas that is jammed, pushes inflation and is contrasted by social policies which hold unemployment quite low.

We examine also the correlation between IHDI and the GDP per capita. Baltic countries are at the top and very near the regression line. Some countries, particularly Ukraine and Belarus, are above the line, showing high IHDI, in comparison with their GDP per capita, whereas Kyrgyz Republic and Tajikistan are under the line. Also Russian Federation is above the regression line; in this case, and even more in the cases of Belarus and Ukraine, education (and, perhaps, health: but it is not the case in Russia) is quite good in comparison with personal income.

The construction of a couple of indexes allows going deeper in the analysis. FSD conveys information about economic and social performance and allows a classification in four classes. The first class is formed by Baltic Republics, which, again, are the most European countries. Russia is in the second class, which is far from the first, and is penalised by inflation, inequality and life expectancy. Again, Russia shows relevant weak points in its economic and social model. At the bottom we find Tajikistan and Kyrgyz Republic, together with Moldova, which has a very high rate of unemployment.

FSG conveys information about the quality of governance. It has robust correlation with FSD (around 71%), confirming the generally accepted relation between governance and socio-economic development. Remarkably, in this classification Russia falls in the last class: the weak points we have seen can find here further explication. On the other hand, Baltic Republic are at the top again.

Interestingly, FSG is correlated with IHDI: quality of life and good and fair institutions go together. On the contrary, FSD is not correlated with GDP growth: growth and human development are not strictly linked each other.

Finally, we can say that, from our study, emerges the portrait of a group of countries heterogeneous. A part of them looks at the EU and is really near it. Other countries have inner weaknesses, due to political turmoil, institutions not affordable or fair, economic growth based on the export of fuels and raw materials. Russia shows inequality, inflation and bad governance. According to our results, its leadership could be jeopardised in the medium – long period.

# APPENDIX 1

|  | GDP per capita (current US$) | Exports of goods and services (% of GDP) | GNI per capita, PPP (current international $) | GINI index (World Bank estimate) | Inflation, consumer prices (annual %) | Internet users (per 100 people) | Imports of goods and services (% of GDP) |
|---|---|---|---|---|---|---|---|
| Armenia | 3499,80 | 29,73 | 8720 | 31,54 | 3,73 | 46,3 | 41,26 |
| Azerbaijan | 5496,34 | 37,81 | 17140 | 16,64 | 4,17 | 61 | 34,82 |
| Belarus | 5740,46 | 60,07 | 16840 | 26,01 | 13,53 | 59,02 | 59,12 |
| Estonia | 17295,36 | 79,76 | 27510 | 33,15 | -0,46 | 84,24 | 75,67 |
| Georgia | 3795,97 | 45,04 | 9410 | 40,03 | 4,00 | 48,9 | 64,91 |
| Kazakhstan | 10508,40 | 28,63 | 24260 | 26,35 | 6,72 | 54,89 | 24,68 |
| Kyrgyz Republic | 1103,22 | 37,45 | 3300 | 27,37 | 6,50 | 28,3 | 87,68 |
| Latvia | 13664,94 | 58,76 | 24220 | 35,48 | 0,20 | 75,83 | 60,18 |
| Lithuania | 14172,22 | 77,29 | 26660 | 35,15 | -0,88 | 72,13 | 77,41 |
| Moldova | 1843,24 | 43,43 | 5350 | 28,53 | 9,68 | 46,6 | 73,73 |
| Russian Federation | 9057,11 | 29,53 | 23790 | 41,59 | 15,53 | 70,52 | 21,21 |
| Tajikistan | 925,91 | 19,18 | 3320 | 30,77 | 5,71 | 17,49 | 68,33 |
| Ukraine | 2114,95 | 52,77 | 7810 | 24,55 | 48,72 | 43,4 | 54,76 |

## Growing Market Economy and Institutions 165

|  | Life expectancy at birth, total (years) | Adult literacy rate, population 15+ years, both sexes (%) | Unemployment, total (% of total labor force) (modelled ILO estimate) | Poverty headcount ratio at national poverty lines (% of population) | Agriculture, value added (% of GDP) | CO2 emissions (metric tons per capita) | Central government debt, total (% of GDP) |
|---|---|---|---|---|---|---|---|
| Armenia | 74,68 | 99,74 | 17,10 | 30 | 19,35 | 1,67 | 27,83 |
| Azerbaijan | 70,76 | 99,79 | 5,20 | 6 | 6,79 | 3,65 | 6,39 |
| Belarus | 72,98 | 99,62 | 5,90 | 5,1 | 7,80 | 6,68 | 25,22 |
| Estonia | 77,24 | 99,86 | 7,70 | 21,8 | 3,50 | 14,05 | 0,63 |
| Georgia | 74,67 | 99,75 | 13,40 | 14,8 | 9,19 | 2,05 | 32,53 |
| Kazakhstan | 71,62 | 99,73 | 4,10 | 2,8 | 5,01 | 15,81 | 13,22 |
| Kyrgyz Republic | 70,40 | 99,24 | 8,10 | 30,6 | 15,94 | 1,20 | 99,33 |
| Latvia | 74,19 | 99,90 | 10,00 | 22,5 | 3,27 | 3,79 | 41,59 |
| Lithuania | 73,97 | 99,82 | 11,30 | 19,1 | 3,44 | 4,54 | 43,76 |
| Moldova | 71,46 | 99,17 | 3,40 | 11,4 | 13,83 | 1,40 | 24,33 |
| Russian Federation | 70,37 | 99,68 | 5,10 | 13,4 | 4,63 | 12,65 | 12,68 |
| Tajikistan | 69,60 | 99,75 | 10,90 | 32 | 27,41 | 0,36 | 79,80 |
| Ukraine | 71,19 | 99,74 | 7,70 | 8,6 | 14,04 | 6,26 | 33,70 |

|  | Control of Corruption: Estimate | Government Effectiveness: Estimate | Political Stability and Absence of Violence/ Terrorism: Estimate | Regulatory Quality: Estimate | Rule of Law: Estimate | Voice and Accountability: Estimate |
|---|---|---|---|---|---|---|
| Armenia | -0,44 | -0,17 | -0,21 | 0,22 | -0,32 | -0,55 |
| Azerbaijan | -0,92 | -0,34 | -0,50 | -0,29 | -0,61 | -1,44 |
| Belarus | -0,32 | -0,50 | 0,12 | -1,04 | -0,81 | -1,45 |
| Estonia | 1,27 | 1,05 | 0,76 | 1,67 | 1,36 | 1,17 |
| Georgia | 0,74 | 0,48 | -0,23 | 0,93 | 0,20 | 0,23 |
| Kazakhstan | -0,76 | -0,02 | 0,05 | -0,27 | -0,55 | -1,16 |
| Kyrgyz Republic | -1,11 | -0,84 | -0,78 | -0,42 | -0,94 | -0,53 |
| Latvia | 0,34 | 0,97 | 0,55 | 1,17 | 0,87 | 0,83 |
| Lithuania | 0,48 | 0,99 | 0,78 | 1,20 | 0,91 | 0,96 |
| Moldova | -0,85 | -0,38 | -0,10 | 0,02 | -0,27 | -0,02 |
| Russian Federation | -0,87 | -0,08 | -0,84 | -0,40 | -0,71 | -1,04 |
| Tajikistan | -1,00 | -0,75 | -0,68 | -1,01 | -0,96 | -1,44 |
| Ukraine | -1,00 | -0,38 | -1,93 | -0,63 | -0,79 | -0,08 |

## APPENDIX 2

|  | FSD | FSG | GDP growth | AHDI |
|---|---|---|---|---|
| Armenia | -0,45 | -0,11 | 3,00 | 0,73 |
| Azerbaijan | -0,28 | -0,67 | 1,10 | 0,75 |
| Belarus | -0,04 | -0,66 | -3,89 | 0,80 |
| Estonia | 2,11 | 1,88 | 1,07 | 0,86 |
| Georgia | -0,20 | 0,77 | 2,77 | 0,75 |
| Kazakhstan | 0,23 | -0,36 | 1,20 | 0,79 |
| Kyrgyz Republic | -1,19 | -0,86 | 3,47 | 0,66 |
| Latvia | 1,04 | 1,31 | 1,89 | 0,82 |
| Lithuania | 1,34 | 1,43 | 1,59 | 0,84 |
| Moldova | -0,98 | -0,17 | -0,50 | 0,69 |
| Russian Federation | 0,25 | -0,63 | -3,73 | 0,80 |
| Tajikistan | -1,22 | -1,08 | 4,20 | 0,62 |
| Ukraine | -0,59 | -0,86 | -9,90 | 0,75 |

## REFERENCES

Assembly, U.G. (2012, April 25). *Resolution adopted by the Human Rights Council,* n° A/HRC/RES/19/20. The role of good governance in the promotion and protection of human rights.

Berkhin, P. (2006). *A Survey of Clustering Data Mining Techniques.* In J. Kogan, C. Nicholas, & M. Teboulle, Grouping Multidimensional Data: Recent Advance in Clustering (p. 25-71). Springer.

Bugnacki, J. (2015, April 06). *Critical Issue Facing Russia and the Former Soviet Union: Governance and Corruption.* American Security Project: http://www.americansecurityproject.org/critical-issues-facing-russia-and-the-former-soviet-union-governance-and-corruption/

Cattel, R. (1966). The screen test for the number of Factors. *Multivariate behavioural research,* Vol.1, Issue 2, 245-276.

Ciborra, C., & Navarra, D. (2005). Good governance, development theory, and aid policy: Risks and challenges of e-government in Jordan. *Information Technology for Development,* Vol. 11, Issue 2.

Fabrigar, L., Wegener, D., MacCallum, R., & Strahan, E. (1999). Evaluating the Use of Exploratory Factor Analysis in Psychological Research. *Psychological Methods,* Vol. 4, n° 3, 272-299.

Gorsuch, R. (1983). *Factor Analysis* (2nd ed.). Hillsdale, NJ: Lawrence Erlbaum Associates.

Hogan, J., & Tchernis, R. (2004). Bayesian factor analysis for spatially correlated data, with application to summarizing area-level material deprivation from census data. *Journal of the American Statistical Association,* Vol. 99, Issue 466, 314-324.

Ivaldi, E., & Soliani, R. (2014). Is economical and social development really linked with the shift of labour from secondary to tertiary sector? Evidence from the Italian case. *International Journal of Economics and Finance,* Vol.6, n°5, 26-32.

Ivaldi, E., Bonatti, G., & Soliani, R. (2016a). The construction of a synthetic index comparing multidimensional well-being in the European Union. *Social Indicators Research,* 397-430.

Ivaldi E., Bonatti G., Soliani R. (2016b) *The measurement of Well-Being in the Current Era.* Nova Publishers ISBN: 978-1-53610-005-1

Kaiser, H. (1960). The application of electronic computers to factor analysis. *Educational and Psychological Measurement,* Vol. 20, 141-151.

Kaiser, H. (1960). The Application of Electronic Computers to Factor Analysis. *Educational and Psychological Measurement,* Vol. 20, 141-151.

Kaufmann, D., Kraay, A., & Mastruzzi, M. (2010). *The Worldwide Governance Indicators: Methodology and Analytical Issues.* World Bank Policy Research Working Paper 5430.

Landi S., Ivaldi E., Testi A. (2017) *Identifying Change over Time in Small Area Socio-Economic Deprivation and Health in an urban context.* Social Indicator Research online DOI 10.1007/s11205-017-1720-3 ISSN 0303-8300.

Myer, S., & Jencks, C. (1989). Poverty and the distribution of material hardship. *Journal of Human Resources,* Vol. 24.

Nardo, M., Saisana, M., Tarantola, S., Hoffman, A., & Giovannini, E. (2005). *Handbook on constricting composite indicators: methodology and user guide.* N° 2005/3. Paris: OECD Publishing.

Osborne, J. (2015). What is Rotating in Exploratory Factor Analysis? *Pratical Assessment, Research & Evaluation,* Vol. 20, n° 2, Available online: http://pareonline.net/getvn.asp?v=20&n=2.

Petrovsky, V. (2004). Growth, Governance, and Human Development: Post-Soviet Transition in North and Central Asia. In Y. Sato, *Growth & Governance in Asia* (p. 155-164). Honolulu: Asia-Pacific Center for Security Studies.

Pituch, K., & Stevens, J. (2016). *Applied Multivariate Statistics for the Social Sciences.* New York: Routledge.

Ranis, G. (2004). *Human Development and Economic Growth.* Center Discussion Paper n° 887, Yale University.

Rechel, B., Richardson, E., & McKee, M. (2014). *Trends in health system in the former Soviet countries.* United Kingdom: European Observatory on Health System and Policies.

Rodrik, D., Subramanian, A., & Trebbi, F. (2004). Institutions Rule: The Primacy of Institutions Over Geography and Integration in Economic Development. *Journal of Economic Growth,* Vol. 4, Issue 2, 131-165.

Rule of Law and Economic Development Research Group. (2012). *Rule of Law and Economic Development: A Comparative Analysis of Approaches to Economic Development across the BRIC Countries.* Montreal: McGill.

Santagata M., Ivaldi E., Soliani R. (2017) Development and Governance in the Ex-Soviet Union: an Empirical Inquiry. *Social Indicator research online* DOI 10.1007/s11205-017-1815-x ISSN 0303-8300,

Shirley, M. (2005). Institutions and Development. In C. Ménard, & S. MM., *Handbook of New Institutional Economics* (p. 611-638). Netherland: Springer.

Smith, B. (2007). *Good governance and development.* Shangai: Palgrave McMillan.

Soubbotina, T., & Sheram, K. (2000). *Beyond Economic Growth: meeting the challenge of Global Development.* Washington, D.C.: The World Bank.

Stevens, J. (1986). *Applied multivariate statistics for the social sciences.* Hillsdale: L. Eribaurn Associates Inc.

UNDP. (1990). *Human Development Report.* New York Oxford: Oxford University Press.

UNDP. (1996). *Human Development Report.* New York Oxford: Oxford University Press.

UNDP. (2015). *Human Development Report 2015: Work for Human Development.* New York: PBM Graphics.

Ward, J. (1963). Hierarchical Grouping to Optimize an Objective Function. *Journal of the American Statistical Association,* Vol. 58, Issue 301, 236-244.

In: Progress in Economics Research
Editor: Albert Tavidze

ISBN: 978-1-53615-120-6
© 2019 Nova Science Publishers, Inc.

*Chapter 5*

# SOME ASPECTS OF TAXATION IN THE FORMER SOVIET UNION

### *Sergei V. Jargin*
Peoples' Friendship University of Russia, Moscow, Russia

### ABSTRACT

According to Russian legislation, the income-tax is collected from funds obtained from selling of securities. There have been exemptions, depending on the time the property had been owned by a taxpayer, and newly also on the date when it was acquired. The legislation has been modified several times being hardly transparent for non-professionals. The aim of this report was to demonstrate that exemptions from taxation can be arbitrarily denied by fiscal authorities under invented pretexts. A stockholder and investor should know that, even in the course of simple transactions, he or she can encounter decisions of authorities contradictory to the law, misquoting of the legal codes by civil servants in their correspondence, backdating of official letters, embezzlement of registered letters etc. Stockholders receive numerous letters and telephone calls from brokers prompting to sell the stock sometimes at prices below the market value. Brokers dispose of confidential information about stockholders: not only their names, addresses and telephone numbers but also names and quantities of their securities etc., which indicates that they have access to databases of depositaries. Besides, some aspects of taxation of immobile property (owner-occupied apartments) are discussed.

# INTRODUCTION

The aim of this report was not to overview Russian tax legislation, which would be unfeasible in a short article, but to demonstrate that an investor or taxpayer can encounter decisions of authorities contradictory to the law, misquoting of the codes of law by civil servants in their official correspondence, backdating of official letters, embezzlement of registered letters from taxpayers, and red tape even at simple transactions. The following report is based on the author's experience. The controversy lasted about 6 years, and cost to the author, a medical doctor, considerable loss of time.

According to the Tax Code of Russian Federation (RF) as of 2004, the income-tax (13% for residents; 30% for "non-residents" or those who have resided in RF less than 183 days during a financial year) was to be collected from the funds obtained from selling of property including real estate and securities. However, if the property had been owned by the taxpayer longer than three years, the amount received by the sale was allowed to be exempted from taxation (Article 220 section 1 of the Tax Code of RF, as of 2004). Since then the law has been changed several times. At the moment, the critical period of possession is 5 years (Tax Code, Article 217, section 17.2) but, according to the Federal Law No. 395 of 28.12.2010, article 5, section 7, the exemption is not permitted if the shares had been acquired before 2011. So the matter is regulated not only by the Tax Code but also by other laws and regulations, being hardly transparent for non-professionals.

# CASE REPORT

In October 2003 I sold a certain amount of stock of the corporation Unified Energy System of Russia (UESR). The stock had been in my possession since 1995, being deposited according to instructions at the Central Moscow Depositary. Despite the above-cited provisions by the Tax Code, I was requested by the fiscal authorities to pay income-tax from the whole amount acquired by the sale. My argumentation was dismissed under the pretext that the stock was in my possession allegedly not since 1995 but since 11 July 2003 as a result of the "Unification of the Shares". It turned out that the governmental agency "Federal Commission for the Securities Market of RF" performed unification of different types of UESR stock, while names of some shares were changed. In my rebuttal letter I pointed out that the ownership cannot be changed without consent of the proprietor or a court decision. Therefore, the act of the governmental agency had no impact on the ownership and was in fact nothing else but renaming of the shares. My objection was disregarded by fiscal authorities of all levels.

In May 2005, the arguments of the authorities changed. They acknowledged the fact that the period of uninterrupted ownership started in 1995. The new reasoning was as follows. According to the Tax Code of RF (article 214, section 3, as of 2004), if a stockholder has no documentary evidence of his or her expenditures for the purpose of acquisition and upholding of the securities, he or she can exempt from the taxable income the whole amount acquired by selling of securities, provided that he or she owned them longer than three years. The Deputy Head of the Federal Tax Authority, quoting the Tax Code in his official letter dated 06 May 2005 (Figure 1), inserted the word "only", thus stipulating that a taxpayer is entitled to exempt from taxation the amount received by selling of securities only if he or she has no documentary evidence of his expenditures (Figure 2). From the misquoting resulted nonsense: if a taxpayer has no documentary evidence of his expenditures, he is entitled to exempt from taxation the whole amount; if he has a receipt for a minimal sum - he is not entitled to the exemption. Without the word "only" the meaning of the law is clear: if there is no documentary evidence of expenditures, the exemption from taxation is permitted; if there is such evidence - the taxpayer may choose between the tax exemption and calculation of the taxable income as a difference between gain and loss.

On 23 August 2006 I received a new payment order dated 08 August 2006 (sent according to the postal stamp on 10 August; the backdating of documents is not unusual for Russian official correspondence), requesting to pay the whole amount of the tax plus penalty fees accumulated in the meantime - about 30% in addition to the original amount. I paid the requested amount but wrote a rebuttal (Figure 3). After six years of correspondence and considerable loss of time, the paid amount of the tax was reimbursed, however, without adjustment for inflation. The fiscal authorities acknowledged by a letter dated 31 March 2010 that their preceding decisions had been wrong.

This is, however, not the whole story. On 1 July 2008, the UESR gave up its formal existence and was subdivided into 24 daughter companies. Correspondingly, the stockholders now possess shares of up to 24 denominations instead of one. The market value of the stock decreased as a result of this act. The shares are now deposited not in one but in 7 different registries (depositaries); and a stockholder must visit them during working hours to complete formalities. The volume of correspondence increased considerably. Between numerous useless letters there was also an important one, which could be missed in the ample correspondence: this letter informed that the shares of the corporation TGK-8 had been compulsorily purchased by LUKOIL-Volgogradneftepererabotka. The letter (without signature) contained a questionnaire, which a stockholder had to complete. I travelled from Moscow to Astrakhan to settle formalities and receive the money for my compulsorily sold TGK-8 shares. There were queues in waiting rooms. It turned out that according to the Federal Law Nr. 208 (Article 84.8), a stockholder possessing more than 95% of shares of a corporation may purchase the rest of the stock compulsorily not below the market value determined by an assessor. Whether this provision is always observed is unknown; according to some estimates, my shares could have been sold at a higher price. Stockholders receive numerous letters and telephone calls from brokers prompting them to sell their shares below the market price. The brokers persuade to sell the stock as otherwise it can be bought out compulsorily according to the above-mentioned Law, which sometimes happened indeed. Remarkably, many brokerage firms dispose of confidential information about stockholders: not only their names, addresses, telephone numbers but also denominations and quantities of their securities. All details are discussed on telephone, although calling individuals don't know with whom they are actually speaking. This indicates that unauthorized persons not bound by professional secrecy have access to databases of securities registries (depositaries). Moreover, it has become usual practice also for bank employees to call to mobile phones, despite the clients' repeated protests, also when the latter are in public places, promoting some services and also discussing the clients' bank accounts, so that the banking secrecy can be compromised.

A few words should be said also about immobile property. The growth of Russian economy during the last decades has been accompanied by considerable elevation of prices for real estate. Big investors purchase apartments in old houses in the center of Moscow, perform major repairs sometimes damaging neighboring rooms, and hire them out. Mechanisms of compensation for damage often do not function, while insurance compensates certain amounts disregarding e.g., historic and esthetic value - damaged ancient parquet, stucco moldings etc. This process is accompanied by pressing former inhabitants out of the city center. With communal flats, which had prevailed in the center of Moscow during the Soviet time, it went rather smoothly. The relocation was facilitated by rumors that old houses would be demolished or undergo major repairs with compulsory relocation of inhabitants. To stimulate the decision making, threats and violence by "unknown hooligans" occurred as well [1, 2]. After a majority of communal flats had been cleared, new tactics came to the fore. In the houses, particularly those having high commercial value, appear initiative groups, aimed at breaking-off from existing house managements and foundation of TSJ (ТСЖ - Russian abbreviation for the Association of Apartment Owners). From the beginning, the initiative groups applied inappropriate methods: collected considerable amounts of money without giving receipts, collected signatures under various pretexts (for example, to inform about a forthcoming meeting) on separate sheets of paper, making them suitable to endorse an application made as if from apartment owners e.g., a consent to placement of firms and offices in the house, in basements or other rooms outside private apartments, which are, according to the Housing Code of RF, in condominium of all apartment-owners. The latter do not participate in profits from hiring out of the premises. It should be also mentioned that repairs of electricity, heating, water supply and sewerage appliances also within apartments (except for terminal devices), external repair/maintenance of window frames etc., must be performed free of charge by the house management, being included in the monthly maintenance fee (Regulation No. 170 of 27 September 2003 by Rosstroi - the governmental agency for construction, residential and utilities services). In fact, lodgers are sometimes manipulated towards paid services or have no other choice as to pay for the works. Moreover, the TSJ management can perform reconstructions or repairs at the costs of apartment owners, even if some of them want to preserve historic buildings in their original conditions. The TSJ management can make payments unpredictable, collecting money for different kinds of repairs, renovations and reconstructions (Figure 4). Even wealthy apartment owners are cautious because of inappropriate acts already committed by the "initiative groups": one would rather abstain from dealing with those, who had acted inappropriately. Financial uncertainty is a tool of pressing original inhabitants out of the city center and, at the same time, of reconstruction and rebuilding of old houses. Both mechanisms act synergistically: to reconstruct an old building for commercial purposes, original inhabitants must be removed, while the reconstruction with accompanying costs helps removing them. In this way, the old city of Moscow loses its historic architectural image together with original inhabitants of the city center [1].

Since 2015, the property tax for the real estate has been considerably elevated especially in historic city centers, being now calculated on the basis of the cadastral value of apartments or houses determined on the basis of their market prices. The tax basis and rate depend on the market price and location of the apartment, which can become a motive for some owners to move out of the city center. Municipalities of Moscow, Saint Petersburg and Sevastopol are entitled to additionally enhance the property tax rate for the real estate for "physical persons" (normally 0.1%) up to threefold (Article 406 section 3 of the Tax Code, last amended 2015). Admittedly, pensioners are currently exempted from the property tax for a share in one apartment or house. War veterans are also exempted; however, there are misgivings that the veteran status has been awarded gratuitously to some privileged individuals. The tax calculations are sometimes arbitrary or overtly wrong (double taxation of the same rooms). Fiscal authorities do not respond to some taxpayers' letters while penalty fees are accumulating (Figure 5). Inadequately calculated cadastre values can be contested in court, which is costly and time-consuming. Reportedly, in 2014 there were around 4800 litigations of that kind; in 2015 - 7500 [3].

## DISCUSSION AND CONCLUSION

Investors, taxpayers, owners of Russian securities or immobile property should know that, even in the course of simple transactions, they can encounter red tape, tricks, misquoting of legal codes by civil servants in their correspondence, backdating of official letters etc. Registered letters from citizens may be left without response or attention (Figure 6). Moreover, it is not unusual for Russian postal services to deliver registered letters several days after the date stamped on the envelope as a date of delivery. The Russian post is notoriously slow: the delivery of letters within the country can last weeks, and to a foreign country – over a month (there may be some improvement tendency). There is apparently cooperation between accelerated mail delivery services (courier delivery) and postal employees, whereas the latter e.g., fill in a postal receipt for a registered letter sent abroad in Cyrillic letters with mistakes. At the same time, gossip about allegedly poor services of foreign courier delivery services is sometimes spread by their domestic analogues. Disregard for small stockholders is expressed also by scarcity of dividends paid by some corporations, or by total absence of dividends. The tax legislation is frequently changed, voluminous and non-transparent. According to the author's experience and general knowledge, courts tend to be inefficient. It is known that transaction taxes and their unpredictability, insufficient transparency and credibility, manipulative and deceptive tactics, can have negative impact on the liquidity and lead to reduction in market efficiency [4-6]. In conclusion, the gap between laws, regulations and everyday life is sometimes quite broad in Russia.

## DOCUMENTARY EVIDENCE

Figure 1. (Continued)

## Some Aspects of Taxation in the Former Soviet Union 179

При этом положениями пункта 3 статьи 214.1 Кодекса предусмотрено, что налогоплательщик вправе воспользоваться имущественным налоговым вычетом, предусмотренным абзацем первым подпункта 1 пункта 1 статьи 220 Кодекса, только в случае, когда его расходы не могут быть подтверждены документально.

К указанным расходам относятся:
-суммы, уплачиваемые продавцу в соответствии с договором;
-оплата услуг, оказываемых депозитарием;
-комиссионные отчисления профессиональным участникам рынка ценных бумаг;

(a)

-биржевой сбор (комиссия);
-оплата услуг регистратора;
-стоимость ценных бумаг, полученных безвозмездно, с которых уплачен налог;
-другие расходы, непосредственно связанные с куплей, продажей и хранением ценных бумаг, произведенные за услуги, оказываемые профессиональными участниками рынка ценных бумаг в рамках их профессиональной деятельности.

Если расходы налогоплательщика на приобретение, реализацию и хранение ценных бумаг не могут быть отнесены непосредственно к расходам на приобретение, реализацию и хранение конкретных ценных бумаг, указанные расходы распределяются пропорционально стоимостной оценке ценных бумаг, на долю которых относятся указанные расходы.

Таким образом, в Вашем случае налоговая база за 2003 год в отношении доходов по операциям купли-продажи ценных бумаг определяется как разность между суммами, полученными в данном налоговом периоде от продажи ценных бумаг и расходами на их приобретение (договор купли-продажи от 14.12.1995 №4741/315), хранение (оплата услуг депозитария) и реализацию (договор купли-продажи от 07.10.2003 №Ц/2955). В связи с чем из полученного Вами дохода от реализации ценных бумаг вычитаются фактически произведенные Вами расходы, связанные с приобретением, хранением и реализацией ценных бумаг.

Изменения действующего порядка определения налоговой базы по операциям с ценными бумагами возможно путем внесения соответствующих изменений и дополнений в налоговое законодательство.

Приложение: письмо Яргина С.В. на 1 л. (во второй адрес).

И.Ф.Голиков

(b)

Figure 1a,b. A letter on two pages, dated 06 May 2005, signed by the Deputy Head of the Federal Tax Authority, containing a misquoting of the Tax Code (2004): the arbitrarily added word 'only' (1$^{st}$ page, 7$^{th}$ line from the bottom) causing distortion of the meaning. According to the false citation, a taxpayer is entitled to exemption from taxation of the amount received by selling of securities only if he has no documentary evidence of his expenditures (commented in the text).

**ФЕДЕРАЛЬНАЯ
НАЛОГОВАЯ СЛУЖБА**

ЗАМЕСТИТЕЛЬ РУКОВОДИТЕЛЯ

Неглинная, 23, Москва, 127381
Телефон: 913-00-09; Телефакс: 913-00-05;
E-mail: mns@nalog.ru; www.nalog.ru

22.06.2005 № 04-1-04/432

На №

О налогообложении доходов физических лиц

Яргину С.В.
Климентовский пер., д.6, кв.82
г.Москва, 115184

Управление ФНС России по г.Москве

Уважаемый Сергей Вадимович!

Федеральная налоговая служба, рассмотрев Ваше повторное обращение, сообщает, что по данному вопросу в письме от 06.05.2005 № 04-1-04/272, направленном в Ваш адрес, дан конкретный ответ.

Дополнительно разъясняем, что в соответствии с пунктом 2.1 Постановления ФКЦБ России от 01.04.2003 № 03-18/пс объединение дополнительных выпусков эмиссионных ценных бумаг осуществляется путем аннулирования государственных регистрационных номеров, присвоенных дополнительным выпускам эмиссионных ценных бумаг, и присвоения им государственного регистрационного номера выпуска ценных бумаг, к которому они являются дополнительными. При этом пунктом 2.3 данного Постановления предусмотрено, что принятие решения об аннулировании государственных регистрационных номеров дополнительных выпусков эмиссионных ценных бумаг без принятия решения о присвоении дополнительным выпускам эмиссионных ценных бумаг государственного регистрационного номера выпуска ценных бумаг, к которому они являются дополнительными, не допускается.

Таким образом, объединение выпусков ценных бумаг не предусматривает аннулирования самих выпусков ценных бумаг. При изменении государственного регистрационного номера дополнительного выпуска эмиссионных ценных бумаг сами ценные бумаги не аннулируются, а права владельцев ценных бумаг, закрепленные ими, не прекращаются и не прерываются.

Исходя из изложенного при объединении дополнительных выпусков ценных бумаг срок нахождения ценных бумаг в собственности налогоплательщика не прерывается на дату объединения и исчисляется с даты приобретения ценных бумаг.

Следовательно, при реализации ценных бумаг, по которым к моменту продажи было проведено объединение выпусков, налогоплательщик вправе воспользоваться имущественным налоговым вычетом, исходя из соответствующих сроков приобретения ценных бумаг до их объединения, в случае, если отсутствуют документально подтвержденные расходы, связанные с приобретением, реализацией и хранением указанных ценных бумаг.

(a)

Figure 2. (Continued)

> Поскольку у Вас имеются документально подтвержденные расходы от операций с ценными бумагами (согласно Вами приложенных к запросу документов, это: договор купли-продажи от 14.12.1995 № 4741/315, расходы по оплате услуг депозитария и договор купли-продажи от 07.10.2003 № Ц/2955), то право на получение имущественного налогового вычета в размерах норматива, установленного статьей 220 Кодекса, по указанным операциям купли-продажи ценных бумаг Вы не имеете.
>
> Приложение: письмо Яргина С.В. на 1 л. (во второй адрес).
>
> И.Ф.Голиков

(b)

Figure 2a,b. Another letter with the same signature, dated 22 June 2005, acknowledging the fact that the uninterrupted period of possession of the stock started in 1995. On the basis of the misquoting illustrated by Figure 1, the exemption from taxation was denied because of the following reasons (translation from the last paragraph on the 2$^{nd}$ page): "As you had documentarily confirmed expenditures from operations with securities [listed], you have no right for tax exemption according to the Article 220 of the Tax Code for the operations of selling and purchase of securities". Later it was acknowledged by the fiscal authorities that the above decision had been unlawful.

> 01.07.2005
>
> **Жалоба**
>
> 08.12.2005 я обратился с письмом в Федеральную Налоговую Службу с просьбой пересмотреть решение ИМНС № 5 по ЦАО Москвы об отказе в предоставлении мне налогового вычета на сумму, полученную от продажи ценных бумаг, которые находились в моей собственности без движения с 1995 года. В письме была изложена суть дела, были приложены все имеющиеся документы.
>
> Переписка с Налоговыми органами по данному вопросу ведется с октября 2004 года. Сначала отказ в предоставлении налогового вычета основывался на неправильном утверждении, что акции находились в моем владении менее трех лет. Затем факт нахождения акций в моей собственности с 1995 года был признан, а отказ в предоставлении налогового вычета подкрепляется новым аргументом. В письме № 04-1-04/272 от 06.05.2005, подписанным г-ном И.Ф. Голиковым, (приложение 1) указано: "налогоплательщик вправе воспользоваться имущественным налоговым вычетом, предусмотренным абзацем первым подпункта 1 пункта 1 статьи 220 Налогового Кодекса только в случае, когда его расходы не могут быть подтверждены документально" (пункт 3 статьи 214.1 Кодекса). Г-н И.Ф. Голиков неверно цитирует Налоговый Кодекс: он вставил слово "только", которого в тексте Кодекса нет. В результате получилась бессмыслица: если расходы не могут быть подтверждены документально, налогоплательщик вправе воспользоваться налоговым вычетом на сумму, полученную от продажи имущества. Если же имеются документально подтвержденные расходы на сумму один рубль - он теряет право на налоговый вычет. На самом деле текст Кодекса (без вставленного г-ном Голиковым слова "только") имеет ясный смысл: при отсутствии документов,

Figure 3. (Continued)

(a)

подтверждающих расходы, налогоплательщик вправе воспользоваться имущественным налоговым вычетом, предусмотренным абзацем первым подпункта 1 пункта 1 статьи 220 Кодекса, а при наличии таких документов - вправе выбирать между налоговым вычетом и определением налоговой базы как разности между полученной при продаже суммой и произведенными им расходами.

**Таким образом, с сотрудники Налоговых органов прибегают к ложному цитированию текста Законов с целью нарушения прав налогоплательщиков.**
Налогооблажение сумм, полученных от продажи имущества (в том числе недвижимости и ценных бумаг) напралено на то, чтобы от налогов не ускользали доходы, поучаемые от спекуляции. Именно поэтому в Налоговое Законодательство вводится временной критерий. По российским Законам налоговому вычету подлежат суммы,

(b)

полученные от продажи имущества, которое находилось в собственности налогоплательщика более трех лет (пункт 1 Статьи 220 Кодекса). Этот срок превосходит принятые в зарубежной практике временные параметры. Например, в Германии не облагается налогом выручка, полученная от продажи любого имущества, находившегося в собственности более одного года. Требование оплатить подоходный налог на сумму, полученную от продажи ценных бумаг, находившихся в собственности владельца без движения восемь лет (как в моем случае), беспрецедентно в мировой практике. Если о подобных случаях появятся публикации за рубежом, это неизбежно сократит приток инвестиций в российскую экономику.

С учетом изложенного, прошу предоставить мне имущественный налоговый вычет на всю сумму, полученную от проданных акций. Кроме того, в соответствии со статьей 141

Figure 3a,b. My rebuttal letter of 01 July 2005 pointing out the misquoting of the Codes of Law by civil servants in their official correspondence.

Главе Управы «Замоскворечье»
С.Н. Носкову

Уважаемый Сергей Николаевич!

В доме №6 по Климентовскому переулку сложилась крайне напряжённая ситуация с электроснабжением, а именно: дом подключён к трансформаторной подстанции с устаревшим оборудованием; силовой кабель ветхий, т.к. эксплуатируется без замены уже более 50 лет. Следствием этого является постоянная угроза отключения электроэнергии (последняя авария, обусловившая замену 8-метрового участка кабеля, произошла 27 и 28 января с.г., когда третья часть квартир дома в течение почти 6 часов оставалась без электричества), повышается пожароопасность. Кроме того, в связи с тем, что данный кабель является трёхжильным, использование современных электробытовых приборов жителями дома затруднено.

Просим подключить наш дом к новой трансформаторной подстанции, расположенной на ул.Б.Татарская, а также проложить к дому новый силовой четырёхжильный кабель, рассчитанный на повышенное потребление электроэнергии. Жители дома готовы принять долевое участие в финансировании данных работ в части оплаты увеличения мощности электропотребления по сравнению с нормативом.

Figure 4. (Continued)

(a)

Разрешите Вам напомнить, что данный вопрос был задан Вам на встрече с жителями района 22 февраля с.г., и Вы обещали рассмотреть возможность включения средств на его решение в бюджет района на 2006 г.

По поручению жильцов дома №6 по пер. Климентовский

Старший по дому  A.Р. Сараев.
(тел.:953-11-81)

Приложение: подписные листы жильцов в поддержку данной просьбы
(на ___ листах).

(a)

Главе Управы Замоскворечье
Г-ну Носкову Сергею Николаевичу
от Яргина Сергея Вадимовича
Адрес: 115184 Климентовский пер. д. 6 кв. 82
Тел. 9516788

04.03.2005

Заявление

В нашем доме было проведено несколько собраний собственников жилья с целью создания Товарищества (ТСЖ). Руководитель инициативной группы по созданию ТСЖ г-н А.Р. Сараев планирует на средства жильцов проведение технической экспертизы дома и других мероприятий технического характера (см. приложение). На эти и другие цели собираются крупные суммы денег.

Текст прилагаемого письма заставляет усомниться в его технической обоснованности. Пятьдесят лет назад кабели были рассчитаны на напряжение 127 вольт. Сила тока в проводах при заданной мощности потребителей при этом вдвое выше. Поэтому провода при напряжении 127 должны иметь сечение примерно в 4 раза больше, чем при напряжении 220 вольт. Пожарная безопасность кабеля определяется не числом жил, а их суммарным сечением. Во всяком случае, для принятия решения необходима консультация специалиста.

Ответственность за техническое состояние дома несет ДЕЗ "Замоскворечье". Действия активистов по созданию ТСЖ противоречат "Соглашению об общем владении строением и долевом участии в расходах по его содержанию и ремонту", заключенному нами с ДЕЗ "Замоскворечье" 04.02.1997, согласно которому ДЕЗ переданы права по управлению домом, обеспечение его надлежащего содержания и ремонта. Кроме того, их действия противоречат Жилищному кодексу РФ, согласно которому многоквартирный дом может управляться только одной управляющей организацией (Статья 161, пункт 9). Мы придерживаемся соглашения с ДЕЗ и регулярно вносим плату за техническое обслуживание.

(b)

Figure 4. (Continued)

**Просим Вас провести проверку законности действий активистов по созданию ТСЖ и сбора ими денежных средств.**

**С уважением,**

**Яргин С.В.**

**Приложение: копия заявления активистов по созданию ТСЖ от имени жителей дома**

5.03.05г.

Figure 4a,b. a - Letter from the leader of an initiative group asking for replacement of an external electric cable and declaring that apartment owners are ready to participate in the payment. However, according to the law, such works must be financed by the house management being covered by monthly maintenance fees; b – my rebuttal letter.

ФГУП "ПОЧТА РОССИИ"
131000, г.Москва Варшавское ш. д.37
Москва 101000
Адрес: Москва, ул .Мясницкая, д. 26
Телефон: 8(495)624-95-29
Касса № 10100017
КАССОВЫЙ ЧЕК
ПРИХОД
Прием
Внутренняя почта
Население, Наличные рубли
Заказное письмо
Квитанция № 37185
Отправитель: ЯРГИН С В
Оплачено 22,00 руб,
РПО № 10100020371856
Способ пересылки: НАЗЕМН.
Вес, гр.: 14
Кому: УПРАВЛЕНИЕ ДЕЛАМИ ПРЕЗИДЕНТА РФ
103132, МОСКВА

В Управление делами Президента Российской Федерац
103132, Москва, Никитников пер., д. 2, подъезд 5, E-ma
от Яргиной Елены Евгеньевны, Яргина Сергея Вадимо
проживающих по адресу: Климентовский пер. д. 6 кв. 8
+74959516788, электронная почта yargina_kb83@mail.r

06.03.2018

**Почему мы не пойдем на выборы**

ОТКРЫТОЕ ПИСЬМО

По поводу двойного налогообложения нашей квартиры налогом на имущество физических лиц и непредставления льгот пенсионерам мы дважды (19.10.2017 и 28.11.2017) обращались в ИФНС № 5 по ЦАО г. Москвы, а затем 15.01.2018 на имя руководителя Управления ФНС России по г. Москве (письмо прилагается) с просьбой дать письменный ответ. Ответ не был получен ни в письменном, ни в электронном виде.

Суть дела подробно изложена в прилагаемом письме и предшествующей переписке. В связи с ошибкой в Едином государственном реестре недвижимости, налог на имущество физических лиц на нашу квартиру был начислен дважды: на всю квартиру и еще раз на 2 комнаты в той же квартире. Поскольку комнаты в той же квартире рассматривались как «вторая» недвижимая собственность, на них не была предоставлена льгота пенсионерам (Яргина Е.Е. пенсионер с 2002 г., Яргин С.В. – с 21 августа 2016 г.). Ошибка в Едином государственном реестре недвижимости была исправлена по нашему заявлению, все документы были представлены в ИФНС № 5 с нашими письмами от 28.11.2017.

Налог за квартиру был оплачен Яргиным С.В. (пенсионер с 21 августа 2016 г.) в сумме 5588 рублей и Яргиным Д.С. в сумме 9579 рублей 27.11.2017 в соответствии с уведомлениями, соответственно, № 72003552 и 71662640, оба от 21.09.2017. Яргиной Е.Е. налог на квартиру не оплачивался, поскольку она является пенсионером с 2002 г. Налог, начисленный дополнительно за комнаты в той же квартире, нами не оплачивался.

Figure 5. (Continued)

## *Some Aspects of Taxation in the Former Soviet Union* 185

> При повторных проверках личных кабинетов (последний раз 04.03.2018) мы обнаружили, что налог пересчитан не был, требуемые к уплате суммы остаются в соответствии с требованиями об уплате налога от 18.12.2017. Кроме того, начислены пени. По данным из наших личных кабинетов и требованиям об уплате налога от 18.12.2017. невозможно понять, за какой период и на какое имущество начислен налог.
>
> В связи с тем, что государственные налоговые органы игнорируют наши письма, касающиеся нарушений налогового законодательства, просим Вас помочь в решении данного вопроса.
>
> Яргина Е.Е. (врач-рентгенолог)
> Яргин С.В. (кандидат мед. наук)
> Яргин Д.С. (Яргина Е.Е. по доверенности)
>
> Приложение: Наше письмо на имя руководителя Управления ФНС России по г. Москве от 15.01.2018

Figure 5. Open letter to the Presidential Office of RF about inappropriate acts by fiscal authorities.

> Мировому Судье участка № 101
> от Яргина С.В.
>
> 10.07.2007
>
> Объяснение
>
> Ваша Честь,
>
> Подсудимый утверждал, что я напал на него, а проходившие по лестнице двое незнакомых мужчин стали защищать его от моего нападения. Между тем, в момент нападения обвиняемый находился на лестнице надо мной и перегнулся через перила, чтобы достать до моей головы. Нас разделяли перила и разница по высоте около 1 метра. Я не мог напасть на подсудимого, просто не дотянулся бы до него. Избиение происходило внизу, где я находился изначально. Это значит, что я не поднялся по лестнице, чтобы напасть на подсудимого, а он с сообщниками спустился вниз, чтобы напасть на меня.
>
> Объяснение мотивов нападения (якобы, я не впустил в подъезд знакомую подсудимого) несостоятельны: я действительно стараюсь не пускать в подъезд незнакомых лиц, но всегда при этом обращаюсь вежливо и предлагаю позвонить по домофону в квартиру, в которую они пришли. Спонтанные хулиганские действия под влиянием алкоголя также исключены: повторные угрозы в мой адрес продолжались около года. Признаков опьянения у нападавших я не заметил. Это значит, что имелись другие мотивы.
>
> В 2004-2006 годах в нашем доме работала инициативная группа по созданию ТСЖ (Сарзев А.Р., Панкратова О.И. и др.), которая ставила в качестве одной из своих целей расторжение существующего соглашения с ДЕЗ и взятие на себя управление домом. Активисты по созданию ТСЖ собирали крупные суммы денег, а также, обманным путем, под видом сбора платы за домофон, собирали подписи жильцов дома под фиктивными протоколами собраний. Деньги собирались на проведение повторных экспертиз технического состояния дома под предлогом того, что дом включен в списки аварийного жилья; однако на наш запрос в Префектуру ЦАО был получен ответ, что дом в подобных списках не значится. Кроме того, деньги собирались на ремонт (замена кабеля), хотя согласно имеющемуся соглашению с ДЕЗ расходы на все виды ремонта включены в плату за техническое обслуживание и отдельно оплачиваться жильцами не должны. Инициативная группа отказывала в доступе к соответствующей документации.

Figure 6. (Continued)

На собраниях руководителя инициативной группы говорили о планах реконструкции дома, в частности, о строительстве дополнительных этажей (надстройки). Я выступил на собрании против реконструкции дома, сославшись на его историко-архитектурную ценность. Кроме того, я высказал сомнение в обоснованности сбора денег инициативной группой. В ответ на это присутствующий на собрании молодой человек сделал замечания угрожающего характера (угроза физической расправы с теми, кто не будет платить).

Со слов строителей, выполнявших ремонт в кв. № 85, нам стало известно, что квартиры в доме покупает банк. К нам неоднократно приходили неизвестные лица, называвшие себя представителями фирмы по торговле недвижимостью, и убеждали продать нашу квартиру; соответствующие материалы часто бросали в почтовый ящик.

В расположенной над нами кв. № 85 в 2005 году выполнялся капитальный ремонт, в ходе которого в нашей квартире возникли повреждения потолка. Мы обратились с жалобой в ДЕЗ; в результате вопрос был улажен после того, как в нашей квартире был выполнен ремонт ванной комнаты и туалета. Примерно в это время (лето-осень 2005 года) я, выйдя из подъезда, увидел группу молодых людей, которые шумели и раскачивали стоявший около подъезда мусорный контейнер. Я сделал им замечание, после чего один из молодых людей напал на меня и нанес несколько легких ударов и толчков (очевидно, с целью напугать, а не нести повреждение). Я обратился в милицию; по прибытию наряда милиции молодых людей у подъезда не оказалось. Сейчас я вспоминаю, что напавший на меня в 2005 молодой человек был в числе нападавших 13.03.2007.

С учетом изложенного, у меня возникло подозрение, что имевшие место угрозы в мой адрес и нападение на меня в подъезде 13.03.2007 могли быть организованы с целью подтолкнуть нас к решению продать квартиру и сменить место жительства.

В ходе следствия я предоставил эту информацию следователю и просил допросить участницу инициативной группы, старшую по подъезду г-жу О.И. Панкратову (Климентовский пер. д.6 кв. 86), однако этого сделано не было.

Таким образом, дело не расследовано до конца: не найдены сообщники, не проработана версия, что группа лиц, заинтересованных в покупке нашей квартиры и недовольных моими жалобами, направила действия подсудимого и его сообщников.

С уважением,

Яргин С.В.

В Московскую городскую прокуратуру
Новокузнецкая ул. 23а
От Яргина Сергея Вадимовича
Климентовский пер. д. 6 кв. 82; 115184 Москва
Телефон: 95167888

18.11.2009

Уважаемые господа,

Настоящее заявление я подаю в Московскую городскую прокуратуру в связи с тем, что описанные в нем явления, очевидно, наблюдаются в разных районах и касаются всей Москвы. У Мирового судьи участка № 101 района «Замоскворечье» (ул. Пятницкая д. 53/18 с. 1) разбиралось дело об избиении меня 13.03.2007 в подъезде нашего дома № 6 по Климентовскому переулку. К делу была приобщена моя объяснительная записка и другие материалы, суть которых состоит в следующем. В 2004-2006 годах в нашем доме работала инициативная группа по созданию ТСЖ (Сараев А.Р., Панкратова О.И. и др.), участники которой утверждали, что ставят своей целью расторжение действующего соглашения с ДЕЗ и взятие на себя управления домом.

Figure 6. (Continued)

Активисты собирали крупные суммы денег, а также, обманным путем («распишитесь, что Вы сдали деньги за домофон» или «распишитесь, что мы Вас пригласили на собрание») собирали подписи жильцов дома под фиктивными протоколами или решениями собраний, что фактически равноценно фальсификации подписей. Деньги собирались на проведение повторных экспертиз под предлогом того, что наш дом включен в списки аварийного жилья; однако на мой запрос в префектуру ЦАО был получен ответ, что наш дом в подобных списках не числится. Деньги собирались на ремонт наружного кабеля (приложение 1), хотя согласно действующему соглашению с ДЕЗ расходы на все виды ремонта включены в плату за техническое обслуживание и отдельно оплачиваться жильцами не должны. В связи с этим я дважды направлял письма с подтверждающими документами в Управу «Замоскворечье»; копия одного из этих писем (приложение 2) была приобщена к судебному делу.

На собраниях руководители инициативной группы (А.Р. Сараев) говорили о планах реконструкции дома, в частности, о строительстве дополнительных этажей (надстройки). Я выступил на одном из собраний против реконструкции дома, сославшись на его историко-архитектурную ценность, а также высказал сомнение в обоснованности сбора денег. В ответ на это, присутствовавший на собрании молодой мужчина сделал замечание угрожающего характера в смысле угрозы физической расправы с теми, кто не будет платить.

В расположенной над нами квартире № 85 в 2005 году выполнялся капитальный ремонт с перепланировкой, в результате которого в нашей квартире возникли повреждения потолка. Мы обратились с жалобой в ДЕЗ. Вскоре после этого (лето-осень 2005 года), услышав шум и крики около нашего подъезда, я вышел на улицу и увидел группу молодых людей, которые шумели и раскачивали стоявший около подъезда мусорный контейнер. Я сделал им замечание, после чего один из мужчин напал на меня и нанес несколько легких ударов и толчков (очевидно, с целью напугать, а не нанести повреждения). Я обратился к сотрудникам милиции, но к моменту их прибытия молодых людей у дома не оказалось.

Со слов прораба (Светлана), руководившей ремонтом квартиры 85, квартиры в нашем доме скупал банк с целью их сдачи в поднаем. К нам неоднократно приходили неизвестные лица, якобы от фирмы по торговле недвижимостью, и убеждали продать квартиру; соответствующие материалы часто бросали в почтовый ящик.

С учетом изложенного у меня возникло подозрение, что имевшие место угрозы в мой адрес и нападение на меня в подъезде 13.03.2007 были организованы с целью подтолкнуть к решению продать квартиру и сменить место жительства. Эти соображения я высказывал в ходе следствия и в письменном виде представил Мировому судье.

В результате следствия был найден только один из троих нападавших на меня 13.03.2007 мужчин: опознанный мной Финогенов Денис, проживавший (возможно, временно) в кв. 74 в нашем подъезде. Во время судебных заседаний Финогенов утверждал, что это я напал на него, а двое спускавшихся по лестнице незнакомых мужчин защитили его от моего нападения. На самом деле, в момент нападения Финогенов находился на лестнице надо мной и перегнулся через перила, чтобы достать до моей головы. Я не мог напасть на Финогенова снизу через перила. Избиение происходило внизу, на нижней площадке, где я находился изначально. Это значит, что Финогенов

с сообщниками спустились вниз, чтобы напасть на меня. Все это видела и подтвердила в суде моя жена Яргина Е.Е.

Мировой судья несколько раз откладывал заседание, причем мне было сказано, что мое присутствие необязательно. Я присутствовал на трех (как минимум) заседаниях, а на дальнейшие заседания не приходил, поэтому я не знаю, чем закончилось разбирательство. После суда я несколько раз встречал Финогенова около подъезда.

После избиения, с синяками на лице, я встречал старшую по подъезду, участницу описанной выше инициативной группы, О.И. Панкратову (кв. 86), которая также сама заходила к нам в квартиру. Во время первой после избиения встречи она сказала: «Теперь Вы должны разговаривать со мной более адекватно». Осенью 2009 года я обратился к Панкратовой по поводу ключа от двери в подъезд, она ответила не по существу вопроса приблизительно следующее: «Финогенов отказывается расписаться за домофон, а если (Панкратова) не дам ему ключ, то Финогенов будет ломать дверь».

17.11.2009 около 22.45 Панкратова пришла к нам в квартиру вместе с соседкой из кв. 79 (Татьяна) с целью сбора подписей в связи намерением произвести ремонт фасада нашего дома (приложение 3). Как всегда, на листах с подписями не было указано, под чем подписываются жильцы. Панкратова требовала расписаться «за уведомление об участии в собрании по поводу ремонта фасада». 18.11.2009 Панкратова передала мне дополнительно 3 экземпляра бланка (приложение 4) и настаивала на их заполнении всеми членами семьи. В бланках требуется указать данные конфиденциального характера, которые могут быть использованы посторонними лицами с противозаконными целями.

Figure 6. (Continued)

С учетом изложенного, у меня возникло подозрение, что **в нашем доме в интересах определенных коммерческих структур действует организованная преступная группа**. Имеются признаки того, что нападение на меня 13.03.2007 было совершено организованной группой по чьему-то указанию. В ходе следствия и судебных заседаний была установлена личность только одного из троих нападавших; личности организаторов и лидеров остались неустановленными. Очевидно, что показания Финогенова были сформулированы таким образом, чтобы воспрепятствовать выяснению личностей соучастников.

На вопрос о характере предстоящего ремонта, о проведении которого должны просить жильцы дома, Панкратова ответила, что это ей неизвестно. По примеру соседнего с нашим домом здания бывшего радиокомитета (ул. Пятницкая 25) и многих других зданий в Москве, я предполагаю, что речь идет об облицовке фасада плиткой. Об этом свидетельствует фраза из Уведомления (приложение 1) о ремонте за счет рекламы на строительных сетках. Для покраски фасада установка сеток (на продолжительное время) не требуется. **В выполнении работ по облицовке фасадов плиткой заинтересованы определенные строительные фирмы, в интересах которых, по-видимому, действует «инициативная группа»**. По словам Панкратовой, вопрос о ремонте фасада будет решаться в Управе «Замоскворечье», в связи с чем ею была названа фамилия Громова.

Наш дом, построенный в 1912 году, имеет большую архитектурно-художественную ценность, является неотъемлемой частью архитектурного пейзажа старой Москвы. Облицовка плиткой приведет к необратимой утрате подлинного облика. Кроме того, имеются данные, что некоторые применяемые сегодня при реконструкции Москвы стройматериалы китайского производства, в частности, облицовочная плитка, имеют низкое качество, и работа с ними вызывает у персонала и жильцов аллергические реакции. Техническая необходимость ремонта фасада в настоящее время отсутствует; косметический ремонт (покраску фасада) лучше было бы выполнить позже, когда уляжется нездоровый строительный ажиотаж.

С учетом изложенного, прошу Вас возбудить уголовное дело в связи с недостаточным расследованием дела об избиении меня 13.03.2007, в связи с появлением новых обстоятельств дела, а также в связи имеющимися признаками деятельности организованной преступной группы, которая прибегает к мошенничеству, угрозам и организации нападений с нанесением телесных повреждений.

С уважением,

Яргин С.В.
Приложение на 4 страницах.

---

В Комитет по борьбе с коррупцией
Москва 127000, Зубовский бульвар д.4
От Яргина Сергея Вадимовича
Адрес: Климентовский переулок д. 6 кв. 82, Москва 115184
Телефон + 7 495 9516788 Электронная почта sjargin@mail.ru
07.08.2017

ИНФОРМАЦИЯ

Уважаемые дамы и господа!

Ранее я сообщал в правоохранительные органы о предполагаемых коррупционных взаимодействиях между государственными учреждениями, строительными фирмами и новыми владельцами квартир в нашем доме № 6 по Климентовскому переулку (приложение 1). Дом признан объектом культурного наследия. Почти во всех квартирах нашего подъезда № 3 был выполнен или проводится капитальный ремонт с перепланировкой и/или заменой перегородок из дранки на стены из блоков или кирпича. Работы сопровождаются сильными ударами, что вело к повреждению соседних квартир, в том числе, нашей. Повреждались предметы охраны объекта культурного наследия: лепнина на потолке, паркет. Удары и изменение нагрузки на деревянные перекрытия могут повысить риск аварии.

Figure 6. (Continued)

Последний пример. Начиная с 2012 года, в расположенной под нами квартире № 79 производился
капитальный ремонт. Владельцы кв. 79 отрицают кладку перегородок из блоков, но я видел новые
стены из блоков через дефект в стене кладовой (отмечена красным цветом на плане - приложение
2); вход в кладовую с черного хода, уровень пола кладовой по середине между кв. 79 и 82. В кв. 79
завозили большое количество блоков (фото – приложение 3). В 2013 г. во время работ с сильными
ударами в кв. 79, в нашей квартире в подсобном помещении (отмечено желтым цветом на плане -
приложение 2) возник провал пола (описан в письме Префектуры ЦАО города Москвы от
09.10.2013, приложение 4; фото – приложение 5). Провал был показан собственнице кв. 79 с
повторной просьбой прекратить удары и снос перегородок. Также возникли неровности
паркетного пола в комнатах, где проводились работы с сильными ударами. Несмотря на
многократные просьбы, управляющая компания (ранее ДЕЗ Замоскворечье; в настоящее время –
ГБУ «Жилищник») не выдала нам акт с описанием провала, хотя страховая компания была готова
принять случай к рассмотрению при наличии акта. В настоящее время срок для получения
страхового возмещения пропущен.

Опасаясь за состояние перекрытий, мы сообщали о провале в управляющую организацию, затем в
управу района Замоскворечье и префектуру ЦАО (приложение 6). 24.07.2017 для обследования
провала приходил сотрудник ГБУ «Жилищник» Виктор Яковлевич, который предложил нам
самим выполнить ремонтные работы по провалу, по-видимому, чтобы переложить на нас
ответственность. Он также просил меня произвести замеры выступа в результате перепланировки
кв. 80, на 43% сужающего ширину лестницы черного хода. В письме префектуры ЦАО от
04.08.2017 (приложение 7) со ссылкой на обследование, проведенное ГБУ «Жилищник», провал
пола в нашей квартире не описан; речь идет только об отслоении плитки и трещинах стяжки. См.
также приложения 8,9.

С уважением Яргин С.В.

Приложения: 1. Письмо МВД РФ от 30.12.2011
2. План кв. 82, Климентовский пер. д. 6
3. Доставка блоков в кв. 79
4. Письмо Префектуры ЦАО города Москвы от 09.10.2013
5. Провал пола в кв. 82
6. Наше письмо в Префектуру ЦАО от 17.07.2017
7. Письмо Префектуры ЦАО от 04.08.2017
8. Статья о реконструкции исторического центра Москвы. Искажение архитектурного наследия.
Журнал «Посев» 2012 г., № 12 (1623).
9. Наше письмо в Департамент культурного наследия города Москвы от 30.10.2012.

Figure 6. Letters reporting inappropriate and illegal acts submitted to the court and various authorities.

# References


[1] Jargin S. Moscow reconstruction: some mechanisms. *Domus Magazine* 2010; 934:125-6.

[2] https://www.researchgate.net/publication/273178996_Moscow_reconstruction_some_mechanisms.

[3] Jargin S. *A roof: not only an architectural term.* Domus 11 April 2010.

[4] https://www.researchgate.net/publication/275018741_A_roof_not_only_an_architectural_term (accessed 14 March 2018).

[5] Apevalova EA. State cadastre evaluation: theory and practice. *Nalogi (Taxes)* 2016; (5):3-6 (in Russian).

[6] Habermeier K, Kirilenko A. *Securities transaction taxes and financial markets*. International Monetary Fund, working paper 01/51; 2001.
[7] Soulier J-L, Best M. *International securities law handbook* (3rd edition). The Hague: Kluwer Law International; 2010.
[8] Loss L, Seligman J. *Fundamentals of securities* (5th edition). New York: Aspen; 2004.

In: Progress in Economics Research
Editor: Albert Tavidze

ISBN: 978-1-53615-120-6
© 2019 Nova Science Publishers, Inc.

*Chapter 6*

# EVOLUTION AND TRENDS IN A SPANISH FISHERY OF ANCHOVIES

### Raquel Fernández-González, PhD, Marcos Pérez-Pérez, PhD, Ana Lemos Nobre, PhD and M. Dolores Garza-Gil*, PhD

Department of Applied Economics, University of Vigo,
Vigo, Spain

## ABSTRACT

Anchovy (*Engraulis encrasicolus*) is a widespread pelagic species in the East Central Atlantic, the Mediterranean and the Black Sea. It is a species of great commercial importance, which presents great fluctuations depending on environmental conditions. Spain is the EU country with the largest catch of anchovy, and there is also an important processing and canning sector in this country, where some fishing ports have specialized in preparations such as salting or marinating. The Spanish fisheries for anchovy include ICES sub-area VIII (Bay of Biscay), where the French fisheries also operate, and Division IXa (Iberian Atlantic waters), where the Portuguese fleets also operate. It is important to note that the Spanish

---

* Corresponding Author Email: dgarza@uvigo.es.

fisheries operate mainly with purse seiners in Sub-area VIII and with purse seiners and trawlers in Division IXa. Anchovy is the target species in Sub-area VIII and Sub-area IXa-S, while occasionally it is targeted (when abundant) in the northern part of Division IXa (southern Galicia), where sardine is the target species. The management of this type of fisheries has also presented challenges for the Spanish fishing community, for example, when the fisheries in the Bay of Biscay were closed between 2005 and 2009, due to extremely poor stock conditions. This chapter studies the Spanish fishing and processing sector of anchovy, analyzing with special attention its trade balance and prices for preparation to characterize the current situation of this sector at national level. Production and economic performance are analyzed in the local, European and global context to define trends affecting the management of this species.

**Keywords:** Anchovy, Bay of Biscay, trade balance, processing industry

# 1. BIOLOGY AND HABITAT

The European anchovy (*Engraulis encrasicolus*) is a marine pelagic fish species belonging to the order Clupeiformes and to the family Engraulidae. The distribution include the Eastern Atlantic, from about Bergen, Norway (the Baltic Sea is not included), to East London, South Africa (perhaps reaching Durban), the whole Mediterranean and Black and Azov seas, and stray individuals in Suez Canal and Gulf of Suez. It has also been recorded from St. Helena and from Estonia. The southern limit of the species was formerly considered to be Morocco, with accidental strays south to Cape Blanc (CLOFNAM, 1973:112). Whitehead (1964c) extended the range to West Africa as far south as Angola and St. Helena. Anchovy is mainly a coastal species, forming large schools. It can be found at a depth range from 0 to 400 m. It tends to move into more northern waters and into surface waters in Summer, retreating and descending in Winter (to 100-150 m depth in the Mediterranean). It is euryhaline, tolerating salinities of 5 to 41°/oo and in some areas entering lagoons, estuaries or lakes, especially during spawning season, in the warmer months. It is a short-lived fish. The maximum reported age is five years, but it generally lives less than three years. Many authors have suggested that anchovies reach their first sexual maturity at 1 year old (Furnestin, 1945; Cort et al., 1976; Lucio and Uriarte, 1990; Uriarte et al., 1996). The average length at maturity is 13.5 cm, and the oldest specimens will grow to as much as 20 cm, but usually to about 12 to 15 cm. Those in tropical waters are smaller than those in northern waters. It feeds on planktonic organisms, especially calanoid copepods, cirrepede and mollusk larvae, and fish eggs and larvae. Anchovies are pelagic spawners. The spawning period extends from April to November, with peaks usually in the warmest months, which makes this species a spring-summer spawner. The spawning season limits depend on temperature, and thus they are more restricted in northern areas. Gametogenesis is continuous. The eggs are ellipsoidal to oval, floating in the upper 50 m, and hatching in 24 to 65 hours. The sex ratio is: 45% female, 55% male. The recruitment is very variable depending on environmental conditions, which, combined with the short life cycle, leads to violent fluctuations in stock size from year to year.

The anchovy inhabiting the Bay of Biscay (ICES Subarea VIII) is the short-lived pelagic fish with the greatest importance to fishing in Spain and France, and it is considered as a stock isolated from other small anchovy populations located north and south of the Northeast Atlantic, with the following characteristics: intense growth, early sexual maturity (from its first year of life), seasonal migrations, formation in shoals (above all, in the spawning season in spring), and the space it occupies depending on its abundance (the greater the abundance, the larger the spawning ground). One of its important characteristics is the enormous interannual fluctuations in the abundance of its population, with high and variable natural mortality. These fluctuations are due to the great variations in recruitment, driven mainly by environmental factors. As spring and summer progress, anchovies migrate from the interior of the Bay of Biscay towards the north along the French coast and towards the east along the Cantabrian Sea, where they spend the autumn. In winter, they migrate in the opposite direction towards the east and southeast of the Bay of Biscay (Prouzet et al., 1994). Pelagic habitats within the Bay of Biscay are dynamic and characterized by the presence of a variety of mesoscale physical features such as river plumes, upwelling areas, gyres, eddies, and fronts, with the strength of these features depending upon the season and climatic conditions (Koutsikopoulos and Le Cann, 1996). The cool waters of the Iberian Atlantic coasts limit the distribution of anchovy outside of the relatively warm waters of the Bay of Biscay (Junquera, 1986). Therefore, the larger population of this area would be related, among other factors, to the warmer and more stable waters of the bay compared to those existing either to the north or to the west and south (Uriarte, et al., 1996).

There is no sufficient knowledge on the anchovy inhabiting the Gulf of Cadiz (South of IXa) as to state whether it corresponds with a single or several small stocks of anchovy or even to assure that the Northwest African population off Morocco does not mix with the anchovy population. Despite all this lack of knowledge, the fishery in Subarea IX is being treated as a single fishery unit for management purposes and a precautionary TAC is being set by the EU (Uriarte, et al., 1996). The distribution of anchovy in the Division IXa is mainly concentrated in the Spanish waters of the Gulf of Cadiz (Subdivision IXa-South), where the main part of the catch is normally taken. The stock biomass in Subdivision IXa South is variable because it is largely composed of one-year-old fish. The observed harvest rates for anchovy in Subdivision IXa South (10–49%) are considered low, since they result in 50–90% of the potential spawning biomass being allowed to spawn. In the central and northern parts of Division IXa the anchovy abundance has been generally low, showing occasional outbursts of biomass, such as in 2011, 2015, and 2016. In 2017 there is an increase of biomass in IXa North, which is a small part of the western area. Recent studies on genetics suggest that the stock inhabiting Subdivision IXa South (Algarve and Cadiz) is different genetically from the one inhabiting the remaining parts of Division IXa (Zarraonaindia et al., 2012). However, after revision of all the available evidence (Ramos, 2015), the ICES Stock Identification Methods Working Group (ICES, 2015) recommended that the current stock structure and spatial explicit monitoring remain as they currently are until new evidence is available.

## 2. Spanish Fisheries for Anchovy

Spain is the EU country with the largest catch of anchovy, with an annual production of about 50,000 tons, and with the most important processing and export industry for this species. Catches have increased 75% since 2010. Italy, which until 2012 was the first European producer, has decreased its catches by 82% since 2010, ceding in 2013 the first position to Spain. The Spanish fisheries for anchovy include ICES Sub-area VIII (Bay of Biscay), South of Division IXa (Gulf of Cadiz) and the Mediterranean. The anchovy catches in the Atlantic are determined by the TACs (Total Admissible Catches), set for each year by the EC Council of Ministers. The 2018 quota of anchovy (25,000 tons) is divided into two semesters. Before July, 90% could be fished, and 10% would be reserved for the second semester. The catches in the Mediterranean are not regulated by quotas. The main EU anchovy fishery is the Bay of Biscay, where the main fleets concerned are in north-west Spain and south-west France. Most European anchovy are caught by pelagic trawlers. The anchovy catches in EU waters declined from almost 85,000 tons in 1965 to less than 4,500 tons in 1982 and only 950 tons in 2005, so that the anchovy fishery in the Bay of Biscay has been closed from 2005 to 2009 due to the extremely poor condition of the stock. In the last years, the European production of anchovy has raised. In 2013, 90,551 tons were caught, 101,652 tons in 2014 and 129,763 tons in 2015.

The Spanish fisheries operate mainly with purse seiners in Sub-area VIII and the Mediterranean, and with purse seiners and trawlers in Division IXa. Spain shares with France the Sub-area VIII anchovy fishery, and with Portugal the Division IXa fishery. In the Bay of Biscay, the fishery takes place in summer and autumn. In 2016, total catches of anchovy in Sub-area VIII were 20,628 tons. 92% of the total catches were landed by purse seiners and 8% by pelagic trawlers. Discards were negligible (0.2%). In the northern part of Division IXa (southern Galicia), sardine is the target species for the purse seiners, but anchovy is occasionally caught, when it is abundant. In subdivision IXa south, the fishery yields yearly catches of about 7-4 thousand tons, mainly in spring and early summer. In 2016, Spanish landings of anchovy in subdivision IXa were 6,803 tons, and Portuguese landings were 6,937 tons. 99% of the total catches (13,583 tons) were landed by purse seiners and 1% by other gear types. Discards were 156 tons.

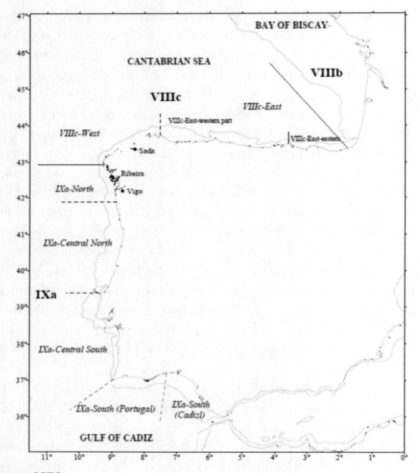

Source: ICES.

Figure 2.1. Anchovy in Division IXa. ICES divisions and subdivisions in southern Europe. The terminology "IXa West" refers to the geographical area from Subdivision IXa North to Subdivision IXa Central-South, whereas "IXa South" refers to the rest of Division IXa.

Anchovy is the main target species of the purse-seine fleet in Northern Alboran Sea (south-west Mediterranean), due to its high economic value, although its abundance is low and very local. In the early twenties of the last century, anchovy was fished all around the Alboran Sea, but currently Málaga Bay is the only area where anchovy is fished throughout all the year and where more than 80% of catches are located. Catches in the period 1990–2014 has been highly variable, with a minimum of 157 tons in 1993. Higher catches occurred in 1996 and 2001–2002 and 2013 they were caught between 2000 and 3200 tons. The whole period average is 888 tons. Anchovy is the main target species of the purse-seine fleet in Spanish Northwest Mediterranean. Catches in the period 1990–2015 has been highly variable, with a minimum of 2,800 tons in 2007 and an average of 12,000 tons. Higher catches occurred in the period 1990–1994, they were caught between 17,000 and 22,000 tons. Thereafter it has been continuously decreasing with three recoveries in 2002, 2009, and 2012. In 2014 and 2015 shows higher catches 16,000 t, a similar value to the one in 1990, but it is still not close to the peak of the landings occurred between 1991 and 1994. Years with higher landings are usually correlated with a successful and high recruitment period, while unsuccessful recruitment in a given year is correlated with a low level of landings.

## 2.1. MSC Assessment

On June 12, 2014, the Marine Stewardship Council (MSC), an international non-profit organization that sets standards for sustainable fishing and supply chain traceability, announced that several fishing associations had come together to prove the sustainability of the Cantabrian Sea (Bay of Biscay) anchovy fishery, entering it into full assessment. This was the first time that European anchovy was assessed against the MSC standard for sustainable fishing and also the first Cantabrian Sea fishery to enter the program. On April, 2015, the Cantabrian Sea anchovy fishery was awarded MSC certification for sustainability. The certification was awarded after an independent assessment by accredited certification body, Bureau

Veritas, against the MSC Fisheries Standard. The fishery was evaluated for stock sustainability, minimizing of environmental impacts and effective management. The certification report highlighted that anchovy fishing operations in the Cantabrian Sea were conducted using purse seine nets, a surface fishing method with low bycatch. The certification covered 58 boats, which in 2013 had a total catch of 7000 tons.

## 3. TRADE BALANCE

The anchovy *Engraulis encrasicoulus* is, in Spain, one of the most appreciated species not only for its nutritional value, but also for its various conservation systems that give it a high added value. Its consumption dates back to ancient times, with the influence of the Greeks and Romans, who already used it as an ingredient in *garum* sauce.

Spain, as a member country of the European Union, must comply with the catch level indicated by this supranational body. In this case, the TACs (Total Allowable Catches) determine the level of anchovy catches in the Atlantic. The TACs are adopted annually by the Council of Ministers of the European Community on the basis of the Commission's proposal.

The trade balance for the *Engraulis encrasicoulus* anchovy, in all its presentations, shows that during the period 2007-2016 it has had a negative trajectory for Spain. However, there has been a sharp increase in the coverage rate, driven by the progressive decrease in imports and the considerable increase in exports since 2014. It is also important to qualify the improvement in the coverage rate by providing significant data: in 2016 the value of one ton of imported anchovy cost €3,639, while each ton exported amounted to €4,122. This figure shows us the greater added value of Spanish exports with respect to their imports (MAPAMA, 2017).

Within the anchovy processing industry in Spain, there are two well differentiated modalities with their own characteristics. On the one hand, the artisanal industry of anchovy in semi-preserved or salted form, this uses anchovy from the Cantabrian Sea as raw material and aims to offer a high quality product with added value. This type of industry competes both internationally and nationally for the differentiation of its product. On the other hand, the canning industry uses mostly imported raw materials whose final product competes in prices (Fernández Polanco, J. M. et al; 2012).

## 3.1. Tariff Regime

In general, the tariffs stipulated in Spain for anchovies differ according to the type of presentation: 15% for fresh anchovies, 10% for frozen anchovies and 25% for canned anchovies. However, there are exceptions in the form of bilateral agreements, duty suspensions and special contingencies with third countries that abolish or lower tariffs (MAPAMA, 2013):

- European Free Trade Association (EFTA): The current EFTA countries that have ratified the Agreement on the European Economic Area (Norway, Liechtenstein and Iceland) have a reduction which, depending on the type of quota imported, is 4.5% or total.
- Preferential agreements: the countries that have signed this type of agreement have improved tariffs and, at the same time, improved access for their fishery products to the European Union. Among the countries with preferential treatment for imports of anchovy are Mexico, Chile, Moldova, South Korea and Falkland Islands.

Within these preferential agreements, it is worth highlighting the ones made with the Mediterranean countries. Since the conclusion of the 1995 Euro-Mediterranean Agreements, these countries have been granted more favorable measures for certain fishery products. In fact, with the exception of Syria and Jordan, zero rights for trade in anchovy are granted to: Algeria, Tunisia, Morocco, Egypt, Lebanon, Turkey, Cyprus, Serbia, Malta, Israel, Macedonia and Albania.

**Table 3.1. Trade balance for the Engraulis encrasicoulus anchovy, in all its presentations (metric tons and thousand euros) 2007-2016**

| Year | Importations | | Exports | | |
|---|---|---|---|---|---|
| | MT | Thousands of euros | MT | Thousands of euros | Coverage ratio % |
| 2007 | 45,027 | 100,688 | 8,296 | 33,473 | 33.24% |
| 2008 | 42,295 | 92,453 | 6,259 | 28,849 | 31.20% |
| 2009 | 38,307 | 87,489 | 5,814 | 29,091 | 33.25% |
| 2010 | 40,029 | 90,976 | 7,818 | 35,673 | 39.21% |
| 2011 | 34,997 | 85,780 | 9,776 | 42,826 | 49.93% |
| 2012 | 29,125 | 75,225 | 8,907 | 43,658 | 58.04% |
| 2013 | 20,530 | 77,277 | 8,835 | 46,325 | 59.95% |
| 2014 | 24,275 | 81,073 | 15,249 | 61,523 | 75.89% |
| 2015 | 26,541 | 100,371 | 20,694 | 81,126 | 80.83% |
| 2016 | 27,105 | 98,639 | 19,158 | 78,974 | 80.06% |

Source: Dirección General de Aduanas.

Moreover, there are also specific agreements for the Balkan countries, which apply to prepared and preserved anchovies:

- Montenegro: 200 MT of imports of prepared and preserved anchovies with a 12.5% tax, this tax being a 50% reduction with respect to the general tax. From 2012 onwards, it may be increased to 250 tons provided that at least 80% of the previous tariff quota has been used by 31 December of the previous year at the latest. RCE 497/2008.
- Bosnia and Herzegovina: 250 mt. of imports of prepared and preserved anchovies with a 12.5% tax. RCE 354/2011.
- Albania and Croatia: 1000 tons of imports of prepared and preserved anchovies with a 0% levy. From 2007 onwards, it may increase by 200 tons provided that at least 80% of the previous tariff quota has been used by 31 December of the previous year at the latest, up to 1600 tons. CERs 1916/2006 and 2088/2004.
- Generalized systems of preferences: these European Community tariff systems are a tool used to establish reduced or zero taxes for developing countries. This promotes industrial and commercial

growth in the most disadvantaged countries. There are three types of regimens: general and two special. The applicable legislation for each of these types of management is found in RCE 978/2012, the European regulation in force until December 31, 2023 (MAPAMA, 2014).

- General regime: a reduction of 3.5 percentage points is applied to each type of preparation imported by the countries concerned.
- Special arrangements for the least-developed countries: under these arrangements, countries enjoy, for the majority of fishery products, anchovy being one of them, a total suspension of the ad valorem duties of the Common Customs Tariff. The countries included in this regime are: Afghanistan, Angola, Bangladesh, Burkina Faso, Burundi, Central African Republic, Benin, Bhutan, Democratic Republic of the Congo, Democratic Republic of the Congo, Djibouti, Eritrea, Ethiopia, Gambia, Guinea, Equatorial Guinea, Guinea-Bissau, Haiti, Cambodia, Kiribati, Comoros, Comoros, Lao People's Democratic Republic, Liberia, Lesotho, Madagascar, Mali, Myanmar, Mauritania, Maldives, Malawi, Mozambique, Niger, Nepal, Rwanda, Solomon Islands, Sudan, Sierra Leone, Senegal, Somalia, Sao Tome and Principe, Solomon Islands, Chad, Togo, East Timor, Tuvalu, Tanzania, Uganda, Vanuatu, Samoa, Yemen and Zambia.
- Special incentive arrangement for sustainable development and good governance: all countries that comply with, or undertake to comply with, certain international governance arrangements are eligible for the arrangement. All countries included benefit from the abolition of customs duties on fishery products. Countries eligible for this agreement are those that show special interest in the fight against drug trafficking and are not relevant to international trade. Currently, the beneficiary countries are: Armenia, Bolivia, Cape Verde, Georgia, Kyrgyzstan, Mongolia, Pakistan, Paraguay, Philippines, Sri Lanka and Cape Verde.

## 3.2. Imports

In the period 2007-2016, imports of anchovies *engraulis encrasicoulus* fell by 36% in quantitative terms. The reasons for this decrease are varied, so for a more in-depth analysis, we are going to study the behavior of the different types of anchovies imported by Spain (MAPAMA, 2016).

Anchovies salted or in brine: The consignment of salted or in brine anchovies has decreased from 23% in 2007 to 14% of total tones imported in 2016. Similarly, their value in total imports decreased by 7 percentage points in the period, a progressive decrease.

Frozen anchovies: The most constant presentation during this period has been that of frozen anchovies. Its share of total imports has only increased by four percentage points in these nine years (from 5% to 9%). In any case, it remains the smallest of the four existing items. Also in the total value of imports, the consignment of frozen anchovies remains stable, since in 2007 it represented 3% of the total value and in 2016 it reached 4%, without substantially changing these data during the period analyzed.

Semi-preserved or canned anchovies: This type of preparation has experienced the most notable increase. Starting from 9% of total imports in 2007, it has managed to represent 29% of them since 2004. Between 2010 and 2013 it doubled its share of total imports, peaking in 2013. But if its increase in tons has been large, it has been greater in the total value of imports. Its increase from 19% to 62% of the value in only nine years shows that it has not only increased in the number of tons imported, but also that it is one of the preparations with the highest €/Kg ratio.

Fresh or chilled anchovies: Although their importance has decreased from 2007 to 2016 by 13 percentage points, this type of preparation is still the most important in the calculation of imported tons with 49% of the total in 2016. However, the greater its decline in the total value of imports has been a process inverse to that experienced by canning. It has gone from representing 58% of the value of imports to only 23% in 2016.

By analyzing the evolution of the different preparations of anchovy, we can characterize the import market. To this end, the following observations are necessary: In 2016, 49% of Spain's imports were fresh or chilled. Even though this presentation is the one with the highest number of tons imported, the trend in Spain is that the types of anchovies that involve a greater processing increase in imports to the detriment of fresh or frozen products. From 2007 to 2016, fresh or chilled anchovies decreased by 13 percentage points their importance in the overall calculation, while canned anchovies increased by 20%. The analysis of these figures shows us how part of the industry is increasingly focusing on the treatment and finishing of semi-finished products (Fernández Polanco, J.M. et al; 2012).

### Table 3.2. Imports of anchovies *Engraulis encrasicoulus* (metric tons). 2007-2016

| Presentation of imports. MT. | Fresh and chilled anchovies | Frozen anchovies | Anchovies salted and in brine (not dried or smoked) | Semi-preserved and canned anchovies | Total |
|---|---|---|---|---|---|
| 2007 | 27,952 | 2,303 | 10,528 | 4,244 | 45,027 |
| 2008 | 25,909 | 2,987 | 8,543 | 4,856 | 42,295 |
| 2009 | 25,243 | 2,576 | 5,867 | 4,621 | 38,307 |
| 2010 | 24,696 | 3,102 | 6,145 | 6,086 | 40,029 |
| 2011 | 19,634 | 2,749 | 6,111 | 6,503 | 34,997 |
| 2012 | 15,799 | 1,497 | 4,903 | 6,926 | 29,125 |
| 2013 | 8,757 | 1,460 | 3,727 | 6,586 | 20,530 |
| 2014 | 12,747 | 1,070 | 3,464 | 6,994 | 24,275 |
| 2015 | 11,278 | 2,327 | 5,283 | 7,653 | 26,541 |
| 2016 | 13,235 | 2,318 | 3,778 | 7,774 | 27,105 |

Source: Dirección General de Aduanas.

As far as the origin of imports from Spain is concerned, those of an intra-Community nature are greater than those from outside the Community, but this trend is not unanimous for all presentations. The majority (97%) of anchovies salted or in brine come from countries outside the EU, with Argentina by far the largest importer, followed by Peru and Morocco. However, Peru and Morocco are the two main countries from which prepared or preserved anchovies are imported. If we analyze this, at European level, the consignment of frozen anchovy, the imports are only representative for Spain and Germany and, in this case, the origin of the same is 88% intra-Community. Similarly, the intra-Community origin is the majority when fresh anchovy imports are analyzed. Portugal, Italy and France are the countries that contribute the most to the largest imported presentation from Spain (36% of the total in 2016) (EUMOFA, 2018).

## 3.3. Exports

If, as we analyzed in the previous section, imports fell by 36%, exports had an opposite trend and increased by 130% between 2007 and 2016. It is important to note that, in the case of exports, all presentations increased in quantitative and monetary terms (MAPAMA, 2017).

Anchovies salted or in brine: Since 2007 it has been the first item in volume of exports, but during nine years its relative weight in the total preparations has decreased by 44%. Its evolution has been uneven, alternating stages of growth and setting minimums in 2009 and 2013. As for the total value of exports, anchovies salted or in brine occupy the second place in importance, representing 18% of the total value.

Frozen anchovies: this presentation is characterized by its volatility. Although it grew by 18% from 2007 to 2016, this growth was not sustained until 2013. In spite of this increase, this item is one of the least important in terms of both tons (20% of the total) and value (8% of the total).

Semi-preserved or canned anchovies: Whether we analyze this preparation by tonnage or by relative weight of the volume exported, prepared or canned anchovies have gone from being the second largest batch in 2007 to the last in 2016. This is reflected in the fact that its relative importance in exports has decreased since 2009 (43% of the total) to reach the current 17%. This decrease in comparison with the increase in the presentation of fresh anchovies and the subsequent increase in the number of frozen anchovies, both of which benefited most from the lifting of the veto on the fisheries in the Bay of Biscay in 2010. However, as a consequence of its high price, the consignment of prepared anchovies remains the first in importance, both in relative value (57% of the value of exports in 2016) and absolute value (45,774 million euros out of the 78,974 million euros of exports in 2016).

Fresh or chilled anchovies: this presentation had a spectacular increase from 2010, with annual growth rates of 10% until 2014. The explanation for this evolution lies in the opening of the anchovy fishery in the Bay of Biscay, which was banned from 2005 to 2010. Its large increase was also reflected in the millions of euros raised by the export of this item: from 1,132 million euros in 2007 to 15,018 million euros in 2016.

**Table 3.3. Exports of anchovies *Engraulis encrasicoulus* (metric tons) 2007-2016**

| Presentation of exports. MT. | Fresh and chilled anchovies | Frozen anchovies | Salted anchovies and anchovies in brine (not dried or smoked) | Semi-preserved and canned anchovies | Total |
|---|---|---|---|---|---|
| 2007 | 758 | 220 | 5,008 | 2,310 | 8,296 |
| 2008 | 144 | 297 | 3,342 | 2,476 | 6,259 |
| 2009 | 360 | 435 | 2,516 | 2,503 | 5,814 |
| 2010 | 768 | 845 | 3,486 | 2,719 | 7,818 |
| 2011 | 976 | 476 | 5,507 | 2,817 | 9,776 |
| 2012 | 1,818 | 53 | 4,584 | 2,452 | 8,907 |
| 2013 | 2,949 | 450 | 3,088 | 2,348 | 8,835 |
| 2014 | 5,859 | 1,804 | 4,560 | 3,026 | 15,249 |
| 2015 | 7,205 | 3,912 | 5,866 | 3,711 | 20,694 |
| 2016 | 5,373 | 3,937 | 6,411 | 3,437 | 19,158 |

Source: Dirección General de Aduanas.

An analysis of the markets to which the anchovy is exported in 2016 shows that there are different scenarios depending on the presentation studied. For fresh or chilled anchovies, Italy is the main destination country with 47% of exports, followed by France with 9%. Among the non-EU countries, Morocco stands out with 34%. For anchovy salted or in brine, the European Union is linked to 19% of the tons exported, while 81% come from third countries. The three main exporters of salted anchovies are: Morocco (35%), Albania (31%) and Italy (15%). By contrast, the Community market accounts for the majority of exports of prepared or preserved anchovies (68% of the total), with Italy (18%), the United Kingdom (16%) and France (11%) being the three main intra-Community markets. The United States

(7%) and Switzerland (6%) should also be considered for their exports in this presentation (EUMOFA, 2018).

## 4. PRICE TRENDS

In the anchovy sale process, three main differentiated steps involve different agents. The price at source, determined at the time of downloading; the price determined by the wholesaler, the MERCASA platform; and the Retail Price, which is finally paid by the consumer after passing through intermediaries.

The price at source increased considerably in 2007 and 2008, because of the scarcity of anchovies due to the veto of the fisheries in the Bay of Biscay since 2005. Since 2009, the price of anchovies has been on a downward trend. The factors that contributed to this decline were the renewed agreements on commercial sizes and the new exploitation regime for anchovy in the northwest Cantabrian Sea (MAPAMA, 2013). Although prices at source have not reached 2.5 €/kg since 2009, it was not until 2015 that they fell from 2 €/kg.

The average price of anchovy on the central markets is significantly higher than the price at source. In spite of the fact that in the last five years parallel businesses have proliferated that have competed for MERCASA's market share, this platform continues to be the most important in the marketing of fresh fish and seafood in Spain (Fernandez Polanco et al., 2010). With respect to the price at origin, MERCASA follows a parallel trajectory, but with a margin of difference, that exceeds, even in its lowest figures, 20%. The trend that follows the difference between the prices of first sale and those of MERCASA tends to increase when there are low quotations in the price of origin, as can be observed in the data for the years 2009, 2015 and 2016. It can be concluded that, even if there is a reduction in prices at source, they are not passed on to intermediaries, much less to consumers. The explanation lies in the fact that retail establishments show a rigid behavior, even more than MERCASA (MAPAMA, 2013).

As regards the other types of anchovy preparations, it is important to note that all of them, except fresh and frozen, are labor-intensive. This is due to the use of production techniques in filleting and salting, both in barrels and packaged. This characteristic makes the price of the product more expensive and, on 14% or 16% of the final price, is due to the labor factor (Fernández Polanco et al., 2010).

**Table 4.1. Evolution of the average annual prices of fresh and chilled anchovies (euros). 2007-2016**

| Year | Origin | MERCASA (Wholesaler) | Retail (RRP) | % MERCASA/ origin | % RRP/ Merca | % RRP/ Origin |
|---|---|---|---|---|---|---|
| 2007 | 2.87 | 3.69 | 7.36 | 29% | 99% | 156% |
| 2008 | 3.26 | 3.98 | 7.5 | 22% | 88% | 130% |
| 2009 | 1.91 | 3.07 | 6.74 | 61% | 120% | 253% |
| 2010 | 2.23 | 2.99 | 6.59 | 34% | 120% | 196% |
| 2011 | 2.16 | 3.09 | 6.3 | 43% | 104% | 192% |
| 2012 | 2.32 | 3.59 | 6.49 | 55% | 81% | 180% |
| 2013 | 2.48 | 3.77 | 6.55 | 52% | 74% | 164% |
| 2014 | 2.24 | 3.51 | 6.38 | 57% | 82% | 185% |
| 2015 | 1.97 | 3.32 | 6.07 | 69% | 83% | 208% |
| 2016 | 1.95 | 3.75 | 6.09 | 92% | 62% | 212% |

Source: MAPAMA, 2013, 2016, 2017.

As regards the average value of anchovy exports, they grew by 5.5% between 2007 and 2016, while imports increased much more, by 33%. This is because the average value of the kg of anchovy imported went from €2.6/kg in 2007 to €3.53/kg in 2016. Despite this growth, the average price of €/kg imported is not close to its export equivalent, which is 4.87 €/kg. Except for the consignment of salted or in brine anchovies, Spain has a higher value €/kg for its exports than for its imports.

Prices of imports of anchovies are largely due to processed products. Anchovies salted, in brine or canned present a growth in prices of more than 45% in nine years. However, although export prices have stagnated, the high price of prepared and preserved anchovies (€13.32/kg) has increased the coverage rate of the anchovy market in Spain. Analyzing the profitability of this preparation, prepared and preserved anchovies, we must point out that its profitability, not its price, has been reduced over the years. The explanation lies in the fact that this processing activity uses imported products that have become more expensive.

## 5. ANCHOVY PROCESSING INDUSTRY IN SPAIN

The anchovy processing industry in Spain has a long tradition. It is currently a consolidated sector, with two different types of activities: canning and semi-canning or salting. But its beginnings go back much further, being Cantabria the region that began and still perpetuates this activity.

Several historians have managed to identify the beginning of the semi-conserve sector in 1250, when King Alfonso XI granted the town of Laredo the possibility of developing a salting industry to supply the rest of Castile. There is also evidence to prove that around 1500, Laredo, Colindres and Castro-Urdiales continued with this activity. However, it was not until 1800 that the modern canning industry developed on the Cantabrian coast (Castro-Urdiales, Laredo, Santander and San Vicente de la Barquera) (García Cobo, 1998).

Later was the introduction of salting of anchovies, another type of semi-preserved fish. In 1880, due to the high quality and quantity of raw material for canning and its scarce commercial exploitation by the local inhabitants, the Italian initiatives to exploit anchovies began (Escudero Domínguez, 2008). One of the first companies to settle in Cantabria was Angelo Parodi fu Bartolomeo, who hired Sicilian personnel and settled first in Bermeo and then in different locations on the Cantabrian coast. In view of the good results obtained by this pioneering company, several Italian companies involved in the processing of anchovies decided to set up gradually in Cantabria, some of which are: Societá comerciale de Alessandría e Genova, Domenico Pelazza, Vicenzo Gribaudi, Eugenio Cardini & Co. and A. Pontecorboli (Escudero Domínguez, 2012).

This wave of Italian settlements on the Cantabrian coast is classified as the first phase (1986-1904) of the anchovy processing industry in the

Cantabrian Sea. The second stage (1905-1919) is characterized by the incipient capitalist investment coming from other sectors towards the anchovy sector, which shows us the not inconsiderable profitability of the sector and its definitive settlement in Spain.

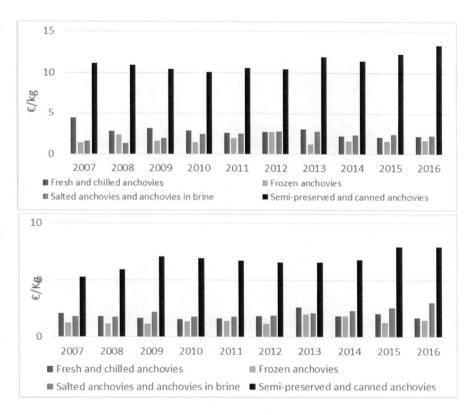

Figure 5.2. Price per type of anchovy presentation imported.

From 1920 to 1936, the phenomenon of the emancipation of the pioneering managers of the industry, with the purpose of founding their own businesses, became urgent and the emergence of commission companies broke out. It was in 1925 when the Federation of Cantabrian Coast Manufacturers was established in Santoña (Cantabria), the first proof of the institutional organization of the sector (García Cobo, 1998). The fourth phase began, after the Spanish Civil War, from 1939 to 1950, when some historic companies went bankrupt and the sector underwent a period of restructuring and maintenance linked to the technological innovations of the time. But the real changeover between companies with a long tradition and others newly founded occurred in the last stage (1951-1980). This period was the one with the highest production, with the "golden age" of Cantabrian anchovy occurring between 1963 and 1970, when the greatest number of catches (85,000,000 kg) were recorded in 1965 (García Cobo, 1998).

From 1965 onwards, the level of anchovy catches in Spain decreased slowly but progressively. This fact is accentuated in the nineties, being one of the problems causing the closure of part of the industries associated with anchovy. In the same decade, in addition to the problem of low catches, the anchovy sector faced the consequences of the signing of the Treaty of Accession to the European Union. The incursion into this European Community area led to the application of high reducible taxes. This fact constituted a barrier to the export of anchovy products to the traditional European market (Escudero Domínguez, 2007). Furthermore, the entry into the European Economic Community implied the imposition of new health and hygiene measures for the entire sector, determined in Council Directive 91/493/EEC and included in national legislation through Royal Decree 1437/92. These regulatory changes posed a major problem for the sector. The modernization of the facilities required a large investment that many companies did not have available. This problem was most acute for small and medium-sized enterprises, most of which were engaged in salting and filleting. The anchovy canning companies, on the other hand, had greater financing capacity and were therefore able to cope with the restructuring of the sector in almost all cases. In fact, the strategy of the anchovy canning industry was to abandon its old facilities and settle in what would be called "canning estates," which are industrial estates in fishing towns such as Laredo, Santoña or Ondarroa-Berriatua. This process arose both in Cantabria and in the Basque Country. The first territory to adopt this strategy was the Basque Country, when in 1991, the canneries Astorkiza and Campos opened in the Landabaso industrial estate in Bermeo. A year later, in 1992, three companies from Ondarroa and a fourth from Gardotza moved to the industrial estate of the latter city. Cantabria followed suit years later, in 1997, when aid from the European Union had already been granted (López Losa,

2008). That year, thirteen companies set up in the Marismas de Santoña industrial estate and seven more did so the following year in the La Pesquera industrial estate located in the town of Laredo (Escudero Domínguez, 2007).

The late relocation of Cantabria with respect to the Basque Country is explained by the strategy followed by this community, which waited for the approval of the financing funds from the European Union. In 1993, the Structural Funds FIFG were set up to provide aid to the European fisheries sector. The different regions of the European Union (EU) could benefit from them to a greater or lesser extent, being classified on a scale depending on their Gross Domestic Product (GDP). Asturias and Cantabria were classified as Objective I regions (which have a GDP per capita of less than 75% of the EU average), which is why the FIFG financed 45% of the sector's investments (López Losa, 2000). In the case of Cantabria and Asturias, the government of the community and the state also financed 15% of the expenses, so that 60% of the total investments were paid by the public administrations. The Basque Country was classified as an Objective II region, thus its public funding was structured in 20-22% by the FIFG and 8-10% by the Basque regional government (Escudero Domínguez, 2000).

As mentioned above, another major problem facing the sector was the shortage of raw materials. Traditionally, local fishing ports supplied the sector, but from the 1970s onwards, imports of anchovies became necessary in view of the decline in catches and the increased demand for fresh fish. Although these imports were of lower quality, they ensured the necessary supply of anchovies at affordable prices.

The consequences of these two major problems, the reconversion of the sector by European legislation and the lack of catches, led to the closure of companies of former foundations was restarted in 1996. This phenomenon was mainly concentrated in Cantabria, where companies such as SAPEMSA, Pergisa, Almar and Diego y Fernández in Laredo, Andrés Lo Coco in Santoña, Nicola Lo Coco in Castro and Echevarría de Colindres closed down.

In the last ten years, the anchovy sector has not undergone any major changes. The Autonomous Community with the greatest presence of this sector continues to be Cantabria, followed by the Basque Country and with the anecdotal contribution of Asturias. In fact, Cantabria is the Autonomous Community with the largest number of companies, 60 in total, and 2,800 direct jobs. The presentation with the highest turnover is the semi-conserve, with 150 small companies located in coastal areas with a long tradition of fishing. The anchovy sector continues to be an economic engine in the area where its industry is located, as its activity generates 4,000 direct and 16,000 indirect jobs, 95% of which are occupied by women. (MAPAMA, 2013, 2014).

The problem of under-harvesting remains. In the last five years, it is estimated that 25% of the tons caught by Spain are destined for this type of local industry, which, however, only meets 20% of its needs with the national product. The remaining 80% of its demand is covered by third countries, both intra-Community and extra-Community. Imports for the industry can be classified according to their preparation: half of them are fresh chilled anchovies and the other half are salted anchovies without drying. In relation to the latter, Argentina is the main supplier country for its quality and stable production. Being able to meet the need for raw materials is vital in this industry. This has been one of the biggest problems he has faced in the last 15 years. The ban on the anchovy fishery in the Bay of Biscay between 2005 and 2010 aggravated this situation. In order to alleviate this situation, the European Union approved the establishment of autonomous Community quotas for un-dried salted anchovy, the vast majority of which was intended for Spanish industry. It should be noted that, in order to maintain the quality of the product, the anchovy processing industry in Spain needs an import volume of approximately 10,000 tons. (MAPAMA, 2013, 2014).

This analysis shows that the anchovy sector is still dependent on imports. A problem that will continue to drag on in the coming decades according to estimates of catches on the Cantabrian coast. Despite the challenges facing the sector, it is still an important economic driver for coastal towns, offering a high quality product with a high added value.

## REFERENCES

CLOFNAM (1973): Check List of the Fishes of the North-eastern Atlantic and of the Mediterranean. *Engraulididae*, 112.

Cort, J. L., O. Cendrero and X. Iribar. (1976). La anchoa, Engraulis encrasicholus (L.) del Cantábrico. Resultados de las campañas de 1974, 1975 y 1976. *Bol. Inst. Espa. Ocean.*, 220: 1-34. [The anchovy, Engraulis encrasicholus (L.) of the Bay of Biscay. Results of the 1974, 1975 and 1976 campaigns. *Gazette of Spanish Oceanographic Institute*, 220: 1-34].

Escudero Domínguez, L. J. (2000). The fishing processing industry. Implementation, development and consolidation in the Basque Country: 1841-1905. *Journal of Maritime Studies of the Basque Country*. 3:289-327.

Escudero Domínguez, L. J. (2007). Canned, semi-preserved and salted fish in the Cantabrian Sea. Analysis and situation of the sector in recent years (1993-2004). *Zainak, anthropology-ethnography notebooks.* 29: 171-196.

Escudero Domínguez, L. J. (2008). From splendour to crisis: evolution of the salting industry through Italian manufacturers (1920-1936). *International Science Journal. A century of fishing in Spain: new perspectives, new contributions*. 27: 105-115.

Escudero Domínguez, L. J. (2012). Italians in the Cantabrian Sea. Identities and histories of a particular migration. *Journal of Maritime Studies of the Basque Country*. 7: 315-324.

EU Market Observatory for Fisheries and Aquaculture products (EUMOFA) (2018). *Anchovy processed in Italy*. https://www.eumofa.eu/documents/20178/111808/La+anchoa+procesada+en+Italia.pdf/487fe9ea-b718-49c6-afdb-b0abd0609516.

European Commission. Anchovy (*Engraulis encrasicolus*). https://ec.europa.eu/fisheries/marine_species/wild_species/anchovy_en.

FAO. Engraulis encrasicolus (Linnaeus, 1758). Species Fact Sheets. *FAO.* http://www.fao.org/fishery/species/2106/en.

Fernández Polanco, J. M., Llorente, I., Luna, L. and Fernández, J. L. (2012). The fisheries products market in Spain: effects of the crisis on production and consumption. *Globefish Research Programme*. 106. Rome, Italy: FAO.

FishBase. The SPECIES Table. *Engraulis encrasicolus* (Linnaeus, 1758). *FishBase*. European anchovy. www.fishbase.org/summary/66#.

Furnestin. J. (1945). Note préliminaire sur l'anchois, *Engraulis encrasicholus* (L.), du golfe de Gascogne. *Rev. Trav. Off. Sci. Tech. Pêches Marit.*, 13(1-4):197-209. (CLOFNAM, 1973:112). [Preliminary note on anchovy, *Engraulis encrasicholus* (L.), from the Bay of Biscay. *Rev. Trav. Off. Sci. Tech. Maritime Fishing*, 13(1-4):197-209. (CLOFNAM, 1973:112)].

García Cobo, J. L. (1998). Importance of the canning sector in the economy of Santoña and Cantabria. *Mount Buciero*, 2: 95-100.

ICES (2017). Report of the Workshop on Age estimation of European anchovy (*Engraulis encrasicolus*). *WKARA2 2016 Report 28 November - 2 December 2016.* Pasaia, Spain. ICES CM 2016/ SSGIEOM: 17. 223 pp.

ICES (2017). Anchovy (*Engraulis encrasicolus*) in Division 9.a (Atlantic Iberian waters). *ICES Advice on fishing opportunities, catch, and effort Bay of Biscay and the Iberian Coast Ecoregion ane.27.9$^a$*.

ICES (2017). Anchovy (*Engraulis encrasicolus*) in Subarea 8 (Bay of Biscay). *ICES Advice on fishing opportunities, catch, and effort Bay of Biscay and the Iberian Coast and Oceanic Northeast Atlantic Ecoregions ane.27.8*.

Junquera, S. (1986). Pêche de l'anchois (*Engraulis encrasicholus*) dans le golfe de Gascogne et sur le littoral atlantique de Galice depuis 1920. Variations quantitatives. *Rev. Trav. Inst. Pêches Marit.*, 48: 133-142. [Anchovy (*Engraulis encrasicholus*) fishing in the Bay of Biscay and on the Atlantic coast of Galicia since 1920. Quantitative variations. *Rev. Trav. Inst. Pêches Marit.*, 48: 133-142].

Koutsikopoulos and Le Cann (1996). Physical processes and hydrological structures related to the Bay of Biscay anchovy *SCI. MAR.*, 60 (Supl. 2): 9-19.

López Losa, E. (2000). Fishing in the Basque Country: a long-term vision (19th and 20th centuries). *Journal of Maritime Studies of the Basque Country*. 3: 239-276.

López Losa, E. (2008). Fishing in the Basque Country during the 20th century: modernisation, tradition and crisis. *International Science Journal. A century of fishing in Spain: new perspectives, new contributions*. 27: 7-25.

Lucio, P., and Uriarte, A. (1990). Aspects of the reproductive biology of the anchovy (*Engraulis encrasicholus*, L. 1758) during 1987 and 1988 in the Bay of Biscay. *ICES Document*, CM 1990/H: 27.

Ministry of Agriculture, Food and the Environment (MAPAMA) (2013). *The anchovy market in Spain*. http://www.mapama.gob.es/es/pesca/temas/mercados-economiapesquera/INFORME_ANCHOA_2013_tcm 7-304823_tcm30-285581.pdf.

Ministry of Agriculture, Food and the Environment (MAPAMA) (2014). *The anchovy market in Spain*. http://www.mapama.gob.es/es/pesca/temas/mercadoseconomiapesquera/informeanchoaoct20 14actualizado _tcm30-290987.pdf.

Ministry of Agriculture, Food and the Environment (MAPAMA) (2016). *The anchovy market in Spain*. http://www.mapama.gob.es/es/pesca/temas/mercados-economiapesquera/informeanch oaene2 016-5agosto_tcm30-291087.pdf.

Ministry of Agriculture, Food and the Environment (MAPAMA) (2017). *The anchovy market in Spain*. http://www.mapama.gob.es/es/pesca/temas/mercados-economia-pesquera/informeanchoa2017_tcm30-4407 64.pdf.

Prouzet, P., K. Metuzals and C. Caboche. (1994). *L'Anchois du Golfe de Gascogne. Caractéristiques biologiques et Campagne de pêche française en 1992. Rapport CNPM- IMA-IFREMER*. [*The Anchovy of the Bay of Biscay. Biological characteristics and French fishing campaign in 1992. Rapport CNPM- IMA-IFREMER*].

Uriarte, A.; Prouzet, P. and Villamor, B. (1996). *Bay of Biscay and Ibero Atlantic anchovy populations and their fisheries*. SCI. MAR., 60 (Supl. 2): 237-255.

Whitehead, P. J. P. (1964c). (New data extending the range of the bipolar 'antitropical' anchovy genus *Engraulis* into the 1964c tropics - in Russian). *Zool. Zh.*, 43(6):879-88.

Zarraonaindia, I., Iriondo, M., Albaina, A., Pardo, M. A., Manzano, C., Grant, W. S., Irigoien, X., et al. (*2012*). Multiple SNP markers reveal fine-scale population and deep phylogeographic structure in European anchovy (*Engraulis encrasicolus* L.), *PloS One*, 2012, vol. 7 pg. e42201 doi: 10.1371/journal.pone.0042201.

# CONTENTS OF EARLIER VOLUMES

**Progress in Economics Research. Volume 41**

| | |
|---|---|
| **Chapter 1** | Economic Growth and Human Capital Development<br>*Mohamed Aslam and Marina Maharoff* |
| **Chapter 2** | Modernization Logics and Principles of Designing a New Generation of Regional Economic Policies: Findings for Recent Ukraine and Eastern European Countries in Transition<br>*Igor Dunayev* |
| **Chapter 3** | Reviewing the French Economy<br>*Geeta Nair* |
| **Chapter 4** | New Technology and Employment in Mexico<br>*Humberto Merritt* |
| **Chapter 5** | The Integration of Big Data Analytics, Data Mining and Artificial Intelligence Solutions for Strategic E-Commerce Retail and Logistics Business-IT Alignment: A Case Study<br>*K. H. Leung, C. C Luk, K. L. Choy and H. Y. Lam* |

| | |
|---|---|
| **Chapter 6** | Inequality of Opportunities and Distribution of Accessibility to Basic Education in Cameroon<br>*Paul Ningaye and Fourier Prevost Fotso Koyeu* |
| **Chapter 7** | Harvest Costs and Manmade Capital in Renewable Resource Based OLG Models<br>*Karl Farmer* |

**Progress in Economics Research. Volume 40**

| | |
|---|---|
| **Chapter 1** | Exploring Economic History:<br>Dutch Governmental Structure and Foreign Trade Policy Success, 1602-1672<br>*Ralf Fendel and Nicholas Welsch-Lehmann* |
| **Chapter 2** | Economic Growth and Development:<br>An Opportunity for Tourism<br>*Pablo Juan Cárdenas-García and Juan Ignacio Pulido-Fernández* |
| **Chapter 3** | Combining Economic and Tourism Indicators to Position Tourist Destinations via Perceptual Maps<br>*Oscar Claveria* |
| **Chapter 4** | Tourism Destination Competitiveness:<br>Comparative and Competitive Advantage<br>*Ernest Azzopardi and Robert Nash* |
| **Chapter 5** | Export Opportunity, Economic Growth and Structural Change: A Case for Industrial Policy in the Republic of Macedonia<br>*Darko Lazarov and Goce Petreski* |

| | |
|---|---|
| **Chapter 6** | The Political Economy of Global Health Efforts from Australia to Papua New Guinea: Addressing Development, Diplomacy, and Development Constraints<br>*Sebastian Kevany and Amy Gildea* |
| **Chapter 7** | Financial Development, Institutions and Economic Growth: Evidence from Sub-Saharan Africa<br>*Ekpeno L. Effiong* |

**Progress in Economics Research. Volume 39**

| | |
|---|---|
| **Chapter 1** | Perceived Employability, Job Insecurity, and Well-Being<br>*Lisa Fiksenbaum, Zdravko Marjanovic and Esther Greenglass* |
| **Chapter 2** | Efficiency, Technology, and Productivity in Australian Urban Water Utilities<br>*Andrew C. Worthington* |
| **Chapter 3** | On the Analysis of Price Dynamics in Agricultural Markets<br>*Fabio Gaetano Santeramo and Leonardo Di Gioia* |
| **Chapter 4** | An Overview of Interstate Gas Pipeline Regulation in the United States<br>*Matthew E. Oliver and Charles F. Mason* |
| **Chapter 5** | The Concept of Global Currency and Global Government<br>*Pavle Jakovac, Eni Dekovic and Matea Udovicic* |

| | |
|---|---|
| **Chapter 6** | What Drives Restaurants Bankrupt? A Survival Analysis Perspective *Soo Y. Kim, Nan Hua and Arun Upneja* |
| **Chapter 7** | The Nexus of Economic Growth, Stock Market Development, and Globalization: A Panel VAR Approach *José Alberto Fuinhas, António Cardoso Marques and João Mota* |
| **Chapter 8** | Is the Chinese Financial Market Integrated with the US Market? Evidence from Asymmetric Approaches *Abdulnasser Hatemi-J and Alan Mustafa* |
| **Chapter 9** | Nonlinear Dependence between Stock Prices and Exchange Rates in Nigeria *Ekpeno L. Effiong* |

**Progress in Economics Research. Volume 38**

| | |
|---|---|
| **Chapter 1** | Solow Growth Model with Network Production Functions: Theoretical and Empirical Explorations *Juan M. C. Larrosa, Lorena Tedesco and Cecilia Bermúdez* |
| **Chapter 2** | Government Sector and Regional Corruption: Evidence from Italian Regions *Monica Auteri* |
| **Chapter 3** | An Investigation into the Development of Aberdeen as a Leading Leisure Destination *Katie McFarlane, Andrew Martin and Robert Nash* |

| | |
|---|---|
| **Chapter 4** | Romania's Study Case: National Benchmarking Counties Regarding a Sustainable Economic Growth Profile Using the World Bank JoGG's Model<br>*Cristina Lincaru, Vasilica Ciuca and Speranţa Pirciog* |
| **Chapter 5** | China's Urbanization: Acceleration, Transformation, and Expectation<br>*Weilin Zhao* |
| **Chapter 6** | Spatial Analysis of International Tourism Growth in China's Cities<br>*Xi-sheng Hu, Neelam C. Poudyal and Gary T. Green* |
| **Chapter 7** | Public Private Partnership and the Opportunities for Infrastructural Development in Sub-Saharan Africa<br>*Afeez Olalekan Sanni* |

**Progress in Economics Research. Volume 37**

| | |
|---|---|
| **Chapter 1** | The Nexus between the Volatilities of Growth Rates and Crude Oil: Evidence from an Oil-Exporting Economy<br>*Idowu O. Ayodeji* |
| **Chapter 2** | Analyzing the Growth Effect of Transportation Investment<br>*Atrayee Ghosh Roy* |
| **Chapter 3** | The Economic Impacts of A Government Default in a Stochastic Overlapping Generations Model under Homogenous Investor Expectations<br>*Oliver Hann* |

**Chapter 4**  A New Approach to the Estimation of the Total Factor Productivity Dynamics and of the Rate of Disembodied Technical Change in the Context of Cobb-Douglas Production Function with Constant Returns to Scale
*Florin Marius Pavelescu*

**Chapter 5**  Revisiting Investment Dynamics in Solow's Growth Model
*Gregory Gagnon*

**Chapter 6**  Financial Performance and Intellectual Capital: An Empirical Analysis in the Context of the Euronext Market Countries
*Filipe Sardo and Zélia Serrasqueiro*

**Chapter 7**  Financial Integration, House Price Dynamics and Saving Rate Divergence in an Overlapping Generations Model with Intra-EMU and Asian-U.S. Trade Imbalances
*Karl Farmer*

**Chapter 8**  Regional Competitiveness Within the Cluster's Territory: Case of the Volga Federal District's Chemical Industry
*J. S. Tsertseil, V. V. Kookueva and K. V. Ordov*

**Chapter 9**  The Methodology and Implementation of a Knowledge Management System in the Economic Area of a High Polytechnic School: Case Study LABS
*Mariya Gubareva, Orlando Gomes, Maria Margarida Piteira, Anabela Correia, Carlos Proença, Nancy Edith Ochoa Guevara and José Fernando López Quintero*

## Progress in Economics Research. Volume 36

| | |
|---|---|
| **Chapter 1** | On the Harmfulness of Excessive Public Debt Levels in a Zero Lower Bound Framework<br>*Séverine Menguy* |
| **Chapter 2** | Scenario Forecasting After the Great Recession<br>*Camilo Sarmiento* |
| **Chapter 3** | Amartya Sen's Socio-Economic Analysis of Famines: An Overwiew of the Entitlement Approach<br>*Matthieu Clément* |
| **Chapter 4** | Gender Wage Gap from a Social Perspective – Towards Socio Economic Re-Evolution through Mainstreaming Pay Policy: The Case of Cyprus<br>*M. Staboulis, D. Panagiotopoulou and M. A. Matthaiou* |
| **Chapter 5** | The Contribution of Transportation on Socioeconomic Development<br>*Saúl Antonio Obregón-Biosca* |
| **Chapter 6** | Coherence in Policies for Providing and Regulating Global Public Goods<br>*Susana Herrero Olarte* |
| **Chapter 7** | Perceptions of Gold Coast Locals Regarding the Proposed Cruise Ship Terminal<br>*Jodie Wood, Robert Nash and Paul Stansbie* |

**Chapter 8** Tourism Strategies for Rural Economic Prosperity (Case Study: Iran)
*Neda Torabi Farsani, Zahed Shafiei and Babak Saffari*

**Chapter 9** Big Data in the Automotive Industry: Long-Term Challenges and Opportunities in Global Competition
*Alexandra Schulte*

# INDEX

## A

access, xi, 2, 5, 9, 10, 11, 12, 15, 19, 20, 91, 103, 112, 117, 119, 126, 127, 128, 131, 139, 162, 171, 175, 199
accountability, 30, 36, 116, 140, 148
adjustment, 24, 29, 174
advantage, 13, 15, 39, 42, 46, 48, 49, 81, 97, 98, 218
adverse effects, 24, 124, 125
Africa, 77, 101, 131, 133, 134, 135, 219, 221
African Socialism, 102, 131
age, 107, 111, 121, 127, 192, 210
age structure, 107
agriculture, 104, 105, 106, 110, 121, 122, 123, 125, 129, 141, 143, 158
agro-ecological and climatic zones, 103
anchovy, viii, xi, 191, 192, 193, 194, 195, 196, 197, 198, 199, 200, 201, 202, 203, 205, 206, 207, 208, 209, 210, 211, 212, 213, 214, 215, 216
Angola, 69, 76, 192, 201
anthropology, 110, 111, 213
Argentina, 20, 72, 76, 203, 212

arid and semi-arid regions, 103
Armenia, 72, 77, 141, 156, 163, 164, 165, 166, 201
Asia, 30, 36, 78, 79, 140, 168
Asian countries, 79
assessment, 52, 62, 79, 197
assets, 46, 50, 88, 140, 146, 147
Azerbaijan, 141, 156, 163, 164, 165, 166

## B

Bahrain, 74, 77
balance of payments, 121, 122
Bangladesh, 69, 76, 201
banking, 40, 41, 175
banking sector, 40
banks, 91
Barbados, 72, 73, 77
bargaining, 2, 5
barriers, viii, ix, 2, 3, 6, 7, 11, 14, 15, 19, 22, 25, 26, 28, 38, 41, 78, 81, 92
barriers to entry, 11
basic education, 119
basic needs, 121, 126
basic services, 117, 124

Bay of Biscay, xi, 191, 192, 193, 195, 197, 204, 205, 206, 212, 213, 214, 215
Belarus, 142, 145, 156, 163, 164, 165, 166
Belgium, 75, 77, 132
beneficiaries, 26, 118
benefits, viii, 2, 4, 9, 15, 17, 21, 24, 28, 30, 43, 49, 61, 78, 79, 91, 93, 103, 111, 127
Bill of Rights, 117, 119
Bolivia, 8, 11, 12, 16, 20, 71, 76, 201
Brazil, 20, 72, 76, 121
budget deficit, 122, 123
budget surplus, 140
bureaucracy, 91
Burkina Faso, 69, 76, 201
Burundi, 69, 70, 76, 201
businesses, 14, 30, 48, 57, 206, 209

# C

Cambodia, 70, 76, 201
Cameroon, 70, 76, 218
capacity building, 8, 10, 12, 31
capital flows, 44, 83
capital inflow, 61, 87
capital productivity, 51
Central African Republic, 201
Central Asia, 138, 168
Chad, 69, 71, 76, 201
challenges, ix, x, xii, 18, 29, 30, 31, 36, 38, 48, 60, 79, 80, 81, 90, 91, 94, 101, 103, 116, 120, 126, 127, 138, 166, 192, 212
children, 107, 112, 113, 115, 119, 127
Chile, 20, 72, 76, 199
China, v, vii, ix, 13, 37, 38, 39, 40, 41, 61, 72, 76, 78, 79, 81, 82, 83, 84, 85, 86, 87, 88, 89, 90, 91, 94, 95, 96, 221
citizens, x, 45, 61, 93, 101, 103, 117, 118, 121, 138, 148, 177
civil servants, viii, xi, 171, 172, 177, 182
civil service, 124, 148
civil service reform, 124

civil society, 48
civil war, 141, 142, 144, 163
classes, 152, 155, 156, 158, 160, 161, 163
classification, 6, 23, 54, 55, 58, 68, 104, 105, 163, 164
cluster analysis, 152, 155, 158
clustering, 152, 153
Colombia, 20, 72, 73, 77
colonial anthropology, 110, 111
commerce, vii, viii, 1, 2, 3, 4, 5, 6, 7, 8, 9, 11, 12, 14, 15, 16, 17, 18, 19, 20, 21, 22, 23, 25, 27, 28, 29, 31, 32, 33, 34, 35, 36
commercial, xi, 9, 11, 23, 41, 175, 191, 200, 206, 208
comparative advantage, 13, 39, 42, 82
comparative analysis, 6
competition, 8, 17, 19, 39, 41, 46, 49, 61, 91, 92, 93
competitive advantage, ix, 38, 39, 46, 48, 49, 81, 98
competitiveness, v, vii, ix, 37, 38, 39, 40, 41, 44, 45, 46, 47, 48, 49, 50, 58, 61, 62, 67, 79, 80, 88, 92, 93, 95, 97, 98, 99, 100, 218, 222
complex interactions, 83
constant returns to scale, 222
Constituency Development Fund, 126
Constitution, 112, 117, 118, 119, 120, 128, 131
constitutional amendment, 120
construction, 30, 58, 146, 147, 163, 167, 176
consumption, 91, 124, 146, 147, 198, 214
cooperation with UNCTAD, 12
correlation, xi, 9, 138, 140, 150, 158, 161, 162, 163, 164
corruption, 91, 116, 127, 138, 140, 148, 165, 166, 220
cost, 20, 122, 127, 146, 172, 198
crises, x, 38, 60, 66, 81
critical period, 172

# Index

Cuba, 8, 10, 11, 12, 13, 15, 16, 19, 23, 25, 33, 34
Cultural predispositions, 110
culture, 14, 41, 110, 111, 114, 115, 128
Cyprus, 74, 77, 199, 223
Czech Republic, 37, 74, 77

## D

data collection, 6, 25
data gathering, 3
data set, ix, 38, 55, 63
database, 7, 47, 56, 58, 62, 143, 145, 148, 153
debt servicing, 128
decision makers, 61
deconstruct, 103
degradation, 126, 146, 147
dependency syndrome, 113
deregulation, 24, 140
developed countries, 3, 4, 5, 7, 10, 11, 16, 18, 19, 20, 23, 24, 25, 26, 67, 93, 126, 201
developing countries, vii, viii, 1, 2, 3, 4, 5, 6, 7, 8, 9, 10, 11, 12, 13, 14, 15, 16, 17, 18, 19, 20, 21, 22, 23, 24, 25, 26, 27, 28, 29, 30, 31, 39, 41, 93, 122, 200
developing economies, 78, 79
developing nations, 9
development, v, vii, viii, ix, x, 2, 4, 5, 8, 9, 11, 12, 14, 15, 16, 17, 18, 19, 22, 23, 24, 25, 27, 28, 29, 30, 31, 32, 33, 34, 37, 38, 39, 40, 41, 42, 44, 45, 47, 48, 49, 50, 55, 56, 58, 59, 60, 61, 62, 63, 66, 67, 68, 69, 72, 74, 76, 77, 80, 81, 82, 84, 87, 88, 92, 94, 97, 101, 102, 103, 106, 107, 108, 109, 110, 112, 114, 117, 118, 125, 126, 127, 128, 129, 130, 131, 133, 134, 135, 137, 138, 139, 140, 145, 146, 148, 149, 153, 155, 158, 159, 162, 164, 166, 167, 168, 169, 201, 213, 217, 218, 219, 220, 221, 223
development budgets, 127
development policy, x, 30, 101, 115, 126
devolution, 115, 117, 130
devolved funds, 108
digital divide, 12, 15, 25
disadvantage, 39, 109
discrimination, 25, 26, 112, 118, 120, 132
distribution, 61, 92, 105, 121, 145, 146, 162, 167, 192, 194
distribution of income, 146, 162
documentary evidence, 173, 179
Doha, 18, 21, 29, 30, 31, 32
domestic regulatory regimes, 8

## E

ecological conditions, 105
e-commerce, vii, viii, 1, 2, 3, 4, 5, 6, 7, 8, 9, 10, 11, 12, 13, 14, 15, 16, 17, 18, 19, 20, 21, 22, 23, 25, 26, 27, 28, 30, 31, 35, 36
economic activity, 44, 105
economic competitiveness, vii, 39
economic crisis, 60
economic development, ix, x, 4, 5, 19, 24, 27, 28, 31, 38, 39, 48, 80, 81, 94, 102, 103, 106, 107, 108, 109, 110, 112, 117, 127, 128, 164
economic downturn, 60
economic efficiency, 39, 40, 93
economic empowerment, 127
economic growth, vii, x, 2, 24, 40, 44, 50, 60, 61, 62, 80, 82, 87, 93, 95, 102, 104, 107, 108, 121, 122, 124, 127, 138, 162, 163, 164, 168, 217, 218, 219, 220, 221
economic growth rate, 108
economic indicator, 139
economic institutions, 83
economic integration, 41, 91
economic liberalization, 41

economic performance, viii, xii, 41, 49, 121, 140, 145, 159, 162, 192
economic policy, 40, 41, 47, 49, 51, 61, 127
economic potential, 2, 5, 44, 104, 106
economic power, ix, 38, 92
economic progress, 61
economic reform, 41, 83, 123
economic relations, 42
economic resources, 116, 128
economic status, 112
economic theory, 56
economic well-being, 111
economics, 67
economies in transition, 4
economies of scale, 43, 53
eco-system characteristics, 106
education, 14, 44, 59, 60, 62, 67, 88, 92, 108, 109, 113, 116, 117, 119, 122, 123, 124, 126, 127, 134, 139, 145, 158, 162, 163, 218
educational institutions, 119
effectiveness, 39, 40, 49, 50, 68, 98, 140, 148
efficiency, v, ix, 4, 37, 38, 39, 40, 47, 48, 49, 50, 51, 52, 53, 54, 55, 56, 57, 59, 60, 62, 63, 66, 67, 68, 72, 76, 77, 81, 83, 84, 85, 86, 87, 89, 91, 93, 94, 95, 96, 97, 98, 124, 177, 219
emerging markets, 61, 87, 140
employees, 124, 146, 147, 175, 177
employment, 41, 82, 117, 119, 121, 123, 124, 147, 217
employment growth, 82, 124
environment, 11, 39, 42, 46, 50, 59, 67, 83, 93, 112, 123
environmental conditions, xi, 191, 193
environmental degradation, 61, 126
environmental factors, 193
environmental impact, 198
environmental issues, 46
environmental protection, 31
environmental sustainability, 36, 158

equity, 102, 103, 117, 118, 119, 148
Estonia, 74, 75, 77, 144, 156, 158, 159, 160, 164, 165, 166, 192
ethnic groups, 106, 108, 112, 128
European Commission, 98, 213
European Community, 33, 198, 200, 210
European market, 210
European Monetary Union (EMU), 222
European Union, 23, 95, 98, 167, 198, 199, 205, 210, 211, 212
exchange rate, 40, 57, 124
executive political institutions, 116
expenditures, 113, 173, 179, 181
exploitation, 206, 208
export promotion, 30
exports, 5, 14, 19, 46, 56, 78, 79, 81, 91, 123, 141, 142, 198, 204, 205, 207
external environment, x, 101
extreme poverty, ix, 38, 88

# F

factor analysis, 151, 167
factor cost, 147
factor endowments, 47, 56
factor market, 39, 81, 92, 93
family members, 112, 114, 115
family planning, 109
financial, 2, 4, 15, 22, 35, 42, 49, 60, 61, 81, 83, 87, 91, 92, 123, 124, 140, 146, 147, 148, 172, 190
financial condition, 49
financial crisis, 60, 61, 87, 140
financial integration, 222
financial markets, 83, 190
financial performance, 222
financial sector, 91, 124
financial support, 123
fiscal deficits, 124
fiscal policy, 122
fiscal year, 127, 148

fisheries, xi, 191, 195, 204, 206, 211, 213, 214, 215
fishing, viii, xi, 147, 191, 193, 197, 210, 211, 212, 213, 214, 215
foreign direct investment, 40, 61, 87, 88
foreign exchange, 102, 123
foreign investment, viii, 37, 41, 46
formal education, 116
former Soviet republics, v, 137
France, 75, 77, 193, 195, 204, 205
free trade, 81, 140
freedom, ix, 38, 60, 92, 118, 119, 121, 139, 148
freedom of choice, 139
FSD, x, 137, 140, 145, 151, 152, 153, 154, 155, 156, 157, 158, 159, 160, 161, 162, 163, 164, 166
FSG, x, 138, 140, 145, 149, 151, 152, 154, 155, 156, 157, 158, 159, 160, 161, 162, 164, 166
funding, vii, x, 102, 109, 128, 211
funds, xi, 108, 116, 117, 126, 127, 171, 172, 211

## G

GDP, xi, 56, 57, 61, 82, 89, 91, 121, 122, 123, 124, 127, 138, 140, 141, 142, 144, 145, 146, 147, 148, 157, 158, 159, 160, 162, 163, 164, 165, 166, 211
GDP per capita, 56, 57, 141, 144, 145, 146, 158, 160, 162, 163, 164, 211
gender equality, 120
gender equity, 113
gender inequalities, x, 101, 127
general knowledge, 177
Georgia, 72, 77, 156, 159, 164, 165, 166, 201
Germany, 74, 75, 77, 203
Global Competitiveness Report, 40, 47, 99

global economy, 5, 39, 40, 44, 78, 79, 82, 96
global forces, 92
global markets, 47, 49, 61, 92
Global Poverty Index Scale, 125
global recession, 122
global trade, viii, 1, 4, 13, 23, 41, 44, 79, 80
globalization, ix, 30, 31, 38, 39, 40, 41, 42, 45, 49, 81, 92, 93, 94, 220
goods and services, viii, 15, 17, 32, 37, 41, 45, 57, 146, 147, 164
governance, vii, x, 7, 15, 30, 40, 49, 80, 83, 94, 102, 117, 119, 127, 137, 138, 139, 140, 145, 149, 159, 162, 164, 166, 168, 201
government budget, 88
government intervention, 103
government policy, 103, 108
government spending, 116
government strategy, 103
governments, 8, 16, 18, 39, 46, 48, 53, 117
grounded theory, vii, viii, 1, 2, 3, 6, 25, 26, 31, 36
growth, viii, ix, x, xi, 1, 24, 27, 28, 38, 40, 42, 43, 44, 48, 50, 58, 60, 61, 78, 79, 80, 81, 83, 87, 88, 89, 90, 91, 92, 94, 102, 107, 121, 122, 123, 124, 127, 128, 138, 139, 140, 142, 144, 145, 153, 157, 158, 162, 163, 164, 166, 175, 193, 201, 204, 205, 207, 220, 221
growth dynamics, 60
growth rate, 58, 61, 79, 81, 89, 107, 121, 122, 123, 124, 142, 144, 205
Guatemala, 20, 72, 76
Guinea, 69, 76, 201, 219
Guyana, 71, 76

## H

Haiti, 70, 76, 201

health, 46, 62, 109, 111, 115, 116, 117, 119, 122, 123, 124, 126, 127, 145, 162, 163, 168, 210
health care, 117, 126
health indicators, 110, 115
health services, 123
higher education, 91, 129, 134
history, ix, 18, 26, 38, 60, 82, 109, 123
Honduras, 20, 70, 71, 76
Hong Kong, 34, 35, 36, 74, 77
house price, 222
house price dynamics, 222
human development, xi, 138, 139, 145, 162, 164
Human Development Index, xi, 138, 145
Human Development Report, 139, 169
human rights, 30, 116, 120, 166

## I

Iceland, 75, 77, 199
import substitution, 121
imported products, 208
imports, 78, 79, 82, 124, 198, 199, 200, 202, 203, 204, 207, 211, 212
income, ix, xi, 18, 30, 38, 46, 57, 61, 80, 88, 89, 114, 125, 139, 145, 146, 147, 163, 171, 172, 173
income inequality, 61
increased competition, 45, 49
independence, x, 101, 108, 121, 125, 126, 127, 128, 137, 148
index of development, vii, x, 137, 153
index of governance, 140
indigenous peoples, 111
individuals, x, 18, 92, 102, 110, 111, 128, 146, 147, 175, 177, 192
industries, 10, 24, 39, 44, 46, 82, 89, 93, 210
inequality, vii, 117, 127, 130, 145, 146, 159, 163, 164, 218

inflation, 121, 122, 123, 124, 140, 141, 158, 159, 163, 164, 174
information technology, 19
infrastructure, 9, 14, 16, 19, 44, 88, 92, 111, 117, 124
inheritance, 112, 120, 142
institutional change, 31
institutions, vii, x, 47, 58, 81, 83, 108, 110, 114, 116, 119, 127, 135, 137, 139, 140, 158, 162, 164
integration, 4, 9, 12, 41, 42, 44, 78, 79, 82, 96, 120
intellectual capital, 222
intellectual property, 12, 30, 33, 34, 35
intellectual property rights, 33, 34, 35
international competitiveness, 39, 44, 46, 93
international diplomacy, 83
international law, 79
international trade, viii, 9, 20, 23, 24, 27, 28, 31, 37, 39, 40, 41, 42, 44, 45, 46, 78, 79, 82, 96, 201
investment, viii, 10, 14, 38, 39, 44, 46, 48, 60, 83, 90, 93, 146, 147, 209, 210
investment in human infrastructure, 14
investments, 50, 58, 104, 121, 211
Israel, 74, 77, 121, 199
issues, viii, 2, 3, 4, 6, 7, 8, 9, 12, 16, 17, 20, 21, 23, 25, 27, 28, 41, 43, 50, 80, 92, 110, 135, 159, 166
Italy, 74, 77, 137, 195, 204, 205, 213, 214

## J

Jamaica, 72, 76
Japan, 11, 23, 33, 74, 77, 82
job creation, ix, 38, 60, 92, 131
Jordan, 73, 77, 166, 199

## K

Kazakhstan, 69, 70, 76, 156, 159, 163, 164, 165, 166
Kenya, vii, x, 69, 70, 76, 101, 102, 103, 104, 105, 106, 107, 108, 109, 110, 111, 112, 113, 114, 115, 116, 117, 118, 119, 120, 121, 122, 123, 125, 126, 127, 128, 129, 130, 131, 132, 133, 134, 135
kinship, 112
kinship relations, 112
knowledge management, 222
Korea, 74, 75, 77
Kuwait, 71, 76
Kyrgyzstan, 69, 70, 76, 201

## L

labor force, 147, 165
labour market, 17, 108, 135
Latin America, 20
Latvia, 73, 77, 144, 156, 158, 159, 164, 165, 166
laws, 9, 46, 112, 118, 119, 120, 140, 172, 178
laws and regulations, 9, 172
legal system, 8, 119, 162
legislation, xi, 112, 121, 171, 172, 177, 201, 210, 211
less developed areas, 103, 116
levels of development, x, 23, 80, 110, 137, 138
liberalization, 13, 14, 18, 23, 24, 40, 41, 42, 44, 78, 123, 140
Liberia, 69, 76, 201
license fee, 146, 147
life expectancy, 138, 139, 158, 159, 163
literacy, 14, 147, 158, 165
Lithuania, 73, 77, 144, 156, 158, 159, 164, 165, 166
livelihood, 125, 126

Local Authority Transfer Fund, 126
local government, 117

## M

Macedonia, 73, 77, 199, 218
macroeconomic environment, 88
macroeconomic indicators, 140, 141, 158, 163
macroeconomic stabilization, 122, 124, 125
Malaysia, 1, 31, 35, 36, 72, 76
manufacturing, 81, 88, 91, 121
marginalization, x, 102, 111, 128
market access, 8, 79
market economy, 138, 159
market position, 49
market share, 206
market structure, 17, 42
marketing, 123, 206
marketplace, viii, 37, 41, 93
Mauritania, 70, 76, 201
Mauritius, 73, 77, 133
Mediterranean, xi, 191, 192, 195, 197, 199, 213
Mediterranean countries, 199
methodology, 52, 60, 94, 140, 149, 151, 167
Mexico, 20, 72, 77, 199, 217
mixed economy, 102
Mkunumbi, 111
mobile phone, 147, 175
Moldova, 71, 76, 141, 142, 156, 160, 163, 164, 165, 166, 199
monetary expansion, 124
monetary policy, 60, 87, 123
Mongolia, 22, 32, 70, 76, 201
monopolistic competition, 43
Montenegro, 73, 77, 200
moratorium on customs duties, 21
Morocco, 73, 77, 192, 194, 199, 203, 205
Moscow, 171, 173, 174, 175, 176, 189
Mozambique, 70, 76, 201

Mpeketoni, 111
multidimensional, 149, 153, 155, 167
multilateral trading system, 4, 28, 40, 94
multinational corporations, 93
multivariate statistics, 168
Myanmar, 69, 76, 201

## N

national borders, viii, 37, 41
national income, 146
national language, 106
national product, 49, 212
natural resources, 31, 48, 56, 102, 126, 143, 146, 147
Nepal, 69, 76, 201
Netherlands, 75, 77
New Zealand, 74, 77
Nicaragua, 8, 11, 12, 16, 19, 20, 24, 71, 76
Nigeria, 69, 76, 107, 129, 133, 135, 220
non-discriminatory access, 9, 11
nontariff barriers, 79
normal distribution, 63, 149
North America, 95
North Korea, 83
Norway, 74, 75, 77, 192, 199

## O

oil, 121, 122, 159, 163
one dimension, 47, 62, 83
open economy, 81
open-mindedness, 58
openness, 23, 42, 47, 49, 81, 88, 92, 93
operations, 181, 198
opportunities, 4, 5, 29, 48, 61, 67, 92, 114, 117, 214, 218, 221, 224
organizational learning, 36
ownership, 112, 173

## P

Pacific, 30, 36, 168
Pakistan, 69, 70, 76, 201
Panama, 20, 73, 77
Papua New Guinea, 219
Paraguay, 20, 72, 73, 76, 201
patriarchy, 113
per capita income, 62, 124
perfect competition, 43
personal computers, 20
persons with disabilities, 119
Peru, 20, 72, 76, 203
Philippines, 70, 76, 201
policy, vii, viii, x, 2, 3, 4, 6, 7, 8, 9, 14, 15, 18, 20, 23, 26, 27, 29, 30, 31, 32, 35, 36, 40, 41, 49, 50, 81, 84, 101, 102, 103, 104, 107, 108, 118, 119, 124, 126, 128, 148, 149, 166
policy issues, 3, 6, 28
policy making, 149
policy options, 19
policy responses, 84
political ideologies, 116
political instability, 148, 161
political leaders, 120
political participation, 118
political power, 108, 128
political process, 106
political system, 82, 83, 116, 117
politics, 96, 108, 135
population, x, 102, 104, 106, 107, 108, 109, 110, 111, 112, 115, 125, 126, 127, 128, 145, 146, 147, 159, 165, 193, 194, 216
population group, 107
population growth, 107, 108, 111, 128
potential benefits, 2, 17, 19
poverty, ix, 2, 4, 16, 31, 38, 88, 99, 109, 125, 126, 130, 139, 147, 158, 162, 165
poverty alleviation, 31
poverty line, 125, 126, 147, 165

## Index

poverty reduction, 16
preferential treatment, 199
preparation, iv, viii, xii, 192, 201, 202, 204, 207, 212
presidential republic, 117
principal component analysis, 149, 153, 155
private sector, 48, 102, 140, 148
privatization, 124, 134
processing industry, 192, 198, 208, 212, 213
production possibility frontier, 52, 76, 77
production technology, 50
productive capacity, 44
productivity growth, 50, 92
professionals, xi, 171, 172
profitability, 42, 207, 209
profitability ratios, 42
prosperity, ix, 38, 39, 45, 48, 49, 50, 57, 58, 60, 83
protected areas, 105
protection, 20, 118, 120, 166
protectionism, 15, 40, 92, 94
public administration, 211
public affairs, 116
public debt, 127, 158, 159
public health, 88, 110, 114
public interest, 27
public investment, 102
public resources, 107, 108, 109, 110, 114, 117
public sector, 40, 49, 98, 123
public service, 109, 118, 121, 148
purchasing power, 146
purchasing power parity, 146

### Q

quality of life, 93, 139, 145, 162, 164

### R

rainfall, 102, 104, 105, 106
raw materials, 56, 164, 199, 211, 212
real estate, 172, 175, 176
real income, 45
real property, 112
recovery, 40, 49, 61, 124, 138
reforms, ix, 38, 78, 79, 83, 87, 90, 123, 139, 140
regression, 145, 151, 152, 163
regression line, 145, 163
regression method, 151, 152
regression weights, 152
regulations, 15, 18, 148, 178
relevance, 47, 51, 142, 158
relevant technologies, 20
requirements, vii, viii, 2, 3, 6, 7, 8, 25, 27, 28, 78
research online, 168
researchers, 51, 150
resource allocation, 78, 117
resource utilization, 40
resource-poor, 121
resources, 9, 10, 16, 20, 46, 49, 50, 52, 57, 62, 102, 106, 108, 110, 114, 120, 121, 126, 128, 139
restaurants bankrupt, 220
restrictions, 9, 13, 20, 23, 30
returns to scale, 40, 52, 53
revenue, 21, 22, 39
revenue allocation, 109, 111, 129
rights, iv, 9, 18, 114, 116, 118, 119, 121, 128, 199
role of market openness, 24
Romania, 73, 77, 221
rules, 4, 9, 12, 18, 22, 23, 26, 27, 28, 29, 78, 80, 83, 94, 148
rural areas, 112, 113
Rural Electrification Fund, 126
rural women, 127
Russia, 138, 159, 163, 164, 166, 171, 172, 178
Rwanda, 69, 76, 132, 201

## S

Saudi Arabia, 73, 77
saving rate, 222
savings, 140
scarcity, 106, 126, 177, 206
scenario forecasting, 223
school, 109, 111, 114, 115, 116, 127, 192
schooling, 107, 110, 114, 115
scope, 14, 44, 80, 118
secondary education, 126
securities, xi, 148, 171, 172, 173, 175, 177, 179, 181, 190
service provider, 20
services, iv, 9, 10, 11, 13, 17, 18, 29, 48, 49, 81, 82, 91, 114, 116, 117, 118, 146, 147, 175, 176, 177
settlements, 109, 111, 208
Seychelles, 70, 71, 76
Sierra Leone, 35, 70, 71, 76, 201
Singapore, 10, 12, 36, 74, 77
Slovakia, 73, 77
social conditions, 141
social costs, 24
social development, 82, 102, 158, 162, 167
social environment, 112
social expenditure, 124
social learning, 80
social policy, 138
social problems, 93
social sciences, 168
social security, 119
social services, 123
social structure, 112
society, x, 18, 39, 58, 61, 62, 93, 101, 111, 113, 115, 119, 139, 148, 159
socio-economic development, v, x, 101, 102, 103, 107, 109, 110, 112, 128, 164
South Africa, 72, 73, 76, 107, 129, 133, 135, 192
sovereignty, 19, 117

Soviet Union, vii, viii, x, 137, 138, 140, 158, 161, 166, 168, 171
Spain, xi, 75, 77, 191, 193, 195, 198, 199, 202, 203, 206, 207, 208, 209, 210, 212, 213, 214, 215
Spanish fishing and processing sector, viii, xii, 192
Special and Differential Treatment, 13, 14
species, viii, xi, 191, 192, 195, 197, 198, 213
spending, 98, 115
Sri Lanka, 72, 76, 201
stability, 14, 49, 92, 160
stage of economic development, ix, 38, 39, 80, 81
state-owned banks, 91
state-owned enterprises, 91
stock, ix, xi, xii, 38, 88, 148, 171, 172, 174, 181, 192, 193, 194, 195, 198
stockholders, xi, 171, 174, 175, 177
structural adjustment, 122, 129
structural funds, 98
structural reforms, 92
structure, vii, x, 41, 49, 78, 79, 82, 102, 107, 118, 150, 194, 216
super-efficiency, 39, 40, 54, 55, 60, 66, 68, 76, 77, 84, 85, 86, 87, 99
sustainability, 36, 114, 140, 158, 163, 197
sustainable development, 40, 49, 162, 201

## T

Tajikistan, 70, 71, 76, 143, 156, 160, 161, 163, 164, 165, 166
Tanzania, 69, 70, 76, 107, 132, 201
tariff, 24, 78, 79, 92, 123, 200
taxation, viii, xi, 171, 172, 173, 177, 179, 181
taxes, 21, 22, 146, 177, 190, 200, 210
taxonomy, 48
taxpayers, 172, 177

# Index

technical and vocational education and training (TIVET), 108
technological change, ix, 38, 41
technological progress, 42, 82
technology transfer, 10
telecommunications, 13, 20
telecommunications services, 13
telephone numbers, xi, 171, 175
trade, viii, xii, 2, 4, 5, 9, 12, 13, 14, 15, 16, 17, 18, 19, 24, 26, 28, 29, 31, 33, 34, 35, 38, 39, 40, 41, 42, 43, 44, 46, 60, 78, 79, 81, 83, 92, 93, 95, 99, 122, 123, 124, 192, 198, 199
trade agreement, 29
trade balance, viii, xii, 124, 192, 198, 200
trade liberalization, 42, 78
trade policy, 40, 42
trading partners, 13, 46
traditional practices, 112, 114
traditional tenure practices, 112
training, 14, 59, 60, 67, 91, 108, 119
transactions, viii, xi, 18, 171, 172, 177
transfer payments, 146, 147
transformation, 68, 94, 124, 138, 150
transformation processes, 94
transnational corporations, 93
transparency, 40, 83, 177
transport, 44, 88, 98, 102, 146, 147
transport costs, 44
transportation investment, 221
Trinidad and Tobago, 74, 75, 77
Turkey, 73, 77, 199
Turkmenistan, 153

## U

Ukraine, 69, 70, 76, 141, 142, 144, 156, 161, 163, 164, 165, 166
unemployment rate, 141, 142
uniform, viii, 1, 2, 5, 45, 48
United Kingdom, 75, 77, 168, 205

United Nations, 83, 106, 119, 132, 139
United States, 20, 23, 33, 34, 35, 74, 77, 82, 99, 146, 205, 219
universality, 118
universities, 108, 132
urban, 109, 113, 114, 125, 159, 167
urban areas, 109, 113
urban population, 109
Uruguay, 20, 41, 73, 77
USSR, 159, 163
Uzbekistan, 153

## V

variables, 53, 110, 139, 141, 145, 149, 150, 151, 152, 153, 155, 158, 160, 161, 162
varimax rotation, 150
Venezuela, 8, 10, 11, 12, 13, 16, 20, 33, 70, 71, 76
Vietnam, 70, 76
violence, 148, 175
volatility, 143, 204
vulnerability, 126

## W

wages, 56, 81, 90
water, 106, 111, 117, 126, 176
water-scarce, 106
weakness, 58, 59, 67, 159
wealth, 42, 111, 127, 139
WEF, 39, 40, 47, 50, 55, 56, 58, 62, 67, 88, 89, 90, 92, 94, 99
welfare, 45, 49, 50, 102, 139, 162
well-being, 61, 111, 114, 139, 162, 167
working hours, 174
working population, 107
workplace, 113
World Bank, vii, x, 88, 99, 106, 123, 126, 130, 132, 137, 140, 146, 147, 148, 164, 167, 168, 221

WTO, v, viii, ix, 1, 2, 3, 4, 5, 6, 7, 8, 9, 10, 11, 12, 13, 14, 15, 16, 17, 18, 19, 20, 21, 22, 23, 25, 26, 27, 28, 29, 30, 31, 32, 33, 34, 35, 36, 37, 38, 39, 40, 41, 55, 56, 58, 59, 60, 62, 66, 67, 69, 72, 74, 78, 79, 80, 81, 83, 84, 93, 94, 143

## Z

Zimbabwe, 71, 76